My Path to

Dying to self

Spiritual Dynamics

And the struggle of the modern-day Christian

A topic by topic book

By Eric Schmidt

Download full book free at

www.dieingtoself.com

I put this disclaimer in because I was advised to do so. And because I am making this book very public and free on my webpage.

Disclaimers

In this book, I Eric S Schmidt (Writer, I, my) provide information on how to be a better Christian, and I share from my personal experiences. The information and guidance in this book are my opinions, and does not necessarily represent any organization or group. I put a few examples of situations I came across for teaching and learning purposes, identifying information has been removed. Any views or opinions are not intended to malign any religion, ethnic group, club, organization, company, or individual.

Sensitive Content - in this book, I talk candidly about a multiplicity of matters, including but not limited to: demons, lust, suicide, gangsters, and school shootings. There may be details that some might find offensive, triggering, or traumatic.

Everyone is different - The testimonials or experiences in this book are not guarantees and don't reflect how everyone will experience it. User experiences may vary from those depicted in this book.

Errors/Not professional advice - While the writer has made every attempt to ensure that the information contained in the Book is correct, the Writer is not responsible for any errors or omissions, or for the results obtained from the use of this information. The Writer disclaims any liability if the information proves to be inaccurate or incomplete in any way. All information in the Book is provided "as is", with no guarantee of completeness, accuracy, timeliness, or of the results obtained from the use of this information, and without warranty of any kind, express or implied. In no event will the Writer be liable to you or anyone else for any decision made or action taken in reliance on the information in this Book, or for any consequential, special or similar damages, even if advised of the possibility of such damages. The information in this Book is published in good faith for general information purposes only and is not intended to provide any type of professional advice, including but not limited to: financial, medical. Please seek professional assistance should you require it.

Figuratively speaking - Many of the terms represented in this book are spiritual terms and referring to the spiritual and not the natural world and should not be taken literally but spiritually or figuratively.

Fair Use - This book uses minor excerpts from other people's works. The only reason for this statement is I can't remember where I read them. But I did pursue and receive permission from those I do remember. Under the "Fair Use" Act, a copyrighted work can be used, cited, or incorporated within another author's work legally without needing a license if it's being used explicitly for things like news reporting, researching purposes, teaching, commentary, criticism, and other such uses. Title 17, Section 107 of the Copyright Act. These small excerpts fall under the guidelines of fair use because they are for teaching, commentary, or criticism. I am only using them for the betterment of all Christians, and this book is of a non-profit nature. All other appropriate permissions were sought and received.

You acknowledge that you have read these Disclaimers and agree to all its terms and conditions. By accessing and using this Book you agree to be bound by these Disclaimers.

Scripture taken from the New King James Version®. Copyright © 1982 by Thomas Nelson. Used by permission. All rights reserved.
Scriptures taken from the Holy Bible, New International Version®, NIV®. Copyright © 1973, 1978, 1984, 2011 by Biblica, Inc.™ Used by permission of Zondervan. All rights reserved worldwide. www.zondervan.com The "NIV" and "New International Version" are trademarks registered in the United States Patent and Trademark Office by Biblica, Inc.™
Scripture taken from the Holy Bible, Modern King James Version Copyright © 1962 - 1998 By Jay P. Green, Sr. Used by permission of the copyright holder.
Scripture quotations marked (ESV) are from the ESV® Bible (The Holy Bible, English Standard Version®), copyright © 2001 by Crossway, a publishing ministry of Good News Publishers. Used by permission. All rights reserved
The Holy Bible, Berean Study Bible, BSB Copyright ©2016, 2018 by Bible Hub Used by Permission. All Rights Reserved Worldwide. //bereanbible.com
Scripture quotations marked CSB have been taken from the Christian Standard Bible®, Copyright © 2017 by Holman Bible Publishers. Used by permission. Christian Standard Bible·, and CSB® are federally registered trademarks of Holman Bible Publishers.

© Copyright Eric S Schmidt 2021
I Eric S Schmidt, have the copyright for this book, but you may copy in any way or form either partially or fully under the following conditions: you give it for free, it's in its original form, and you attribute me as the source, (download free at www.dieingtoself.com); except for the statements below.

Commercial usage/publishing
In commercial/publishing, you may take what you need out of this book that are my words to be used in your works that you sell without my permission under the following conditions: you credit me as the source, it's in its original form, and my portion used is free (my portion adds no cost to the final price of the book). You may not modify my words or meanings. Paraphrasing is acceptable.
The exception to this would be other people's words or works in my book. You would need to ask

permission of the respective party involved if you use it in your own work; except for that which falls under the fair use copyright law.

Cover photos used described
I personally designed and created the book cover front and back, The photos used on the front cover are pictures from my travels, the words themselves are cut-outs from other personal pictures, the back grass picture is a creative commons picture made by: Mrhayata, Creative Commons license: Attribution-ShareAlike 2.0 Generic (CC BY-SA 2.0) (picture has been modified), and the cut-out words picture is again from my personal picture collection.

My purpose
My intention is only to help people. This book is of a non-profit nature, and I am trying to make it as cheap as possible, but there are basic costs to be covered. That is why I provide the book for free on my webpage, but provide a more official version that is a printed book. Any extra costs involved come out of my own pocket. It is my belief that like the patriarchs of old, they didn't make money off of their writings. I feel I should follow their example and do the same. I am your servant in Christ.

This book is being provided to you at the minimum costs involved

Topics

Introduction	8
Love one another	9
Dying to self	12
Bless and Don't Curse	13
Speak Positive	14
Honor your word, what you say is what you do	15
Foolish Spending	17
Purity	20
Don't Contaminate your Spirit	21
Go and Sin no more	22
The average Christian	23
Faith	26
Waiting for God to come through	32
How Big is God	33
Eternity Past and Future	39
Stay in touch with the Holy Spirit	41
Prayer	42
Basic Training	44
Division	44
Doctrines	45
Willful sins	47
Grace Vs. Responsibility	49
What do you accomplish or become	50
Accountable to what you have been given	51
Levels of Maturity and Obedience	53
Building the Kingdom by Building others	55
Capacities of Heaven	56
A Taste of the Anointing	57
Humility and Wisdom before Power	59
Pride	60
False Voices that Mislead	62
Pseudo anointing	63
The Revival Killers	65

Pastor, The stumbling block	66
Modern-day Pharisee	70
I write to you because you know it	74
The Price of the calling	75
The 5 Ministries	76
Women Should be Free/Women Leaders	77
Mantles	79
Humility	80
Bow down low to receive the next level	82
Obedience vs. works	84
True authority and maneuvering for position	85
I must become lesser so He might become greater	86
The point of Saturation, and The Pain of Correction	87
Too Busy, Don't over plan and miss God	90
Changing God's will out of convenience	91
Spirit of fear	92
Spiritual Suffocation	94
Everybody Speaks The Same Language	95
The "Who's your covering" misconception	97
Arguing, Defense and Walls a better way	99
Relationship and communication	101
The Apology, The Tool of Great Healing	104
Don't Stuff Your feelings in	105
Manipulated out of the calling	107
Boundary setting, why can't you say no!	111
We need another one of you	112
You're better than me, I'm better than you	113
Christian vs. Christian	115
Don't squish what little one has	117
Hidden pains of the past that affect who we are today	118
Actions speak louder than thoughts	120
Don't Worry	121
Stuff happens in life	122
Emotional Pain	123
Follow After Peace	125
Don't Intellectualize, but Spiritualize	126

God doesn't fit in a box	127
Old words, New words	130
Seeing in the Holy Spirit, and the leadings of the Holy Spirit	132
Born in the Spirit with gifts already operating	134
Prayer is a Powerful tool do not retaliate	136
Who me, a Gossiper? Yeah right! and Confidants	137
Revival is Coming	140
Teachable Spirit/Unteachable Spirit	140
Generous with the gift of the Holy Spirit	141
The Purpose of this Life	143
Use your worldly resources to benefit others	144
Worship	145
Worship is slow, less is more	147
Surface Worship/Heart Worship	150
Worship in Spirit and In Truth	151
New Song	151
Layers and Levels of Spiritual sensitivity	152
Worship is the only way to reach some	153
Don't neglect Worship	154
Musician's battle with Pride	155
Equip others	156
Physical healing	157
Physical Ailment of a demonic nature	159
Sticky Emotions and Demonic Pressure	161
Anger, emotion hidden within an emotion	164
Power playing argumenter	165
Rejection Syndrome	167
Exaggeration	168
Mocking Spirit	169
Dominion, and Good and Evil	169
The Devil's on the Outside	172
Devil's last stand and strong demon submission	178
Know your spiritual boundaries, what you have authority over	180
Hidden Demons / Familiar spirit	183
Intercessors	185
I want your Heart, not your religiousness	187

The Harvest	189
Overcoming Lust	191
Suicide	194
Depression	196
Salvation attack	197
The Impressionable mind looking for acceptance/rejection	199
Salvation message	202
Recommended Books	204

Introduction

I am an average person who had an opportunity to go traveling with a ministry and visit home churches around the United States. Starting in late 2002, I have been on this trip to this date full time. No job to go to, I joined this trip as an apprentice, and in that time I have seen a great many Christians from all around the nation in many different situations. I had what I thought Christians were like and what they did and didn't do. But quickly found out that Christians didn't always act the way they should or knew one thing really well, but not another.

I didn't have many opportunities to talk about the things I've seen that repeated over and over again, in many situations. I was frustrated at what I saw, it's not like you can go up to someone and tell them what they are doing very easily. I felt it was better for me to write about what I have seen and what should be. I have also written in this book about my personal struggles to attain godliness.

I view dying to self as a continual process, and that one has never fully arrived; there are many veils peeled away in due process. I believe that there are still levels of maturity that are not even attained yet.

I also didn't get many opportunities to talk about such things, because it's not always the time and place to do so. If I did, it was a quick portion, and they didn't always believe it. I felt I could fully say what I would like all Christians to hear. This is my portion, and it is incomplete, because everybody has a piece to the puzzle. "We need to have humility to take our pieces and to put them together"(paraphrased Rick Joyner). I'm not the all in all who knows all things, and I'm not perfect. If I say something in this book that offends you, I hope you will set that offense aside and understand that I'm only trying to help you as a fellow brother or sister in Christ to attain all that you can be in God.

I am not an intense person, so I try to say things in such a way to try to not offend, but on the other side, I feel that the truth needs to be said. I think we often overlook the simple things Jesus said in the gospels, many things that we often forget about. So I write to you about what I have observed in Christians around the nation.

This is a topic-based, not chapter-based book, so I may repeat what I said in earlier topics because I want each topic to be self-sustaining. This is a strait to the point no filler book, I tried to put the topics in an order that work together, but all the topics were written separately as I felt led to write them. This book was written in spurts all around the nation over a period of about 15 years. If you want to know what the book is about, the easiest way is to go through the chapters list (topics).

I intend for this book to be free or close to it (basic costs) so feel free to copy it or download my book at www.dieingtoself.com under the download link.

Love one another

Did you learn to Love? You are not born with it, you must learn it. Jesus spoke of loving one another, but do we remember His words, it's easy to just brush over this scripture and not think a second thought. The Lord's final words were: "This is my commandment, that you love one another, even as I have loved you" John 15:12. When Jesus was asked what is the most important command, Jesus said, "Love God and Love your neighbor as yourself. That there was no greater commandment than these," Mark 12:30-31. There is an experience that Bob Jones had where He went to see Jesus and was in the line of saints to talk to Him. The only question Jesus would ask each person was did you learn to Love. Each could see their lives and the answer to that question. One had a lot of angels around them and did great things while on earth they said yes and went into heaven and had great rewards, the next one was showed their life and said yes I learned to Love. Then there was a woman who became widowed at a young age. She loved the Lord but never shared that love with others and grew bitter because of it. She said: "only you Lord." Jesus said, you are saved by grace, but have no rewards. (paraphrased)

Bob said you are not born with love. You must learn it, so learn it! Listening to this challenged me, that all Jesus would say is "Did you learn to Love." If your life was measured at this very moment, how would you do? This challenged me to rethink how I related to others. I have read when Jesus said Love one another before, but I didn't really realize what it meant. This challenged me in how I treated people around me, and how I view people that are not commonly accepted. I think how would Jesus treat them? God Loves this person, like in the area of homeless. It made me think why am I like this, so when I see a homeless person I don't think, I hope He doesn't see me, or I can't wait till we're out of here, I feel for them.

Rick Joyner had an experience where he made an off comment about a homeless person. Then had a heavenly experience later in His life where Jesus introduced Him to that same homeless person. He ended up being one of the greatest in heaven because He learned to Love. In His dying moments was trying to keep an elderly woman warm in the cold. This changed His perspective on how He viewed different people. This has revolutionized how I think of other people, not to judge them by their external looks. Love is demonstrated by your actions. Do you help those in need? Actions speak louder than words, and you will be rewarded in heaven according to how great your love was.

I recently had a situation that happened to me. I am a rock collector and I was staying at a condominium. I had picked some local rocks and found many unique rocks; I collected a bit of a bag full. Later the rocks were sitting under the tire of our car, but a worker at the resort took the bag, not thinking much of it. I was a little slow about getting to ask them about it. When I finally did, they looked into it and said they had thrown them in the dumpster, and it was gone already. I was greatly irritated; I didn't say much to them, but I had to let it go. Then a week or two later, I was informed that one of the cleaning people decided to collect some rocks from the area and give from their personal collection. As soon as I heard they did this for me without me even knowing about it, I felt a deep sensation that I don't know if I've ever felt. I felt penetrated with love. It was a moment of clarity, I felt loved. It took me completely by surprise, and I said to myself, I feel loved. This awoke my spirit, this is what love is; it's not the love that takes, it's the love that gives. Willing to go out of our way to love; to go the extra mile, and do something with someone just for love's sake. This is a deep love that Jesus wishes for us to have. Love one another! Love one another by being their servant, involve yourself in what they are interested in, and take the time to help them in their time of need. This is what love is, the love that gives. I can't say that I've mastered this myself, but it was a big wake-up call. The whole reason for this life and what God is interested in is people. So we should realize this and Love one another.

I've heard from many sources that David is your humble servant in heaven. He often shows people things and shows them around, saying we are your servants. This is what love is, the love that serves, the love that gives. These are some of the greatest men who ever lived, and yet they are your servant. Like Jesus said: those who wish to be the greatest should become a servant. There is such humility in that I am astounded.

John 13:12-15 "So when He had washed their feet, taken His garments, and sat down again, He said to them, "Do you know what I have done to you? You call Me Teacher and Lord, and you say well, for so I am. If I then, your Lord and Teacher, have washed your feet, you also ought to wash one another's feet. For I have given you an example, that you should do as I have done to you."

This is probably not referring to literally washing another person's feet. Washing of the feet in the Bible was a necessary thing because they probably wore sandals, and their feet got dusty. It was the lowly servant's job to wash the feet of the people in the house. Peter's response to this was: "You shall never wash my feet!" because he felt this was too lowly for Jesus to do this to him. After Peter understood it, he allowed it. Are you getting it now? The Love that gives. This demonstrates the type of love that we should have.

We are all seeking love, whether you realize it or not. Everyone, young and old, even teenagers, seeks love and acceptance from their fellow peers and will do almost anything sometimes to obtain it, change their entire person, just to be loved. They won't call it that, but this is what it is.

There was this child in Canada whom I spent some time with; all she required was that I spend some time with her. I played in the mud making mud cookies, she did something that I didn't expect; she felt so comfortable with me that she came to me while we were all sitting down and sat near me holding on to me. She without realizing it, wanted love and attention. It is built into us to want love, but when we get older, we don't ask for it. We just accept what we've been given and go on. But we still inside, we need and *require love.*

Dying to self

The Lord longs for His people to come to Him in Spirit and in Truth, and to set a people set apart. He wants a willing heart to rid anything that would get in between you and Him. This is not a mandatory process, but a voluntary one. The Lord will bring you to the door, but you must walk through it. Are you willing to walk the deeper walk with Him? There are great benefits that come with that walk, but it requires dying to self. This is a step-by-step process that by no means will God ask you to do all in one step. He will show you one thing at a time that needs to be dealt with. He will give you time to work it out of your life; then He will show you another thing. The reward is much greater than the sacrifice.

Benny Hinn says: "quit trying and just surrender"! Dying to self is different for each person and will require different things. The closer you get to Him, the purer you will become, and the more intense the light becomes to expose any darkness that might be in you.

It says in Lev 19:2 "You shall be holy: for I the Lord your God am Holy." Jesus says in Matt 5:48 "Therefore you shall be perfect, just as your Father in heaven is perfect." Eph 1:4, Eph 5:27, Lev 20:26. He will not let you progress any further spiritually until you deal with the issue He shows you. God wants you to be Holy as He is Holy. He longs for you to be closer to Him. It pleases Him greatly when you make sacrifices for Him, but don't try too hard, or you will sacrifice things God might not have asked you to. He will reveal it to you.

Dying to self is the prerequisite to true authority. If you are willing to sacrifice your life for Him and live for Him, then He can truly trust you with more. More than likely, He will ask you to give up things that pollute your Spirit, or simply things that are in between you and Him, and things that are more important than Him.

Eph 4:22-24 "That ye put off concerning the former conversation the old man, which is corrupt according to the deceitful lusts; and be renewed in the spirit of your mind; and that ye put on the new man, which after God is created in righteousness and true holiness."

Bless and Don't Curse

If someone says something against you, ridicules you or does evil against you, don't turn and do the same to them. Because you are using the same evil to get them back. It's like trying to fight fire with fire, it only will multiply the damage. That person who did something to you basically has pain in their heart. If you turn around and curse them, you are not affecting any real change but are hurting them further. You are using the enemy's power right back at them. "Two wrongs don't make a right"; it's like throwing gasoline on the fire.

Instead of using the enemy's power, use God's power, which is love and healing. The problem needs to be resolved; the real solution is to get the pain in their heart healed. How do you get your pain resolved? Are trying to resolve it by getting them back and hurting them? This may make you feel better, but what you really need to do is go to the Lord to get your healing instead of multiplying pain in others. If someone curses you, consider it a blessing, because it gives you the spiritual authority in that situation to pray for their pain, that they might be healed. But try to work it out if you can.

It says in Matt 5:44 "I tell you, Love your enemies, bless those who curse you, do good to those who hate you, And pray for those who mistreat you and persecute you, bless those who curse you and pray for those who despitefully use you." Pray for them that their heart would be healed. If you consider this scripture, doesn't it seem that Jesus is suggesting this? I think He knows that trying to hurt someone who is already hurt solves nothing. What resolves this is love and healing. We're looking at the root of the matter and the reason behind it. Some people have had terrible lives, and they strongly need Jesus to heal them because they have pain multiplied in their hearts. Don't make it any worse by doing evil against them. The Lord wants to teach you something that will make you stronger in the Spirit. How to bless those who curse you, and pray for those who despitefully use you.

God's power is infinitely more powerful than the enemy's power. If you curse them, you are only hurting that person more, and they will hurt the next person. Because hurting people, hurt people.

Speak Positive

Many do not realize it, but words do have power, in either a good or bad way. Because we have God-given authority in the earth. What you speak forth can either bring a positive or negative result. If you speak positively, then God can take those words and bless them, because you're professing positive. It's like having faith, you are professing it into reality. If you speak negatively, then the devil can take those words and curse the situation; this is a lack of faith. If out of your mouth you are speaking forth negative, you're then using the enemy's energy over that situation. Because the enemy's power is destruction, and you're cursing the situation with your words. That is why many poor people who speak negatively over everything don't succeed. They have already determined in their mind that it's doomed to failure, and speak accordingly. Because those words are of his energy, he can carry those words out. It says, "Life and Death are in the power of the tongue" Prov 18:21, 1Peter 3:10, Prov 15:4. So don't give the enemy the opportunity, because he will use it.

God gave the authority of the earth to man, this goes in to the spiritual too. So if you're using your authority to give the devil access, then he will have access via your words or actions. What you speak forth, is what you're professing over the situation, whether it's blessing or cursing it. Not only because the enemy can take those words and use them, but because you have given up hope for that situation. If you're speaking positively, the Holy Spirit, who is of a positive nature, and divinely smarter, can think of solutions that you could never have dreamt of.

If you speak negatively, it grieves the Holy Spirit. You are saying your inadequacy is greater than God's adequacy. When you speak positively over a situation, God can take those words and bless the situation. He can't do that if you have already given up by speaking negatively.

It's not just bad situations that negativity can affect. If you speak negatively over something just because it's moving slow or not working as you want it to, you're cursing it, and a curse will come upon it. Bless it instead, praise God for it. You will also have an optimistic attitude toward it, and that is when solutions come. Another thing is don't complain or murmur because that also is negative energy. Don't be a problem finder, be a problem solver.

Honor your word, what you say is what you do

You may be surprised to hear that often, Christians will say they will do something, but will end up not doing what they said, even if it was with good intentions. Leaders of ministries and Christian works often know this fault well, and is more common than not. Sure things can happen in life, but you should go to the person or ministry and get a release from them.

God challenged me one day saying: "honor your word," do what you say. So I try to be careful what I agree to; or be careful how I word it. Matt 5:37 "let your 'Yes' be 'Yes,' and your 'No,' 'No.'"

There are many Christians that work better when they're being paid money. If it's voluntary, then they feel they can treat their word and situation casually, as if their word isn't that important. God wants us to honor our word.

What got me was in a vision someone had who visited heaven. Jesus said He does not say His words casually. He weighs out every word like on one of those old scales. On one side, words said and on the other side the completing of those words, like grains of sand. He also said, "My word will not return void to me; every word I say will be fulfilled," Isaiah 55:11. Do your words return void unto you, do your words fail? What you say is what you should do. If not then get a release from the person you gave your word to.

Be honorable to your word the best you can, even in the smallest detail. I have seen Christians casually say: I will do this or do that, then not do it. Even though it was in their power to do so, making up an excuse why it was okay. Our integrity is failing, we need to be pure and honor our word. There are so many Christians who don't think much about honoring their word; not worrying about if their word fails them. You degrade yourself when your word returns void unto you. You are in effect are being dishonest; this affects your spiritual integrity.

In my earlier walk, I did the same till one day I realized this. So I honor my word the best I can. I also try to word things in a way that if I by chance fail, then my word will not have failed. So perhaps this is the issue. You want to at first, but then something comes up and causes you not to. But still, your word fails, ask for a release from the person you gave your word to.

I have even seen some Christians just lie to you because it's more convenient to say they will do it than later not do it. Some will even make covenants with God and break them.

I read in a book about a man who went before the judgment seat. He said if you will do this for me Lord, then I will do differently. Then God showed him all his covenants with Him in the past and said, "you have promised before." Showing all his covenants in live form in front of him, how he had one way or another managed to break each one. It's one thing to break covenants with man, but another with God.

I have seen one person use it to their benefit in making money, then breaking a covenant. Not intentionally, but making up a justification why he could do that and still be okay with God. It ended up he was concerned more about offending certain people, rather than God. This was not an average person. He walked and talked with God, and God showed him great favor and even small miracles.

Another example is someone saying I'll call you at this time, then fail to call or do it at all. Of course, they have an excuse why not, but still the fact remains that their word failed. And that the other party was expecting you and waiting on you and having to change plans to stay available. Or in other situations, expect that someone is going to do something and then have to compromise because they failed to honor their word.

Yes, some valid things come up, but please release the other person from their expectations of you. Or try to honor your word if you can. You should also be on time; it's like an agreement. If you fail, then others have to compromise on your behalf. Plan ahead and think of all the things that need to be done, and set the appropriate amount of time to get to an agreed time. Yes, things happen but plan for what can be planned for.
Numbers 23:19 "God is not human, that He should lie, not a human being, that He should change His mind. Does He speak and then not act? Does He promise and not fulfill?" Psalm 89:34 "I will not break my covenant, nor alter what my lips have uttered." The point I'm trying to get at is Christians being slippery with their word, being unreliable.

Many times I have seen that people's families trump God. We were with some people, and God wanted to do something in the area, or to minister to them. Their family was coming so that trumped what God wanted to do, so they didn't. Their family coming to town was more important than what God wanted to do. Who is more important, family or God? People often like to fit God in when it's convenient for them, saying: God understands that I need to do this or do that. Sometimes He wants your undivided attention. What if

God has a mission for you to complete that is utterly important to do right now? It could be the enemy sending you the distraction to derail you from God's purpose. You need to get your priorities straight; God will move on from you. You may even miss your high calling because you put other things ahead of Him.

Foolish Spending

It depends on where you are in your financial situation that would determine what's wise and what's not. But what I often see is a person with a lack of finances, spending it unwisely. This may be you! You may even be in a fairly comfortable situation where you have an okay amount to get by on. But what I have noticed in many situations, is a person buying things or services that you could get cheaper or live without. Food is a big one; buying all the name brands or just plain expensive foods. If you're in a financial pinch, you need to determine what you need, not just what you want.

Sure something's are just simply expensive, and to get them you have to pay the money, but do you really need it. You could also save money by not buying the name brands. Some people say they have to buy organic for their health, you could grow a garden. Or go to a farmer's market.

If you're tight on money, you need to examine even the smallest things that you buy in all areas of your life and reconsider if it can be cut out. Do you really need it? Be real, and not after you're broke, but before. You need to project the future financial result. Another thing is that sometimes stores will have a clearance/scratch and dent section. I read somewhere once if you see something you use a lot of, buy extra and stock up for future savings. It's not only food that's an issue, services and items can also. I'm not saying that you can't have fun money, just not excessively so, and to fit your budget.

I know someone who was in a definite financial pinch, that decided he needed to go on a riverboat ride for 200 dollars. Being he was financially limited, this was foolish. He definitely didn't need it! I have heard of this referred to as obsessive compulsive or in other words: I really want it, so I'm going to buy it, Last-minute decisions, and on the spur of the moment compulsive buying. Luke 12:15 (ESV) "Take care, and be on your guard against all covetousness, for one's life does not consist in the abundance of his possessions."

I know another person who had a unique situation with the IRS, and they had made a major error, off of a unique situation that the IRS didn't know all the facts. But the person was too scared of the IRS and decided to just pay it instead of fighting it. This wasn't small either; it took some years to pay. It was a real simple matter and obviously misunderstood, where if it was presented to the IRS, they would have changed it (if you don't know what you're doing then get professional help).

You are poor because you choose to be poor, by poor decisions. Sometimes there are alternatives for what we often pay for, sometimes things are offered for less or free for a similar service. Also, you don't always need to buy things new, you could maybe buy it used. One option is eBay, Craig's list, garage sale, or Goodwill. Sometimes people are giving things away free in your area via Craig's list or Freecycle.

Another problem people have is to be negative; calling things junk, or feel if something slight goes wrong with it, drop it and buy new. Have a positive attitude! Is it possible to still use the old for your needs? Are you mechanical? Try taking it apart and try to fix it yourself (proceed at your own risk). Do you have a cell phone? Do you pay for cable TV, internet? Do you need it? Every small amount helps! Evaluate _every_ monthly cost, do you need it, or can get it cheaper by another means, it will add up!

Do you have a new car or a car payment? I can understand the easiness of having a new car, but it sure costs. If you could afford to buy a slightly older one, maybe you could take the car payment you're paying now and set it aside each month for possible repair costs; just something to consider.

Also, consider the services that you pay for occasionally; do you have to do it in class, or is it possible to consider a cheaper solution. You need to start trusting God's ability to get your needs and wants. Just ask Him for something you need and seek His answer. You have not because you ask not, so ask! I have applied this to my life. I often will put off buying something and just say: God could you get me this. You need to recognize that God works in mysterious ways, so it might come in a way that you might not expect, and it may take some time. You need to trust God's ability to provide for your needs, not trust your ability.

People will often run up their credit cards and say God will pay it off. But what you don't realize is you are using your ability to buy. Maybe God wants to provide in a unique way. I ran across a person that has run their credit to the max, and I heard God say to me, "they do not trust in my ability to provide for them." It's very easy to just buy it, but God doesn't always do it that way. People will say that they are having faith that God will pay off their credit, but maybe God wants to just give it to you in a different way, maybe He wants you to have faith in His ability. Each situation is different, but credit cards are generally your ability. This is not always true, you need to seek God in each situation, and ask Him how to proceed.

This is basic training for you to learn faith and to seek God in each situation, maybe not being so credit-heavy. Some people feel that winning the lottery, or getting millions is the answer. But if you're not wise with what you have now, having millions will be an even bigger mess. God wants to train you in the small before He will give you any larger sum, and He knows if you trust your ability or His. If you have a leaky bucket, is the solution to turn the water on faster? What happens after you take the bucket out of the source? It will all leak out, we need to first fix the leaks, then God can fill it.

Now I'd like to take it one step further, Christian ministries can also mismanage their money. Some have the mindset that all new is needed. That can be good and maybe God would do that, but has He made a way for it, and again that's not using your ability of credit to do it. I heard of a situation where a minister asked for more money to do something, and God's reply was use what you have. They did have the equipment to do what they needed, but his mindset wasn't thinking that way. They didn't think to use what they had, they thought they had to get all new to do it. Can you get by with what you have, or do you have a negative mindset toward it? Use what you have until God provides otherwise.

Don't trust in your ability, like spending money you don't have. I know people who say God's children deserve the best and spend money on their credit, but they really can't afford it at all and put themselves into financial strain. Most often, God hasn't asked you to spend money on your credit, and you put yourself into a situation that you can't handle. There are some cases where He will ask you to trust Him in a borrowed money situation, but it's not always the case. You need to be sensitive to His spirit, make sure He would have you do that. This can easily be confused with you telling you that you can do it, or the enemy telling you to do it (See Topic "False Voices that Mislead" page 62). I think people go with this option because it's an instant solution, but that doesn't make it the right choice. Many will go ahead and borrow and think it's God for them to do this, but in fact, it isn't. God may have very well have been in the process of providing for your needs, but you stepped in front of Him blocking Him with your abilities by borrowing from the bank. So His plans have been replaced with yours.

Purity

One day I was at a church service, and I saw this baby that had just a glow about her; you could just see their purity. Her eyes were so expressive of what she was feeling, you could see pure joy in her eyes. I am an observer of eyes, it says in Matt 6:22-23 "The lamp of the body is the eye. If therefore your eye is sound, your whole body will be full of light. But if your eye is evil, your whole body will be full of darkness. If therefore the light that is in you is darkness, how great is the darkness?"

You can tell how much life a person has just by looking at their eyes. I said to myself, this baby has topped them all. I have nowhere seen any eyes that are purer than those. It was because the baby had Godly parents. But not all babies are like this. When I saw these eyes, I saw the Lord's lips say PURITY. I said, oh, you're right. It is because they have not contaminated their soul with a not so pure world yet.

When a baby is born, that baby has not entered into sin and contamination that clouds the soul. They know nothing of it yet, and if they are raised in a spirit-filled environment, then they will keep that purity. As we get older, we start making choices and start the path of complicating our lives. I have observed the eyes of children. Sometimes what I see is more of a vacuum, because they're in a spiritually lifeless environment, and are unprotected from spiritual dynamics. Some adults haven't even learned this yet! But the child doesn't know better. I'm not blaming children for their state of Spirit, they simply don't know better.

I have seen some children respond to the Holy Spirit automatically. It's quite wonderful to watch some of these in a worship atmosphere. I'm referring to a little girl in specific that is probably about 3-4 years old. Jesus said, "Most assuredly I tell you, unless you turn, and become as little children, you will in no way enter into the Kingdom of Heaven. Whoever therefore humbles

Himself as this little child, the same is the greatest in the Kingdom of Heaven" Matt 18:3-4. Because He knew that when we are young, we have more trust in being taken care of; they don't even think about it, and don't have a worry in the world.

The Lord wants us to come back to being like a child because God will take care of us like our parents did. A child doesn't know the dynamics of how their parents provide for them, even when things are going rough, they have no worries about it. God wants us to be the same way. He provides for us despite us knowing the dynamics of how He is going to. The Lord wants you to become as a child in simplicity and purity. We often let the worries of the world get in our hearts and contaminate our peace. We let the sins of this world also contaminate our Spirits because all have fallen short. God wants us to be Holy, "Ye shall be holy: for I the LORD your God am holy" Lev 19:2 Matt 5:48, Eph 1:4 Eph 5:27 Num 15:40 Lev 20:26. Become as that little child that knows nothing of the sins of this world. Separate from this world and the sins of it. Make your way to the path to become as a child again. It's a step-by-step procedure, so keep making steps toward your goal of being holy even as God is holy. The Lord said to me one day, "you have not fallen down the complete mountain; you have only fallen down one step. Keep trying, and you will get past it. Enter the heavens as a child, and you will know no worries, you will not know the things of this world and the things in it, you will only know purity. He says: come walk the path narrow and steep. I will be there with you, come take my hand, And I will show you the way. Come be Holy as I am Holy. Become as a child, and you will know the way.

Don't Contaminate your Spirit

There are many things in this earth, both good and bad, and many shades of grey. You must ask yourself, do the things that you do or participate in contaminate your spirit. If you want to live a Godly life, you should steer away from these things. Do you feel grieved by the Holy Spirit when you participate in that activity? Because if it's questionable, then there is often a demon behind it, and he has been given permission to be there by your participating in it. You are giving him consent to come into your home, and he will take the opportunity to cloud your spirit because you are participating with it.

Some examples would be watching bad things on TV, movies, video games, or the internet that are of a contaminated nature, but it's not limited to these, it could be anything. Is it something that would grieve the spirit of God? If you're in touch with the Holy Spirit, He will grieve your spirit if it's something He doesn't want you to do, but not everyone is in touch with the Holy Spirit unfortunately, Eph 4:30. If you have chosen to ignore Him, then He will leave you in it. Do you feel yucky when you do it? Do you feel any negative emotion when participating in it? If so, this is an indicator that this is something that you should probably stop. Or if you allow your children to do these things, whatever demon is behind it will be allowed access to your property, Because you have authority over that household and you have allowed it in. Eph. 4:22-24 "That ye put off concerning the former conversation the old man, which is corrupt according to the deceitful lusts; and be renewed in the spirit of your mind; and that ye put on the new man, which after God is created in righteousness and true holiness." 2Cor 6:17, Romans 12:2. 2 Corinthians 7:1

Go and Sin no more

Jesus died on the cross for our sins, and we are forgiven if we're repentant. But many bank on this forgiveness and keep going, it can be hard sometimes to rid of our pesky sins, and there is grace for those who are trying to get out of it. God's grace is not meant that we go on sinning and sinning without trying to work out of it, grace is there so that while we're trying to overcome our sins that He will forgive us if we slip up. Romans 6:1-2, 15 "What shall we say then? Shall we continue in sin, that grace may abound? God forbid. How shall we, that are dead to sin, live any longer therein?" 15 "What then? Shall we sin, because we are not under the law, but under grace? God forbid."

I'm reminded of someone I used to work with that was a Christian and swore all the time. I asked why and he said: "no ones perfect." That was his excuse to keep on, making an excuse why it's okay for him to keep on. The key here is that we're trying to become holy and less sinful. Not that we will make excuses why it's okay for us to keep on going in our sins, not to bank on Jesus's forgiveness purposely. The point of this is to Go and sin no more John 8:11. Sure we may slip into the same sin again, but it's that we're trying to get out of that sin and keep trying to get better at it. The key is that we're trying not to sin, this is where grace comes in.

Now if one participates in an unresolved sin, the sin is like a black ball that grows and grows as the sin is further participated with, darkening the soul. The devil makes it a point to try to grow that sin into greater and greater degrees if he is allowed to. The devil rejoices when he can keep a foothold in one's life, because he is actively seeking to destroy the kingdom of light. We are called to be that kingdom of light. There are many layers of sin, like an onion. It's not that we have to be perfect and solve them all at once, but that we're trying to be better. God reveals new layers of sin to us so that we might draw closer to Him. Because the less sin in our lives, the closer we can get to Him. Romans 6:1-2,6,11-12,15

The average Christian

There are three ranks of Christians: the outer court, inner court, and holy of holy. These ranks are dependent upon the level of obedience, spiritual purity, and spiritual maturity of a Christian. Just like in one of Rick Joyner's final quest books, it mentioned 3 armies. In this topic, I will be talking about the outer court Christian. Which truthfully is most of the church. Like Rick Joyner's 3 armies, the biggest army was the most destructive army, which destroyed everything the first 2 built. These Christians will say that they're close to God, but in reality, they are far from Him. They feel that reading the Bible, memorizing scriptures, going to church, and maybe participating in the church is what's required to be close to God. These could describe someone close to God, but it's more than just these things alone. There can even be pastors that have dedicated their lives to God, and most of what they do is for God. But in reality, they have no real relationship with God. It's based on their intellect and not their heart and spirit.

I have a friend that asked Jesus for a fresh parable. So Jesus told her a parable (paraphrased): God owns a hardware store, and He has many workers in this hardware store outside, inside, and office. The outer group was the biggest, the inner was lesser, and the office was the smallest group. Most were just interested in doing the work of the store. So much so that they never came to the office to see what God really wanted. The inner group walked by and waved, they were just so caught up in the works. But God wanted them to spend time with Him and see what He would have them do, to be personal with Him, rather than just working the store.

People are more wound and worked up about doing the works of God that they lose track of having a personal relationship with Him. One can invent all sorts of things to do for God, but is that what God would have them actually do. The key is to have a real relationship. So the pastor and average Christian alike can be a part of this destructive 3rd army, and be more of a liability than an asset. The reason I say these things is because many Christians think they're deep and wonderful Christians, but in fact, they are part of this destructive 3rd army. Make sure that you're doing works that God would have you do, otherwise, these works could be of your own doing or invention, or even an invention of the church. What you need to do is get in touch with the Holy Spirit, and have Him tell you rather than have you tell you, or your church tell you. Seek and you will find, knock and it will be answered unto you.

Now I would like to talk about the passive or inert Christian, who is content with just be saved and going to heaven. This is not the point of life. What is the point for Him to put us on this earth so we can just barely eek by spiritually and be a stagnated Christian?

Revelation 3:14-22 "And unto the angel of the church of the Laodiceans write; These things saith the Amen, the faithful and true witness, the beginning of the creation of God; I know thy works, that thou art neither cold nor hot: I would thou wert cold or hot. So then because thou art lukewarm, and neither cold nor hot, I will spue thee out of my mouth. Because thou sayest, I am rich, and increased with goods, and have need of nothing; and knowest not that thou art wretched, and miserable, and poor, and blind, and naked. I counsel thee to buy of me gold tried in the fire, that thou mayest be rich; and white raiment, that thou mayest be clothed, and that the shame of thy nakedness do not appear; and anoint thine eyes with eyesalve, that thou mayest see. As many as I love, I rebuke and chasten: be zealous therefore, and repent. Behold, I stand at the door, and knock: if any man hear my voice, and open the door, I will come in to him, and will sup with him, and He with me. To him that overcometh will I grant to sit with me in my throne, even as I also overcame, and am set down with my Father in His throne. He that hath an ear, let him hear what the Spirit saith unto the churches."

Many say that they are okay with the Lord, but as the scripture suggests:

they are in fact wretched, miserable, poor, blind, and naked spiritually. God is looking for a real relationship with you. One where He talks to you personally all day long, and instructs you in even the smallest of matters. You may not think this, but He's more than willing to help you with the dumb stuff. It's the relationship that He's after; He wants a real one with you.

There are many Christians who let the cares of this world wash over them and pollute them. This puts them at a greater distance from the Lord because they have chosen to participate in the unclean thing. When you get closer to Him, these things can not exist. The bad things of this world pollute our spirits. Luke 8:14 "And that which fell among thorns are they, which, when they have heard, go forth, and are choked with cares and riches and pleasures of this life, and bring no fruit to perfection."

Also, their personal time with the Lord could be lacking because maybe if they do have prayer time, they might be excited to get done with it and go onto whatever they had planned next. This isn't good because you're just going through the motions just to satisfy that you did it, with not much heart into it. God is not into us just going through the motions, He wants our undivided attention. He wants to have a real relationship with you. I've had to work on this in some ways myself.

But now there's the Christian who considers themselves serious about God and discuss the things of God here and there, but their lives are super busy with other things. They are so busy doing their own business; even the works that they think are of God, are in fact are their own inventions. The key here is an active and open relationship with God. For them to empty themselves of the world, that they might hear the small voice that speaks. They are deaf to it because their minds are so active with other things. It's never too late in this life to turn and open the door to Him and to even become an overcomer if you were so inclined.

What I'm saying is: wake up lazy Christians! He loves you and wants you to wake up and come into your own Revelation 3:19. It's not too late to wake up and become alive in His spirit. Wake up dead Christians, wake up those who think they have a deep relationship with God but are in fact spiritually sleeping. Wake up you sleepers! Wake up, you who have invented your own path to Godliness. Wake up, you pastors who are more interested in doing the works of God rather than having a live and real relationship with the King. Who are more interested in working in God's hardware store, and doing the works they think God is to have them do rather than checking in with Him to see what He would have them do. Don't be negligent and miss God.

Faith

God's ways are not our ways, His thoughts are not our thoughts. We see what needs to come forth, and we formulate in our mind how it will come forth. Sometimes things work out easily, and sometimes it takes time for it to come forth. We need to be patient with God and His ways. You need to just keep your faith constantly in the faith position, and weed your garden of faith of doubts, because doubts will hinder faith. You need to think outside of the box because sometimes God will do it differently than you think. I think that time is all one to Him and that He exists in time at all points at the same time. Every single moment every single second, Omnipresent. Imagine for a moment if you could see the past, present, and future as God does. Seeing the future and what would happen; being able to maneuver the future to the desired result. This is what He does; you need to view things like this. He takes what would seem like an insignificant factor and can turn it in your favor. God sees all these factors, the entire picture, things that you can't see! God loves faith, He wants you to trust Him; this is a big factor for Him. God gave authority over the earth over to humans; that includes all authority. He likes to do this, but He will not thwart what authority He gave us. If we give up, then He can't do anything, because we have the authority in our hands over the earth. If we don't stand in faith, God will not force it, because He has given dominion over the earth to all mankind. So with this understanding, He requires us to give the authority back to Him, letting Him work through us. We just need to stand in faith, believe, and be patient for His plan to unroll. His ways are not our ways. God can take an impossible situation and use an insignificant factor to turn it around. God sees all and maneuvers whatever factor is required to complete the task. We need to give Him our faith to get the desired result.

A phrase I like to say to myself is step out of the boat and walk on the water. Or jokingly to myself, I like to step out of one boat into another boat, then another, and another. Because I tend to recreate another scenario in my mind of how God is going to do it after the change of events. When that doesn't work out, I have to step out of my newly created boat to another boat that I create for myself. When will you just step on the water and just trust God! It's okay to think about how God might do it, but just don't be disappointed if it doesn't come true. When it doesn't, just keep going even if it seems impossible.

Another thing that people do is try to make it happen for God. They come against a wall then panic, and try to figure out a way to make it work. They haven't given God a chance to come through, so they make their own way. This isn't trusting God, it's trusting yourself, and your means. You might say: well maybe God gave me this opportunity, so I took it. Like one person I ran across ran up their credit card to 100,000; this is them trusting their ability. Or maybe taking out a bank loan, you really have to feel it out, is God in this, or is this your invention. You need to ask God to show you clearly how you are to proceed but be careful there is a fine line in it, you need to make sure God is in it, or you will be doing things in your abilities, not God's. When you do this, God has to step aside until you're willing to seek His way and abandon yours. Then He will have to fix your big mess, where you might have to bend around backward to get back to where you should be. Maybe even uncomfortable decisions like reverse what you just did!

If you trust Him, He might do it in a way that might seem like He's not doing it, but you need to keep trusting that He is doing it in His unique way. He might do it in a completely backward way; He knows what He's doing. If you think about the world around us, if you were able to see the future and possible futures, you could keep trying different possibilities until it worked. Possibly even the weirdest factor could make it happen. It's like when one is trying to invent something, they will try different things until it works; sometimes even funny things make it work. But God doesn't need to keep trying, He knows what will work, it might be funny, but it works!

Think about ancient examples like Moses, David, Joseph, Jacob, Abraham, and probably many more. Moses was at the red sea, we know what happens, but for a moment consider what it would be like to be in that situation. God told you to do a military blunder, go to the sea and wait for instructions; you are cut off from escape. God didn't tell them what he was going to do, but they did what He asked of them. So then next they knew the Egyptians are now on top of them, about to overtake them. This looks like they are defeated, and God messed up, but God had plans for them. If you think about it, if the

Israelites would have gone any other direction, then the Egyptian army would have overtaken them and took them back. But God saw the future and knew that He needed to deal with this army, so God devised how to destroy them. Imagine being at the sea with no escape, it would seem like God had failed and would be unnerving. He didn't tell them what was going to happen; they found out right when the army was right on top of them. Then God at the last possible moment came through. He opened up the sea at just the right moment. It would be unnerving wondering; will this wall of water fall on me? Will the army catch up and get them? I'm sure a few would probably be thinking these things. But God had everything timed out perfectly, and He took care of their pursuers. It was an amazing miracle!

 Now God told David he was going to be the king of Israel, but it sure didn't happen overnight did it. It took longer than you think. First off, Saul is still king, and not willing to budge. David had to be driven into the wilderness away from any power to take over, which wasn't his intention but God's intention. They were banished and pursued by Saul's armies and had to hide in caves, a definite humbling factor. So we all know how the story worked out, God took care of Saul, and now he was out of the picture. But the scripture you may have forgotten or missed is that David only took kingship over Judah and a few others at first. The others were still trying to make Saul's descendants king. David was a king yes, but only over a small portion of Israel. It says that he had to wait 7 years until the rest of Israel came to accept him. Don't minimize this; think about waiting 7 years before God's full plan came through. It sure didn't seem like it was going to come through. It would seem at the time that it wasn't happening. We tend to see the whole story, and brush over this type of detail but imagine what it was like to go through it. There are many examples in the Bible that show the type of faith they required, but because we see the entire story, we may miss it.

 Joseph had dreams of a powerful position when he was a young man. It was symbolism and didn't make sense then, but it made sense later. He was sold into slavery. Imagine the hopelessness of that; it would seem like your life is over, and you're stuck in slavery. God worked the situation around. First off to be purchased by a very top position Egyptian. We're probably talking 2nd in command here I think. Then later to gain favor, and bring him into their house and become the head of his household. This started his reputation of God being with him. Then when things were looking really good for him, he gets thrown into jail for something he didn't do, talk about discouraging. He had to be in that prison for 7 years, he didn't know what God was doing. Would he be there the rest of his life? He didn't know. Be content in whatever situation you are in. Joseph had to trust God that He knew what He was doing. God sometimes has to take us to our wilderness so that we die to self first. Then by a miracle, God made Joseph second in command above his former master Potiphar. That is a miracle beyond miracles. On top of that, he was planning for a drought that was to start in 7 years. Think about the faith that required; wondering, what if God didn't come through? He would probably be hurled from office for being wrong. Joseph had to trust God to come through over circumstances that were out of his control.

How amazing this is to be the lowest slave in the kingdom to becoming 2nd in command of Egypt. God maneuvered Joseph, through various steps, and He can maneuver you as well if you will let Him. If you notice, God knew all of this even before Joseph was even sold into slavery, by the given dream. So God had it all planned out even before it happened!

Now Jacob had to be stripped of all wealth and start from scratch, even be tricked. God weaved Jacob through his circumstances to become very wealthy even though dealing with a crafty and tricky businessman. Then when he came back to his brother, he could have been killed. But His brother had mercy on him and God blessed him and his life after that.

Abraham, think of God asking you to go into the wilderness to a place He will show you. Complete faith in God, not knowing the circumstances. God told him that he would have a son and that He would make a great nation out of him. But Abraham tried to make it happen for Himself and decided to have a child with another woman, but this was a manmade solution. Abraham should have just trusted God to come through. God later had to sort out his mess and come up with the real solution by giving him Isaac. So we need to be careful to not create our own Ishmaels. Trying to work out the details for God. Where it is in fact a big mess that God has to clean up and do it His way anyways.

Also, Think of Israel when they had to fight impossible battles, God told them what do to.

I recently had to go through a major test of faith in major real estate with the ministry I am a part of. God doesn't always do it the way you think. He's going to do it, you just have to be patient with Him! Go with His flow, and He will show you the path. Remember He sees all, you just have to trust in that, be at peace, and try to do what He leads you to do.

    Now we had the opportunity to get a bank loan, but we didn't feel that was the right thing to do. That would be trusting in our ability, not God's. So we skipped that and trusted God to come through. You might be thinking, God was making an opportunity, and you were supposed to take it; maybe, but not in this situation. We all felt it wasn't God's way in this situation. It was the easy way out, but God had other plans. We did ask God if that was what He wanted, but we all felt it wasn't. You need to listen to the feeling of it, do you feel at peace, does it seem like what God would do, are you sure the peace is not just your flesh being happy about an instant solution. You need to listen to your gut feeling, make sure it's not your flesh. There is a fine line between spirit-led and flesh-led; you need to differentiate the difference. Or you may think you know how to be led by the Holy Spirit, but in fact are not, it can be tricky to learn. The enemy wants to confuse the matter, so he always is trying to speak into the situation. You need to learn what voice is speaking, because the enemy wants to thwart anything of God.

    Now I'd like to share a situation that just happened to me recently. I was traveling in ministry, and I was outside in a remote public place. I had my wallet in my pocket, and I was very active. Then I went back and didn't realize I had dropped my wallet in this remote, unpopulated field. We had moved on from that area, but we felt to go to a specific town after a few days, and I then looked for my wallet but couldn't find it anywhere. So I gave up on it and gave it to God to continue looking for it another time. So I went about my day, and then in just about an hour or two, we got a call from the police that they had my wallet. So we arranged to get it, and I got my wallet back. But the thing is, I didn't know I had lost my wallet until just a few hours before the police called. We were also in the exact town that the wallet was delivered, which was about 15-20 miles from where the wallet was lost. It was lost in an area that wasn't very active at all, so it was a miracle that it was found. This situation strengthened my faith, because God knew this was all going on without my knowledge. He was orchestrating all of this in the invisible. And I only noticed that I lost it just a few hours before the police called. It was so well-timed and exactly coordinated, that I was in awe of it. This incident made me believe in God's ability to do things in the unknown to me. It was so well coordinated and timed that I knew that God had it in His hands. So it strengthened my faith that God is able to do things that I am completely unaware of. We all need to become aware of God's abilities to do things for our situation, all you need to do is believe.

Another thing that happened to me is one time I wanted a computer card game, and I was willing to buy it from the internet, but I only had so much money. There was something else that I needed to buy for ministry purposes, so instead of buying that game, I bought the ministry item. The funny thing is soon after that, I saw this exact cd game on a cereal box; all I had to do was buy cereal! So I viewed this as God getting my heart's desire in a very unique way. God is mysterious, He works in the invisible realm.

It's just like when Moses went to the red sea, it didn't make any sense, but since God saw the future, He devised a way to get them out of that mess before it even happened. Think about Joseph he was a slave promoted to head of household, then put in prison, then to become the 2nd in command of Egypt. If you were in these situations; what would you be thinking if you were being dragged away as a slave? It would seem pretty hopeless, and after that, you were falsely accused of something and put in prison. Think about being in that prison, it would seem like your time is done. Yet God was working in the background, working out the details without Joseph even knowing.

What I'm trying to paint a picture of is: God is mysterious, and His ways are mysterious. Even though it might seem like things are not working your way, God is bigger than the circumstance. He can turn things around in mysterious ways. The answer might show up mysteriously and unexpectedly, and in an unconventional manner. Even though you might think you're working with nothing. God is in the mysterious and the invisible. Have some faith, I read that is all you have to do is, only believe.

Mark 11: 23-25 "Truly I tell you, if anyone says to this mountain, 'Go, throw yourself into the sea,' and does not doubt in their heart but believes that what they say will happen, it will be done for them. Therefore I tell you, whatever you ask for in prayer, believe that you have received it, and it will be yours. And when you stand praying, if you hold anything against anyone, forgive them, so that your Father in heaven may forgive you your sins." Psalms 115:16

Waiting for God to come through

There might be something that God said He will do for you. He may have shown you what He is going to do in many ways. And you get your hopes up and are expectant of it happening. And sometimes time passes by, and it hasn't happened yet, but you are still expectant. Each situation is different, and the dynamics as well. Don't make your own invention to solve the problem; we need to be patient with Him. He might be trying to work something else out before it's possible to have it come forth (See topic "Faith" page 26). Only God knows all the dynamics and will do according to those dynamics. I have experience in the matter, because I have been long awaiting something that God has promised to me. He time and time again encouraged me, given dreams, and spoken words to me. Everyone's situation is different, and my situation will probably not necessarily parallel someone else's. He does your situation tailored to you personally. In my situation He wanted me to let it go completely. I had my time of confidence in it, and my time of tears, and my time of getting used to just going on in life, and now my time of completely letting it go. It's a painful thing, but God wanted me to let it go. I have heard of many situations where once someone lets go of that something, then He did it. I'm not saying this is everyone, but it could be you. Some invent their own solution and trust in themselves. God will not stand in your way, but you will have missed the true opportunity. God's ways are not our ways, and His methods are not ours, Isa 55:8. It may take time, He may want you to die to self first before He will do it, or maybe something else, it depends on the situation.

Now I'd like to switch to physical healing. This can be potentially different. I have heard several times about someone seeing a vision of physical healing being delivered by an angel right to the person and was ready to heal them, but they lost their faith in it, and the angel had to take it back. So physical healing could be wavering faith, doubt, or demonic tricks (intensify the issue when they get close to being healed (See Topic "Physical Ailment of a demonic nature" page 159). So the dynamics in healing can be many things, God might be already ready to heal you, but you are getting in the way with your doubts. Or maybe God wants to do it in a different way than what you're thinking; be open to how He would do it. Even if it's an odd way of doing it. Maybe He would heal you slowly. The only job you have to do is "only Believe" I read this in a book about someone visiting heaven and asking about healing, and they said the phrase "only believe" and that it was easier for one to have faith for financial needs than healing. And they just couldn't understand why we doubted it, because it was one of God's promises. Whatever you're asking God to do, your only requirement is to "only Believe" you need to believe and keep believing and stay there.

    He might be waiting on you to do something first, or maybe He's waiting on the situation to be right, to do it, only God knows. You need to keep believing, and try to detach from it as best you can, go on with life, and enjoy it. That's something I had to learn was to just go on with life and let it go. He told me when I let it go, then He can give it to me. I said, okay I let it go in my heart, but now I have literally let it go where I said to God: I give it back to you do with it as you please. Romans 12:12, Psalm 27:14

How Big is God

    This probably can't be measured in a way that we can understand in this lifetime. But I would like to explore His creation, and maybe give you a small glimpse into understanding just how big He is and just how small we really are.

    I would like to start with the super small, then move onto the mind boggling big, then in the next topic, talk about another awesome aspect of God. First off, there is the atom. An atom is a million times smaller than the thickest human hair. Yet it's a very active little thing with all sorts of moving parts and the building blocks of everything. Then there's the ameba, protozoa, bacteria. When I was in school, I brought some swamp water from a pond and looked at it in a microscope. I was mesmerized by the little creatures you could see living in this water that you could only see with a microscope. I watched these things move around and do their thing. Along with many other tiny things you could gaze at through a microscope. That God created the smallest things that all have a purpose and a mind of their own. Then of course there are bugs, one time I saw a set of the tiniest ants that came into the home, and I didn't even realize it was possible. They were 5 times smaller than sugar ants or smaller. There is a reason for all these little creatures. They all serve a purpose in the earth, like earth's little keepers and cleaners.

Everything has a purpose, there is a reason for it all, whether we understand it or not. It all works in unison to keep the earth in balance. If one part of this was missing, it would probably cause problems all the way up the line into big animals and us, maybe even the environment. That God created such tiny little things that move around, and each has their own little mind doing whatever they do.

Then there are plants, take a little tiny seed. How is it possible that this little seed knows how to turn into something super big and knows what to do? It's designed to create whatever its like-kind is. Like a watermelon seed doesn't make a tomato, it always makes a watermelon. The plant that makes these seeds, spits them out like they're nothing. A tiny tomato seed can grow up into a big plant and create hundreds of more seeds and big fruits. How does this little seed know how to do all this? It makes it all out of dirt too. How can dirt turn into this stuff? Dirt also has poisons in it, (like a bad mushroom). This plant knows how to filter out just what it needs and nothing more.

Then moving onto animals, they again all have a purpose and serve the earth in one way or another in the earth's needs, and humans think for a moment how the body works. How is it possible that we remain alive and live? How does a lump of flesh do all this? Can we recreate it? No way! I like to call this God's technology. How is it possible that our brains can store so much information, have our personalities, emotions, and operation of our bodily functions all in just a lump of flesh? It just doesn't make sense how this all works. How is it possible that our hearts keep beating without any thought or concentration on our behalf? How is it possible that just eating food and water gives us all we need to live for 70-100 years? How is it possible that just the nutrients in the food are used to keep us alive? This all seems to have intelligence in itself to know what to do and how to do it. It's because God is amazing and can make stuff like this work. Truly if you think about it, the whole earth is filled with His glory. All of it is glorious, we're just used to it and live with it all the time, but it truly is a glorious creation. Just recently, when I was staring at the stars, I came up with the conclusion that everything everywhere, is a miracle, from the smallest to the largest. Then I had a unique experience just after that, I was cleaning up some papers, and I ran across a tiny piece of paper that had this phrase on it "There are only two ways to live your life. One is as though nothing is a miracle. The other is as though everything is a miracle." - Anonymous. This was amazing, I had just drawn this conclusion, then in a day or so, I run across this paper sitting there for years in a pile of papers. God is amazing how he can make this fragment of a piece of paper come across my path to confirm this to me, immediately after I just made that conclusion.

Now that we have covered the basics, get ready to have your mind blown. You probably have no idea how truly glorious an existence we live in.

Let's move onto earth and space. For a moment, consider if you could drive your car through space at interstate speeds. At this rate, driving 24 hours a day to get to the moon would take 142 days to get there, but if you wanted to sleep and stuff, then probably a year. And it would take a car nearly 4,900 years to get to Pluto, driving 24 hours a day. So that's a little bit too slow so let's go at our current space probe speeds, which I will not include the slingshot effect of going around Jupiter. And I hope you'll forgive me if my math is off, but you get the idea. This time let's make our starting line the sun at rocket speeds of 24,000mph which is 576,000 miles per day and 210,400,000 mpyear. The following is the amount of miles and days it would take for each planet: Mercury (36 million miles) 62.5 days, Venus (67.1 million miles) 116.5 days, earth (92.9 million) 161.3days, mars (141.6 million) 245.8 days, Jupiter (483 million) 2.3 years Saturn (870 million) 4.13 years Uranus (1.1 billion miles) 5.22 years, Neptune (2.8b) 13.3 years and, Pluto 5.9b 28 years. So 28 years to get to Pluto. Now I understand with the Jupiter slingshot, a space probe can get to Pluto in about 9 years.

This is still a little too slow for purposes of traveling outside of our solar systems, so we will have to go a lot faster than this to get anywhere in a timely manner. So the fastest thing that we know of to date, besides God, is the speed of light, which goes 186,282 miles per second, nearly 6 trillion miles per year. It is the current understanding that no one can go faster than the speed of light; time would stand still if you did. The speed limit of the universe.

So let's do a quick warm-up lap around the earth. At the speed of light, we travel around the earth 7.5 times per second. That's around the complete earth in just one second, so you have an idea of how fast we will be moving in space from this point on. Let's make our starting line the sun. The following are the times it takes to get to each planet: 3 minutes to get to Mercury, 6 light minutes to get Venus, 8 light minutes to get to Earth, 12.5 minutes Mars, 43 minutes Jupiter, 1hour 19minutes Saturn, 2hours 40 minutes Uranus, 4 hours 10 minutes Neptune, and 5 hours and 27 minutes to get to Pluto. That's a lot better than 28 years at speeds in our unmanned vessels!

Now let's take a quick look at the sizes of planets and suns in our universe. The following picture is self-explanatory of the grand sizes of objects in the Universe, compared to the size of the earth and our planets. (Picture made by: Dave Jarvis) Creative Commons Attribution-Share Alike 3.0 Unported license.

So in other words, if you shrunk the size of the earth down to the size of one inch and could fit the earth in the palm of your hands, then VY Canis Majoris would be 3.94 miles across and 3.94 miles tall. Do you feel small yet? That's nothing!

Now our solar system (our sun and all our planets) is part of a much grander system called the Milky Way, it's like a massive solar system, but instead of planets, it's other solar systems which are stars with their own planets around them, whirling around at mind boggling speeds. Probably every star you see in the sky has its own solar system.

Let's change it up a bit and pretend we can shrink the size of our solar system down to the size of a quarter (the sun out to Pluto). So it's like you can hold the entire solar system in the palm of your hand. At this scale, the Milky Way galaxy would cover close to 1/2 of the United States.

Take a moment to think about it. Picture a quarter in your hand, then picture half of this United States is the Milky Way, or picture what you would look like on the map to the left. It would literally take 100,000 years to go from

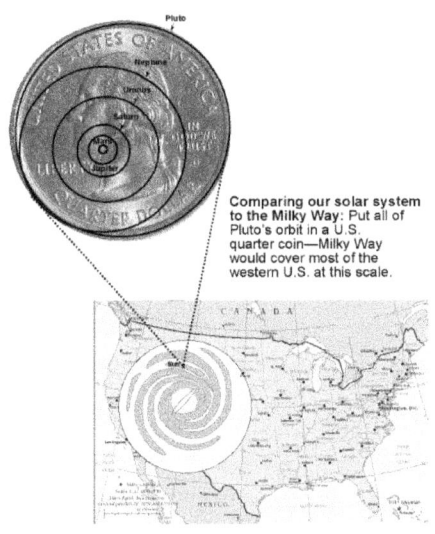

Comparing our solar system to the Milky Way: Put all of Pluto's orbit in a U.S. quarter coin—Milky Way would cover most of the western U.S. at this scale.

one edge of the Milky Way to the other at the speed of light. (This image is courtesy of Nick Strobel at www.astronomynotes.com)

Let's take this one step further and continue moving through the universe. If we shrink the Milky Way galaxy to the size of one inch. Keeping in mind it takes 100,000 years to go that one inch now at the speed of light. At that scale, to travel the distance of your foot, it would take somewhere between 700,000 - 1,200,000 years to travel that distance. At this scale, the entire observable universe, (meaning only what we can see with telescopes, and there is probably a lot more we can't see) would be 14.7 miles. It would take 93 billion years to go from one edge to the other. So for each step you took, it would take you 2.4 million years to travel at the speed of light. Take a walk to the mailbox that took 48 million years. Go for a 1-mile walk, that would take 6.3 billion years to travel. The observable universe is 93 billion light-years across from one edge to the other edge. But we're neglecting one big factor in this 14.7-mile universe; it's not a 2d universe it's a 3d universe, so it's 14.7 miles tall too. It's a 93 billion light-year sphere (3d circle), so it's a lot bigger than you thought. That would be 3,369,282.7 (volume of a sphere) times 93 billion, so 313.3 quadrillion cubic light-years of space. It's kind of like if you were to take a road trip in your car; you're not visiting every inch of the area you're driving through. You're just traveling a 1-dimensional line, and what you can see with your eyes. If you were to travel every single road when you traveled through, it would take you a very long time. On a large scale like this, there could be a billion trillion stars in between the gaps you're not traveling through, or up or down 3 dimensionally.

They say that the objects they see through a telescope could be long gone by now. What we're looking at was something that happened billions of years ago. Even light has trouble traversing these distances. So it's old news, what currently is happening, no one but God and heaven knows.

The reason I write all of this is because this has opened my understanding of God into a whole new realm. He is way bigger and grander than you can possibly imagine. Now think about this, is there a limit to distances in this existence. Can you say the universe is X amount of distance and length across? Is there a limit? Where does it end? Is there an end?

Nasa scanned an area of the sky with the Hubble telescope that is the equivalent to a speck of sand held at arm's length, and what they found is the following picture. What you are seeing in the picture is 10,000 galaxies (each and every light in the picture), not stars but entire galaxies (remember the 100,000-year thing). The area of space appeared dark, so it took the telescope 10 days of exposure to get this picture. (Picture from Nasa)

Astronomers say there are 10 times more suns in the universe than there is sand on all the beaches and deserts on the earth. I also heard if you were to shrink all the galaxies to the size of peas and stacked them on each other, they would fill a basketball stadium full.

If you were to shrink the earth down to the size of a speck of dust (10160 earths in one inch), then the observable universe would be 107.3 billion miles that's like 4.3 billion laps around the earth, or about 11.5 laps from earth to Pluto (23 times the distance). This is still a bit hard to understand, so let's shrink our solar system down to a speck of dust. That would make 1 inch = 12.63 light-years. The observable universe would be 116,184.73 miles, so about 4.6 times around the whole earth. Now, let's put the full universe on your kitchen floor so we get an idea of its distances. If the milky way was a speck of dust, then 1 inch would be 1,016,000,000 light-years (1 billion years to travel 1 inch), then the observable universe would be 7.628 feet. Think about a speck of dust, that it would take 100,000 years to traverse. How many specs of dust do you think you could fit in an area of 7.628 feet?

Like in that picture, if one area of space the size of a grain of sand has 10,000 galaxies. Just think about how many are fully out there. And this is not to mention that this is the observable universe, not the full universe. It could be 10 times larger, or more maybe 1,000,000 times larger. I calculated that you could fit 1,048,772,096,000 specs of dust in a cubic inch (3 dimensions).

Imagine a sphere on your kitchen floor that 7.6 feet tall and 7.6 feet wide, and the Milky Way is a speck of dust. When we think of the universe, we often think 2 dimensionally. It's like trying to fill your bathtub with 1/8 inch of water, but if you think in 3 dimensions, it takes a lot more to fill it. We live in a 3-dimensional existence. Astronomers say there are over 100 billion galaxies in the known universe, and each galaxy contains around 200 billion plus solar systems. Just how Big is our God. If you were to think about His capabilities as in what He created, just that in itself is mind blowing, but I have a feeling that this is just scratching the surface on just how amazing God is.

The Huygens probe landed on one of Saturn's moons in 2005. They discovered drainage channels indicating rushing rivers of methane. To see an image of the surface and a video of its landing do an internet search for Huygens probe landing.

I often like to think about all the stars I see in the sky. Each one of those probably has planets around them, and every single planet is doing its own little thing at this very moment, doing whatever it does. Blowing winds, clouds, rocks sitting there breaking up over long periods of time, rivers, oceans splashing around, maybe even some plant life growing, who knows. It just astounds me to think all this is happening right now, in a billion trillion places all at once, all over the universe!

This topic is intended to be read with the next topic: Eternity Past and Future. Jer 10:12, Psalm 8:3-4, Jeremiah 1:5

Eternity Past and Future

I have been asking God to help me understand Him. I've read that man's mind can't comprehend God; He is not fully understandable. There is no way we can truly in this life understand God. But I asked Him to help me understand the best He can.

He has been showing me a little at a time, and it's still ongoing. But what He has helped me understand so far is this. I will show you by posing a question. Think about eternity past, where is the beginning, was there ever a start? Try to comprehend that! You can't can you? It just seems incomprehensible that there was no beginning. How is this possible? Why doesn't nothing exist? How is it that we exist at all? Can you comprehend it?

Our mind can not! But I believe that God helped me understand it to a point.

God said I AM the beginning and the end. Where did God come from, did something else create Him then who created them, and who created that being, and so on there is no end, it's an endless loop. To make any sense of the matter I had to just simply conclude that God has always existed. It's the only thing that makes sense. But think about it, forever in the past. How is that possible? It just doesn't make sense at all. God doesn't want us to be fearful of it, but to trust Him. It kind of puts me on edge when I think about it. It's a shallow conclusion no doubt, just brushing the surface of the matter. It's much easier to think about eternity future because it hasn't happened yet, but eternity past has already happened. Or has eternity future already happened to? The next conclusion helps you understand this as well.

God exists in time, He lives in time, at least I think He does. He exists in the past, present, and future all at the same time. I AM that I AM, He IS! It's like sitting on a bench; God exists in all of eternity all at once. He exists in every second, minute, hour, century, millennium, eternity. I think He exists at all points in time all at once; at least that's my conclusion, He is time. That's why time is irrelevant because it really doesn't exist in God's realm. If you were able to be in all points in time, would time have any meaning? So perhaps time doesn't exist, we have this bubble of time that we live in, but think of the whole picture of eternity in both directions, perhaps it just is, "I AM," existing outside of time where time doesn't exist, a state of being. So if time doesn't exist, then this explains eternity past better. It's just simply a matter of existing only, not time. I read somewhere God came out of eternity; it's a quality of His character rather than an understanding.

I also believe that God is infinite, which means unlimited everything, no end to His power and majesty. Just like when you think about eternity past that there is no beginning or end to it, He is this way in all aspects of himself. Are you starting to see a small glimpse of God's awesomeness? In someone's heavenly visit, a person in heaven said: you can spend eternities trying to understand God and would just scratch a scratch on the matter. God is so awesome, you can't comprehend Him, at least not yet here in this life, maybe in heaven perhaps. This is why God could see the future even into 400 years into the future for the Israelites. This is why God can see the end of time and speak of it in revelations. Because He is time, He sees it all! Job 37:5

Stay in touch with the Holy Spirit

I have run across someone who said they often don't get to having a prayer, Bible, or God relationship time due to being busy. I know well that time is something that we often have very little of. But what you're doing is setting aside God and going on with your day. I have done this sometimes myself, thinking I'm going onto a project that is God's. Sometimes it's okay under certain circumstances, but generally, you should spend time with Him. Keep in touch with the Holy Spirit, to keep your spirit alive, and receive instructions as well. If we neglect to spend time with Him personally, we will miss Him, and our spiritual life will take a dive. He wants to speak to us, but if we get busy with life, or even busy doing God's work, you set Him aside. We need to have personal time with Him and get to know Him better. It's like having a relationship with your wife or husband, you can do things for them just to do works rather than having a relationship. That doesn't mean you're building the relationship, you are just doing the works of it. It's kind of like buying your spouse jewelry and expecting that to solve your problems.

If you're a super busy person, try to work in some time for God and make it real time with Him, where you are personal with Him, and talk to Him as if He is your friend. Do things that feed your spirit, where you receive life in your heart. Otherwise, you will dry out and get out of touch with Him. He misses you, you know.

You should also have a personal relationship with Him where you talk to Him during the day. Talk to Him as you would a friend. He wants to know you, and for you to know Him. Be open to hearing the Holy Spirit speaking to you at any given moment. Let Him guide you in even the smallest of matters. Someone told me you should be able to hear Him in the small things for you to be able to hear Him in the big things. They were implying that you need to learn to hear Him, nothing is too trivial to hear instructions about, it is training you to hear His voice, and it will be easier to hear Him in the big things. But beware of the enemy's voice, or even your voice can also try to come in and fool you into listening and slowly work a trust in you (See Topic "False Voices that Mislead" page 62)

God doesn't want you working for Him to just do His works, He wants you to spend time with Him, to get to know Him, and see His heart. He wants you to know Him, not to just know about Him. It's one thing to learn and study about someone; it's an entirely different matter to know them personally. And this is what He wants; for you to know Him personally, there is a difference. "I am with you always, even to the end of the age." Matt 28:20, Rev 22:17, Galatians 5:16-18

Prayer

In the beginning, God gave authority over this earth to mankind (men and women). He didn't give it to satan. But through man's authority, satan gained power. Satan has to fool us into using our authority over the earth so that he can have power. If satan wasn't given authority by us, he would have none whatsoever. But this is all mankind, wicked included. This is why witches and warlocks have any influence; they are using their authority in this earth, and are using it for evil. And if they're handing their authority over to satan, then satan has the power to do things.

If satan can use people for bad. Then God can use your authority over the earth for good through prayer. When you pray, you're using your God-given authority in the earth for God. God will not force His way in; He waits upon you to give Him back that authority to do things. He's not going to go around that until He comes back to the earth in the end and sets things straight, but for now, He has given authority over the earth to mankind. When you pray, you're using that authority that God has given you to open up the heavens and work through your prayers to affect change. You are the required ingredient for change to happen because you have the authority.

But there is a limit to this, we have boundaries to our authority, because there are a billion other people in this world that also have authority; each has authority over their properties and their possessions. Like you can't go into the center of New York City and say, I'm speaking to all demons in all of New York you now have to all leave in the name of Jesus, you would get majorly attacked. Sometimes God allows people to do somewhat like things, but it's on God's timing and not before and to a degree. But you have to seek God as to if you're supposed to or not. Because if you do so without authority, you can get what's called backlash. The devil can seriously come against you, potentially physically, so you must be careful what you pray. But sometimes, God will lead someone or a group to do something. And this is strictly off His leading only, not otherwise. This is serious business! But you can pray for people and situations for the betterment.

Prayer is powerful because you're using your authority that God gave to all mankind to work good. You are speaking your authority, and God is then allowed access to come in and do it. Because He's not going to go around that authority He has given you, you have the right to choose. God wants us to pray for one another and situations, then He can come and work in that situation.

Another form of prayer is fasting. This is a much more potent form of prayer, because you're refusing the flesh and seeking the spiritual.

There are also inappropriate prayers, like praying things that are of your will and may not be the Lord's will. You should be careful what you pray and make sure it's not a selfish prayer or your will. Because you're praying contrary to what God would have or want. I am careful about praying my will in prayers, and consider for a moment is this an appropriate prayer. What I do instead is I say to the Lord I request this instead of praying it. If you're speaking to God and asking him to fix it, then that is safe. Because our words do have power, whether to the positive or to the negative.

Another bad type of prayer is one that's implying the power of the enemy or your will, the devil will take the authority that you're granting in that misguided prayer, and will carry out what was said. An example of this is: I was in a church in my youth, and the pastor was talking about a man that did something against them. He literally had the entire church pray a prayer that the man would have physical ailments, and so on; I did not participate. I was disgusted and never went back again. This putrid prayer was witchcraft; witchcraft is using the devil's powers to do bad things. I pray that they will seek forgiveness for such a prayer. I was young in the Lord then, but I might have said something if I was there now.

It's your decision what to proclaim. But whose power are you using God's power of healing, love, and maturing or the devil's power of cursing, and destroying? You are basically using your authority in this earth to release things. That's why witches and warlocks have any power; they're allowing the devil access through their participation to do evil. They are proclaiming bad things with their earth authority. This is also why if you participate in something that you shouldn't, the devil has been given the rights to come in and sit there, because of your participation in it.

If you have prayed or participated in anything that you shouldn't have, then all you have to do is repent of it, and pray for a reversal of your misguided prayer, and stop praying this way.

Eph 6:12 "For we wrestle not against flesh and blood, but against principalities, against powers, against the rulers of the darkness of this world, against spiritual wickedness in high places."

Prayer is powerful because you're releasing God's Power through you in the earth with your earth-bound authority. God wants you to do this so He can come in and do His works here on earth. James 5:14-16

Basic Training

The intention of this topic is to train a Christian who is either new or someone who hasn't been aware of spiritual dynamics. The absolute basics to get by at bare minimum. I'm not referring to salvation basics; I'm assuming this is already understood. The basic training is the following topics in the following order.

1. I want your Heart, not your religiousness, page 187
2. Seeing in the Holy Spirit, and the leadings of the Holy Spirit, page 132
3. Know your spiritual boundaries, what you have authority over, page 180
4. Devil's last stand and strong demon submission, page 178

Division

Division is the tool that the devil uses to divide and conquer. It's one of His greatest tools, and sadly the most successful. It is his main goal to find a weakness and divide people. The devil knows that there is power in numbers. He also knows that if He can divide a group, it will make them half as effective as they were before.

Sometimes individuals will have silly arguments, then divide from each other. Or they don't see things exactly the same way. You can have disagreements; it's what you do after that matters. You should reconcile, or at least agree to disagree. When you stand in division, it gives the devil legal access, a foothold, where he had none before.

It says in Matt 5:23, "If therefore you are offering your gift at the altar, and there remember that your brother has anything against you, leave your gift there before the altar, and go your way. First be reconciled to your brother, and then come and offer your gift." The Lord will not move in the midst of division; it's a stench to Him. God will wait until you settle your differences and come back into unity. Let's say in a small prayer group that everybody is in unity but one person. You will feel the Spiritual friction because God does not like disunity, and will not move as deeply. If there is a prophetic team that's going out to do a task for the Lord and one of them is or gets into division. That person will nullify the effectiveness of that mission, and they will probably come under attack by the enemy because of the legal access the enemy has in division. I travel with a ministry full-time; we have our differences occasionally. What we do is we will say what's on our hearts and think about what was said, then come back into unity. Because if we didn't, then the devil would have legal access, and we would not be effective in ministry. We have become good at this. If you're a team, you all need to be diplomatic and consider change. Mark 3:24-26

Doctrines

Doctrines are man's interpretation of what they think God is. There are so many churches today because of the different variations of beliefs in how they believe. Perhaps a new truth has been revealed, and there's a split in who believes what. So they create separate groups based on their beliefs. And each insists that their way is the only way.

There is grace in doctrinal error. God doesn't care if we understand everything perfectly. In heaven, we will all be one, and not separated by our doctrinal beliefs. God doesn't ignore certain denominations because they believe a certain way. He doesn't look at this; He looks at their heart and their willingness to follow Him. So He uses anyone in any denomination to amount that they are willing to be used by Him. I say we all have a piece of the puzzle, and we must be humble enough to put our pieces together. God will use anybody He can, at the level that they're willing to be used by Him; He works at all levels. The Lord will work with a person or a denomination at what amount they allow Him to.

God does not view one denomination better than another. He looks at the hearts and the willingness of each person. They will have various kinds of veils over their eyes to not see certain truths, but God will still use them if they're willing. Some people think you must memorize scriptures to be mature, but what can happen is they use those very scriptures as whips to whip anybody that might view things differently than them. They think that if you don't view it their way, that you're out of line in the ways of God.

I have seen people divide off for even really simple matters of difference. God will reveal one thing to one person, and something else to another. We all need humility to put our pieces together. God has done this on purpose, that we would be forced to be humble and rely on each other. God is creative. He made every one of us different, every snowflake, tree, bird, insect, and so on. He doesn't want us to be all uniform in the church, all cut from the same cookie cutter. It's possible that He could have us all believing the same about everything, but that would not result in true unity. The Lord is more interested in having us love each other than having us be in doctrinal agreement. We should respect each other's differences, then work from there.

Every person is uniquely different. He wanted us to be different, but we each add a piece to the puzzle. So it doesn't matter if you know all things perfectly. What God looks at is your fruits John 13:34. God wants us to be in unity, but we don't need to make everybody the same to do it. This would not a basis for unity but for division. Realize our differences and be okay with them. Show them Love, they're still growing. It's okay if they don't agree with your truth. You must not hinder their growth by rejecting them. See them at their level, and encourage them on by loving them. God knows each person and what they're capable of, so He does not see them in the condition that they are now. He sees them for what they could become.

Another thing that needs to be realized is that the devil is constantly looking for life and true works of God. When he finds it, he focuses his efforts on trying to stop and stagnate it, because it destroys his kingdom. So he looks for any way to stop or compromise it. If he can't stop it, then he will try to counterfeit it, and replace the real with a counterfeit; so that the real is neglected (See Topic "Pseudo Anointing" page 63). The life that was once there has been replaced by a counterfeit, and that life leaves. Then the devil has them under control so that they do no real damage to his kingdom.

Willful sins

1. Unforgiveness
2. Willful, purposed, and unrepentant sin
3. Blaspheming the Holy Spirit

1. Matthew 6:14-15 "For if you forgive other people when they sin against you, your heavenly Father will also forgive you. But if you do not forgive others their sins, your Father will not forgive your sins."

Mark 11:25 "And when you stand praying, if you hold anything against anyone, forgive them, so that your Father in heaven may forgive you your sins."

Matthew 18:21-35 is a parable talking about a man who owed a lot. He and his family were about to be sold to repay that debt, but he asked for mercy, and the king forgave him. Then later, that same man demanded someone who owed him to pay him back and wouldn't have mercy. Then the king found out and re-demanded his debt. That debt is forgiveness of sins. 35 "So likewise shall My heavenly Father do also to you, unless each one of you from your hearts forgive his brother their trespasses."

2. If you purposely sin and are unrepentant, knowing that it's wrong, or make excuses to do that sin, yet willfully commit it without remorse, then God can't help you if you remain in sin purposely and willfully. Now I'd like to clarify, if after you sin, you are repentant, this is okay. You have a tender heart that wants to do good. It's the unrepentant heart or the one who makes excuses why sin is okay so that they can sin freely.

3. It is my opinion that you would have to have a heart that matches the words. I don't think this can happen by accident or a whoops. It's purposed and thought through thoroughly. So don't be fearful if you think you crossed this line because I think there's a lot more to it than by accident. Mark 3:29 29 "But he that shall blaspheme against the Holy Ghost hath never forgiveness, but is in danger of eternal damnation. 30 Because they said, He hath an unclean spirit." But if you truly think you have done this, then seek God with a repentant heart and ask for forgiveness. God is time, He saw from the very moment you may have done such a thing to the day that you repented; it's all taken into consideration. Just turn from it and change; it's a heart condition. Is your heart hard toward the Lord or now soft? If it's now soft and sorry,

then this is probably what counts! Just like Jonah, God intended for that city to be destroyed, but they turned from their ways and were saved.

I state these things to not scare you, but to remind you of the few scriptures that should be taken seriously. God forgave us a massive debt of sin, like the parable in Matthew 18:21-35. The very least we can do is forgive our fellow brothers and sisters. It darkens your soul to keep unforgiveness. It will remain there until you forgive. God won't forgive your sins if you don't forgive others! This means anybody whatsoever, even if they're a bad person or do bad things. I think He means business, so don't take this lightly.

Now, as far as my second point, there is forgiveness for sins. It's simply the fact that we're trying to get out of that sin that matters. If you are unrepentant and continue in it without being sorry about it and don't care, then that is the difference. We all sin, that's not the issue; it's that we're sorry for our sins and try to stop them even though we repeat them. The fact that we're trying to fix it is what matters. We need to keep seeking forgiveness and truly be repentant for our sins. So don't get stressed out! As long as you're trying and resisting sin the best you can is what matters. But don't make a reasoning in your mind why it's okay to do a sin, then live in that sin; this is where you error.

Now the last one, I have given some thought. I tried once saying to myself, if blasphemies against Jesus and God are forgivable; what would be a blasphemy against God and Jesus be? So I thought about this, and I just couldn't put myself to doing it. I just couldn't think that way. I feel it's the same way with the Holy Spirit. You're not wired to think that way. You would have to have a very hardened heart to be able to do this, and in your heart be purposed to do to it. This is nothing that happens by accident. It is purposeful. If your Christian beliefs are differing in what the Holy Spirit does and doesn't do, just be careful with it. I personally don't know where that line is, just be aware of it.

There are probably some of you who think: oh no, I did it already and feel dread about it, this is harassment from the enemy, so stop thinking this way. Just repent to God with full heart repentance, and I think you're good. The fact that you're concerned about it is a good sign and should feel relieved. Start from this point forward fresh. The past is the past; leave it in the past. Start as a new person today by asking for forgiveness with a true heart.

Now when you die, you want to be as clean as you can under the blood of

Christ, but if you show up to the judgment seat when you die with unforgiveness in your heart or purposed sins, I think you might be in serious trouble. I don't know personally what God does with this, but I sure wouldn't risk it if I were you. Because the consequences are forever and ever! It's not my intention to scare you, but really I don't think it's a big deal to square these few things away. All you have to do is just denounce those, repent, and you're done! Nothing complicated about it. If any of these apply to you, just take 1 minute and be repentant and ask for forgiveness. Then go and sin no more. Don't be tormented about this; we have not the spirit of fear, but that of a sound mind 2 Timothy 1:7. God does not want us to be tormented; just be aware of those things and don't do them is all.

Grace Vs. Responsibility

There are many Christians out there today that are content with being just barely saved. Getting to heaven is their main goal. This is not God's intention, to just get us saved; He wants us to grow in Him! Of course there are many stagnated forms of that as well.

Being saved is a great and wonderful gift from God, but unfortunately, most Christians stop and park at salvation's door. There are journeys in which God wants for us to take in Him. He's very displeased with the lack of motivation in the church today. These are churchgoers who are just content to listen to the pastor preach his message, and that's that. God didn't put us here on this earth to sit around and stagnate. He wants you to pursue your calling, and that's not just being an usher for the church.

This is well and good, but I'm talking deeper than just helping the church out in what it needs. To pursue the path of holiness, to be constantly honing your spirit and flesh, to conform with His Holiness. Everybody has a calling to ministry. God wants you to exercise your gifts. You are one of the fivefold ministries; the apostle, prophet, teacher, evangelist, or pastor. Every Christian on this earth has one or more of those five callings. Find out which is yours and use it!

God is not only love, He's other things also. Many think aw it's okay for me to keep messing up without trying to correct the error. Grace is meant to be a trying process, trying to get better, but many are okay with staying where they are and relying heavily upon the grace of God Rom 6:1-2,15 "What shall we say then? Shall we continue in sin, that grace may abound? God forbid. How shall we, that are dead to sin, live any longer therein?"

God is very displeased with this lazy mentality. You are supposed to be ever trying to be more and holy. To constantly be trying to trim the flesh and grow in Him; becoming a brighter light. He's not looking for lazy Christians that sit around and do hardly anything for Him. As Paul said, I am the chief of sinners. He realized just how much sin really is in the human heart.

As you get closer and closer to Him, you find more and more about the things that need to be changed. God is holy and perfect; any little sins are exposed when you get closer to Him. If you didn't pursue Him, you would think you're just fine and like every other Christian, not growing and become stalemated. You don't really know how much sin you have until you try to get close to Him. God wants you to get close to Him; that requires working out sins in your life.

He will visit you at your level with His anointing, because He loves you. This is probably the main problem. God will touch a person with His anointing in whatever condition they are. Then they think, God must be putting His stamp of approval on me because He's touching me; approving what I do and how I do things, so I must be okay. That's not the statement He's making. He's saying I love you and is healing you. Many Christians will assume this means that everything about them is okay, and they can stay where they are spiritually. It's the process of dying to self, which I consider a never-ending, constant process. At the end of our lives, we will have wished we would have done more.

That is the comment that Paul made in Rick Joyner's final quest series. Paul said he wished he would have done more. So you have never attained the top. Consider it a never-ending mountain in which you have to climb, reaching new levels. You can only see the next plateau of the mountain. Once you get there, then you see another, and another, just like climbing a mountain.

What do you accomplish or become

Rick Joyner said something very interesting, he said: it's not about what you accomplish in this life; it's about what you become. Works versus maturity.

Doing works is good, but if you're not mature, then you have missed the point. The point of this life is to get closer to God, to mature yourself and your fruit. Just doing works because it feels good is not the point. What God really wants is people to get close to Him, and to become holy as He is holy Lev 11:45, 1Pet 1:16.

To obtain holiness is a many-tiered process. It comes in layers and seasons. Concentrate on becoming a better person in the Lord, ridding of your sins, becoming a more mature Christian, and getting closer to the Lord. Becoming more mature is a constant procedure. You can't say, okay I have arrived. I went to school, learned all there is to learn, and now I'm done, no way! Don't ever stop, keep going; get close to the Lord and learn of His ways. I used to work in a shop with an old man and others. He said: "I am learning something new all the time," and he was the most experienced guy there. We will spend eternities trying to get to know God and His ways, yet to have scratched a scratch. Never stop, keep growing in Him. This is more important than many accomplishments or works.

Accountable to what you have been given

Everyone is different, has different callings, gifts, and levels of maturity. One might look at another that has bigger, broader spiritual giftings and ministries, and think they're greater. But the truth is you can be just as great in your own way if you're willing to do His will as He would have you do it. It's not how great, big, and obvious our ministry is. It's about your obedience and will to do what God has called you to do. A person who does the will of God in their life, even if they're never known, is better than a great minister who does the will of God averagely. They may have big ministries, and their names may be known. But the person who does the will of God more wholly is much greater in the kingdom of God. In someone's vision of heaven, it stated, things are not weighed like they are here. Things that are measured here as great, are considered trivial in heaven.

It's not how great and well known you are. It's about obedience and doing the will of the Father in your life, even if it seems insignificant. To God it's not insignificant, it's great because He told you to do it. It's like the scripture Mark 12:41-44 Jesus said, "Truly I tell you, this poor widow has put more into the treasury than all the others. They all gave out of their wealth; but she, out of her poverty, put in everything, all she had to live on." In this situation, the widow was greater than all the others who put in because she gave her everything, and the others gave a small percentage. God looks upon the percentage of obedience, not the greatness or the result. Obedience is the result! So if an unknown person is 100 percent obedient and does all that they're told to do. They are greater than the greatest minister who did 90 percent of God's will. I'm not saying you have to be unknown to be greater. Obedience is what matters. But often unknown people can be some of the greatest.

Now I'm not saying everyone has to be perfect, missing the Holy Spirit in the small ways, like if He warns you of something in your daily life and you miss it. I'm referring to obedience to what you are called to do in your calling; things related to His purpose in your life. It's not the results, it's the obedience that matters. God is very fair in who He makes the greatest in heaven, the most unlikely to be thought as the greatest here, will be the greatest in heaven.

My dad had a dream once where Jesus visited him, and He was talking about various things. In that conversation, Jesus mentioned He has 10,000 josephs that He is working with. I take this to mean that He notices even the forgotten, and works in their lives to do His will. To work the situation around to a beneficial one. So even if you think you're a nobody, God can and will work in your situation. Ask Him to help you know what you're supposed to do, and have a real relationship with Him. It's up to you how deep you will be; you limit yourself.

I am reminded of something that Rick Joyner wrote in one of his books. He talked about a homeless man who found a salvation track and was saved. Then was very faithful to preach about Jesus, and obedient to do God's will. It ended up that he died trying to keep an old lady warm on a very cold night. Rick had seen this man in real life and made a funny comment about him. But later, Rick was shown this man in heaven and found out that he was great in heaven. His level of obedience and love were great, and he was rewarded accordingly. I'm not saying evangelizing is the greatest call. Don't forget there are apostle, profit, teacher, and preacher also, all apply.

It's like the scripture, Matt 20:1-16, about the landowner who hired workers to work in his field. He went in the morning at 9, noon, 3, and even at 5. He called them to receive their payment, and all received the same payment. They were all faithful to do what they were told to do. Even though the amount each did was not the same, all were faithful to do the portion they were given. Even the one who was hired at 5 did very little work compared to the one who did 8 more hours. It's not their fault that they were not hired earlier in the day. If they were hired earlier in the day, they would have worked the full day, because they're faithful. So it's not the quantity, but the quality of the service. But in this situation, all were faithful 100 percent. So in the case of equal percentages, the reward is the same. This could be long-time Christians vs. new Christians. If they're obedient, then their reward will be the same as an equally faithful older Christian. Or one who has a very small ministry that's faithful, will receive the same reward as one who had a great ministry equally faithful. It's about being faithful to what you have been given. If what He has given you is small, and you're faithful in it; you have done your part and will receive your reward according to your faithfulness.

Levels of Maturity and Obedience

God is in the business of training us, working into us various traits, and more and more obedience. He is in a constant process of taming our flesh that would get in the way of our being closer to Him. He also wants us to listen to what He wants us to do. If we listen and tame our flesh, then He will advance us to the next layer of our walk. To more maturity, a higher rank in His army, more of His spirit, and more responsibility. The reason for this life is to get as close to Him as possible Matt 18:1. What you do here on earth will affect what you do in heaven. The closer, more mature, and obedient you are here, the greater you are there forever. The lesser you are here, the lesser you will be there (See Topic "Capacities of Heaven" page 56).

But if we don't listen to Him in His leadings, then it stalls us. We will have to stop our progress until we listen and change. It is the same in what He's telling us to do in our ministry also. If we don't do what He says, then we are stalled or stopped. We will go around the mountain over and over until we get it.

Now I'd like to go one step further into more than any one person. The purposes that God needs to accomplish, and the overall big picture. God has a master plan for what He wants to do for all Christianity of many facets and purposes. It's like an army, not everyone specializes in the same thing. There are many different trainings, purposes, jobs, and different branches in His army. He needs all of the 5 fold gifts to work in unison. Each of these branches in His army does different things. In the big picture, there are a lot of things that need to be accomplished. He is looking for people to fill every one of those purposes. He looks for those who are faithful to listen to Him and are mature in His spirit. He goes through many candidates, often giving each an equal opportunity to fill the position in question. This might be referred to as the high calling of a person. Not everyone qualifies for the high calling due to spiritual maturity and obedience. There are the stalemated, the compromised callings, and high callings.

To fill the important positions, He's looking for those who are willing to fulfill their high calling. So this requires both spiritual maturity and obedience. If one misses their high calling, then they will go into a compromised calling. God can still use them, just not as effectively.

I just saw a video about a man who visited heaven and was prophesied to by Jeremiah. He said: "You think that I stop using my servants after they leave this flesh, and you think wrong. Leaving this flesh is but the beginning of the using of my vessels." In that same video, they talked about 3 realms in heaven; 2 of which were mentioned: the realm of the overcomers, and the realm of the least. So the maturity level you are when you pass from this life is the same level you will be in heaven. Will that be the least or the greatest? Is up to you. Matt 18:1, Matt 23:11.

God will give someone an opportunity to fill one of these high calling positions by calling them to it, and see if they're obedient and mature to fill that position. They might do it, partially do it, or not at all. God will give them time to figure out their way into it. They might do it for a while, but in time might compromise and fail after time. He might warn them they are off, but if they don't listen and stay stuck, God will have to move onto another person to fill that position. If one gets stuck, then God will let them sit there until they figure it out. But in the case of the high calling, they may miss it and have to go into a compromised calling. It's not what God intended, but if they mess up their opportunity for the high calling, God will use them in another way.

In the high calling, there may only be a narrow window of opportunity. If it's missed, then they will have to fulfill a lesser calling. God still loves them of course, and they're still saved. They just missed their highest possible calling.

Depending on their obedience and maturity is what determines what they will be tasked with after that. If the current candidate for filing the position fails to qualify for the position. Then God will look for another obedient person to fill the position to take their place. We're not talking about people who have gone to Bible school as a prerequisite. We're talking about whomsoever God deems is qualified; by His standards, not man's standards.

When it comes to the highest callings, God requires high maturity and obedience to His leadings. What He does for the failed high callings is use them the best He can where they're at; to whatever amount He can work through them in their current state of maturity and obedience. High callings require a high level of obedience and maturity. Only God determines where a person should be or not be, not man.

Building the Kingdom by Building others

I think it's a part of human nature to want to win, be ahead, or be better. Maybe not consciously, but subconsciously. Whether it's on a small or large scale differs from person to person. Like for instance, if you have a gift or a talent in God and are good at it, then see someone who might be doing it better. You in your mind may compare them to yourself, and try to evaluate if they're better, and get frustrated, jealous, or feel bad that you're not doing as well as they are. You might get frustrated and say to yourself, there must be something wrong with me. Or in your mind, you may evaluate them and rate their person to being lesser than your walk.

If you're a ministry that's striving to be on the cutting edge for God, and view yourself as one of God's main Man, Woman or team. Then you hear about someone else doing something for God like a revival, and you get frustrated by it. Wondering in yourself is what they're doing real.

You should view it this way. God has a master plan, and we are all pieces in this plan. No one should try to compete with others. What you should do is be willing to give them what you know from your experiences, in whatever way you can. Not to hold back anything that you can do to help them be a better person for God. Even if that makes them greater than you or gives them the advantage. Why do you compete anyway? God is in control. If someone maneuvered into a position that was not authorized by God, then it's manmade. They didn't wait for God to put them in that position. If that's the case, God is able to put you in your proper place, even if it looks like someone has outdone you. You should still help them if you can. Give all that you are to them, all that you know; surrender it. We should all be on the same team here. Try to not hold anyone back, even if that means they surpass you. Let them be all that they can be, their full potential. If you do this, God will see your love for others and will reward you here on earth and in heaven. Give them your insight and make them greater yet. Few are the laborers. Will you try to stop the few that are there? Luke 10:2. You may lose some of your reward if you're competing and compromising others. Luke 22:24

 We need to build God's Kingdom, not our own kingdom. One example is being a pastor taking pride in their big church building and following that he has. These things are irrelevant in heaven. What is relevant is people and what they become; not how big a kingdom you created for yourself. But how you built others up in God's kingdom. Be happy if someone advances and becomes greater in God, because God's kingdom is advancing by people becoming more mature.

 In fact, what the church should be doing is training people to fulfill their callings rather than just preaching from the front of the room. Training and duplicating themselves in others. Have a team of people to determine and train each type of calling, whatever that might be. Let them try their callings in meetings, and to not be afraid of the results. So what, if they leave the church later. They have been trained and will use that training elsewhere. At least you have duplicated yourself, and that duplication will be multiplied in others. We should be in the multiplication business, not in the plus and minus business. It is better to try and fail, than to not try at all!
1 Thessalonians 5:11

Capacities of Heaven

 I was watching a Rick Joyner Video, and he had an experience where he met with Enoch. He was the most joyful person, and bubbling over with joy. Then soon after, he also met with Elijah, but Elijah wasn't as joyful as Enoch. Rick asked, why are you not joyful? He said "I should be, but on earth I wasn't joyful." You set your capacities here on earth what you will be able to experience in heaven. If you lack on earth, you will also lack in heaven. So don't limit yourself; pick yourself up and be joyful. Don't let the things of this earth get to you. But don't force it and be fakey; there are a lot of fakey people out there.

My Mom heard this from the Lord, "because they don't have life and love in their hearts, they have to put on a fake personality to make up for it." What you need to do is get in touch with your heart and God. If there is any healing that needs to happen. Pursue God to heal you, get healing that is true and real, naturally coming out of your heart.

I had an experience when I was a young Christian in my teen years. I don't remember what I was doing, but I must have been talking or praising God one day when I was laying down, and I felt the Lord give the emotion of joy, but it kept growing to the point where it was beyond my ability to understand it. It went beyond my capacity to experience that emotion. It was overwhelming. I called it joy unspeakable, implying that it was indescribable. I read in a heavenly book that emotions in heaven are much greater and deeper than the ones we experience here on earth.

You also set the capacities of your position and level in heaven here on earth by your obedience and maturity. If you fully do what God has set for you to do, and have gained a lot of maturity in the spirit. Then that will be the capacity that will be set in heaven, but if you do minimal here on earth and are just saved only, then you will be the least in heaven. Because it's not just about getting to heaven, it's about accomplishing what God has for you, and your high calling. God gives positions and authority in heaven based on your level of obedience. (See Topic "Levels of Maturity and Obedience" page 53) Matthew 16:27, Jeremiah 17:10

A Taste of the Anointing

God desires for His people to enter into Him, as far as they're willing. He wants to equip all to the fullest, to the degree they are surrendered to it. Which are giftings, anointings, and commissions given to people. Whether it be commissions to do things for God, anointings that operate within meetings, or whatever it might be. Anointings vary from person to person; each is called differently, Romans 12:6. All are called, no one is left out. It's not just being an usher or helping at the church. It's a dynamic anointing that God has destined for you, unique to your personality and calling. If someone is seeking God, He will give them a taste or a sample of their anointing. But to attain the fullness of that anointing, you have to go through the process of taming your flesh and being obedient to His calling. You need to be sensitive to His spirit, and what He would have you change, each person may be different. The deeper you get in Him, the more tamed the flesh has to be. There are many layers and levels of the anointing.

Consider it that you have never reached the top of the anointing. That you can keep going deeper as you're faithful and trim your flesh. Because if there is flesh in the way, the less effective the anointing will be. Don't contaminate your spirit; the less the contamination, the deeper the anointing. But let Him show you what you're to trim, not you show you. The enemy is also watching and will try to push you; because if he can't stop you, he will try to push you too far. But on the other side, don't miss God's voice by drowning it out with the cares of the world.

This taste of the anointing is not only for new Christians, but for those who are seasoned as well. He's always wanting His people to have more, but they must prove faithful with what they have. God will give that person a taste of more so that they might strive to get it. But often what can happen is the person who is receiving the taste can get puffed up with just the taste of their anointing. They feel that they have already attained the anointing, but God is only giving them a taste of it. Some let their anointing linger and don't pursue it. This taste is meant to draw them up the mountain more, to gain maturity.

God loves you and wants you to know what your anointing could be like. He wants to take you on a path of taming your flesh so that you would be more effective in your anointing. Once you have proven faithful doing that, He will give you a taste of a deeper anointing; the next level. So that you will aspire to that; a continuous process.

Another dynamic in advancing in the anointing is to be humble. If you're not humble, then this can prevent you from advancing as well. God resists the proud. He wants you to be humble in your anointing, because it's not you who's doing it; it's Him through you. He wants to see humility in the anointing; then He will give you more (See Topic "Bow down low to receive the next level" page 82). What people often do is stop with just a taste and stay there. God is life, His river is always moving, going, and doing. He wants us to do the same, to be dynamic, not static.

But beware of the traps that the enemy would try to trap you. He will try to lead you in the wrong direction if you're trying too hard. Let God show you, but seek Him as well. Be willing to do what may not be comfortable.

Humility and Wisdom before Power

If God were to give us power and position suddenly, and we were not mature enough yet, what would we do with it? It's kind of like when someone wins the lottery. If they were poor before, they would probably waste it very quickly. They were probably poor in the first place because they make poor decisions in life, from small to big.

Giving one power, is like a magnifying glass; any issues in our lives will be magnified and multiplied into a much bigger proportion. If He were to give us all position and power upfront before we were ready, we would probably use it foolishly. If we're sloppy with money, it would get wasted. If we didn't hear from the Holy Spirit properly, we would probably be steered in wrong directions. If we lacked maturity, we could get derailed. If we got into pride, it would be a stench to God 1 Peter 5:5.

Basically, anything that is not tamed in our flesh. God needs to work these things first before He can trust us with more. He will probably give it to us in pieces and parts; to give us time to get used to the new part of it and slowly grow into it.

God knows this, so He doesn't give power or resources to those who will waste it with an untamed flesh, or corrupt it with spiritual immaturity. God sees these things in your heart, even before you do, so He has to work them out by tests and trials.

These tests and trials are for your benefit. They're hard; just try to get through them and learn your lessons well. They make you into a more mature Christian; just like a fruit tree needs to be pruned. It probably doesn't feel good to be pruned, but without it, a tree will grow to spread out, and its fruit greatly compromised. I know this to be true because I pruned an apple tree, and its fruit dramatically increased. It was left to grow wild for many years and had a lot of dead branches. Some branches were only half connected because of a lightning strike and producing minimal fruit. But when I pruned it, it immediately had a wonderful amount of flowers right after that smelt good. God needs to hone out anything that would detract from developing good fruits. We will become like that tangled-up tree that has unused portions that are just taking up resources. If we have too much flesh, our spiritual energy will be wasted. He sees what we need and sends us situations that will prune us in those areas. If He gave us any sort of power before we were ready. These deficiencies would be fed and multiplied. Our unpruned nature would waste its spiritual power with spiritual deficiencies. There are a lot of areas that God typically needs to work into us, it's not a presto you're fixed. He looks into your very being and sees exactly what needs to be trimmed. He tries to work on it with you, but you need to change it.

If we were to get into pride, then it would wreak havoc on our ministry, and probably completely derail and stagnate it. God can't put us into position until we're ready to handle it. We may think we're ready, but God might know differently. God doesn't want us taking glory onto ourselves; He wants us to be humble. So He wants us to operate in both wisdom and humility before He can truly trust us with more. James 4:10

Pride

We in ourselves can not produce power or anointing; God brings the anointing. Yes, God has given us our anointing and callings without repentance. God honors the gifts He has given us. But if He doesn't show up, then we are nothing. We need to be humble and realize this. Yes, you may be proficient in your anointing, but if you get into pride, then your anointing turns sour. Because God resists the proud but gives grace to the humble James 4:6.

God puts up with some of our bad behaviors. But if it becomes too much, then He will try to warn you about the issue and give you time to work it out. But if you don't overcome it, then He will move on from you, and your anointing will decrease. Being humble is a big deal with God. We may be very qualified to do His works and might be very good at it, but if we get into pride, it ruins it all, because God does not like pride.

Another thing is one who has many years of experience. There is a tendency to think that they know everything there is to know. They come to a point where no one can tell them anything because they already know it, a stiffness.

Maybe coming to the point where they view themselves on a higher spiritual level than others. Only God can judge this, and it shouldn't be done anyways. There's no amount of knowledge or experience that you can attain that would justify that you are at the pinnacle of understanding of the things of God. You should view yourself as a fellow servant of God and be willing to listen to others. Because we all have been given a different piece; we need to have humility to put our pieces together. God did this so we would rely on each other and not on ourselves. Yes, some people are misaligned in their understanding or hearing, but don't dismiss all because of the few.

God is always moving forward. If you stop and think that you know all things, then you will sit there and stagnate. God likes to grow us deeper and deeper into Him; we need to keep up with Him. But don't get ahead of Him either, because if the devil can't stop you, then he will try to push you too far. We need to neither get ahead of Him nor behind Him.

We should be open to considering new truths, but at the same time be careful of false ones. We should not dismiss someone who is young, thinking they're unable to come up with something from the Lord. Like the scripture says: "thou hast hid these things from the wise and prudent, and hast revealed them unto babes" Matt 11:25, Luke 10:21. So young and old alike can be given things from the Lord.

God can choose to give to whomsoever He desires. We need to be humble before the Lord and follow His leadings; leading implies moving forward, not sitting still. But there can be a pride that arises from the one who thinks they are on the cutting edge of things of the Lord; it's not you, but Him. It's good to be obedient, but pride is a stench to the Lord. He resists the prideful and gives grace to the humble James 4:6.

Pride seeks recognition. I read that man often over emphasizes his importance. It's not us that people should be seeing, but God. We should resist pride as God resists it. Because when we go into pride, we are taking away glory that belongs to God. That is why we should be humble, because He's the one who deserves all glory. When we get into pride, we are trying to take some of that glory unto ourselves. James 4:10

False Voices that Mislead

For every genuine, there's also a counterfeit that the Devil will try to sneak in and fool. It's the enemy's strategy to try to stop God's works by any means necessary. There are 3 possible voices that can be heard in your spirit: your voice, the devil's, and God's voice. As a young Christian, I first learned that I needed to figure out and weigh those 3 possible voices 1 John 4:1. You are trying to hear, and you might make some words within yourself, it's not that you do it intentionally, but in trying to hear, you hear yourself, an imagined voice. Then there's the devil speaking; his voice is often the loudest and easiest to hear. He will pretend like he's God's voice, and if you don't know the difference, he will keep speaking, inserting things.

It's very common for the devil to speak to people. He does it with everybody, including pagans. The devil probably speaks to everyone. Many are probably not aware of it, thinking that it's their thoughts, but it's very common. There is no doubt that many Christians think they're hearing God, but in fact, hearing the enemy. The devil does it in a way where it seems to be right. He might try to steer you down a religious path, because if the devil can't stop you, he will try to push you too far.
I'm not saying people are bad; they can often be very devoted to God. This is something that every single person has to deal with. He tries this with everyone to further his kingdom in any way possible.

We must realize that the devil is very good at what he does. Don't underestimate the enemy; if you do, he will use that to his advantage. You may not realize the devil's tactics; we're all in the same boat. You need to recognize it and filter it out.

So whenever you hear a word, you need to weigh it; was it you, the devil, or God? It's like the wheat and the tares; they're mixed together. The devil comes along and puts his tares in. It doesn't matter how advanced you are; the devil will always try to speak to you. The thing that we need to learn is to recognize it and send him away.

Now going one step further; many people in ministry think they are hearing from God and speaking His words. But are instead hearing the enemy, and saying and doing what he wants them to. Like I said, the devil is very good at deceiving. These people are unaware of it, because the devil managed to trick them into it. They could very well be speaking both God's voice, the enemy's, and their own voice as well, a mixture. I'm not trying to shame people; they just haven't figured out the difference between the voices. That's why the prophet is subject to the prophet. Because often, others can see the errors that we can't.

God's voice sometimes can be difficult to hear in our everyday lives. It can be very soft or in pictures. Sometimes it's so subtle that we think it's our thoughts. The devil isn't always blatant; he can operate in subtle ways too. Because if he were to work on a more blatant level, he would be immediately exposed. So he works at a level where he isn't noticed. 1 John 4:1

Pseudo Anointing

For every real, there's a counterfeit that comes from the enemy. He does this so that he can deceive you from the true. If he can't stop you, he will try to set a trap for you to get you off track. The devil is very resourceful and is very smart. He will do anything and everything to try to stop you. He can even appear as an angel of light, but it's a counterfeit.

Here is an example of the pseudo anointing. A large group I was with worked up an anointing in a building. It was a beyond wonderful anointing, a place where I had some of my most potent experiences. It was several weeks of anointed events, and the spirit of the Lord was in the building and stayed there. One would only walk into the building and strongly feel God's Presence, even in just the entrance. This building was out in the country, and was owned by a church that gave us all permission to use that building; they also participated in the meetings. This was their secondary building to their main church, which was about 30 miles away. This was a country retreat they had set up. They remodeled their main church, so they then came on a Sunday to do their service in the same room as these meetings were. We went in there after they had their church service to have a totally different feeling altogether. It had a feeling that was almost similar to the real anointing, but it was definitely different. It was disturbing because if you had never felt the real anointing, you would mistaken it for this presence, which was a pseudo anointing.

It almost felt like a nice presence, but we all knew it was a counterfeit anointing. God's presence had left, and this counterfeit took its place; we were all very frustrated. The enemy can emit a pseudo-presence in many types of situations. This was my first experience with feeling this, and I was shocked. Yes, it was worship to God, but it had no life in it. Where there's no life, the enemy can come in to deceive, and bring a counterfeit in to fool those he can. This was not a dull church. They were either non-denominational or Pentecostal. They believed in the gifts of the spirit and sang some okay songs, but there was no life in it. I'm not saying these denominations are bad; just this one didn't have much life. They are great people with good hearts, but the enemy has pulled a pseudo anointing on them.

Another example is, I was touring a Christian building, and I didn't know this, but they let out one of the rooms to a Lutheran church. I went into the room without knowing this and felt a strong choking spiritual climate. I wanted out right away; it was spiritually suffocating. This Lutheran church had some sort of suffocation spirit assigned to them. Again I'm not saying any denomination is bad; some people are simply unaware of what the devil is capable of.

No one should look down upon or treat differently any denomination for overlooking such things. You should love them right where they're at; treating them as less will not reach them, but love and life will. Like the Rick Joyner vision about a river and the enemy surrounding it. The enemy ended up being fellow Christians, but all they needed was a taste of the river and were changed. There had to be those willing to take the chance to offer a drink of the river to them! Once they tasted the river, they then realized their extreme thirst and wanted more.

The devil is very smart and resourceful. He will try absolutely anything; nothing is too low with him. As long as it works, he will do it, 1 Peter 5:8. Once he can get a foot in the door, he can use a pseudo anointing or the suffocation spirit to spiritually suck out those involved. He tries to keep you out of God's real presence, fooling those involved. He also tries to dry you out spiritually and suffocate your spirit to keep the life of God away from you. Just like in Rick Joyner's final quest book, they ate the enemy's puking's and felt okay at first but worse afterward, that was the vision of the church.

It's kind of like honey-flavored poison. Whether you believe it or not, it's happening in the church today. It might seem too extreme to be true, but if you're unaware of it, you can be duped by it. Demons are real, and their tactics are also real. Try to be open-minded about just how tricky the enemy can be. And how he will do anything he can whatsoever to sneak in and extinguish any life of God he can. Even to where there's no life, a vacuum or void in its place.

The devil is always looking for anything that disrupts his kingdom. If he sees any light of God in the earth, he will aggressively try to put that light out and will exploit any weaknesses that he can. Because light is contrary to his kingdom of darkness; he will do all that he can to stop it!

The Revival Killers

God starts a revival when the hearts of man are in the right place, humble, and the timing is right. He will often use the unexpected person, like David, a simple sheepherder. It is not contingent upon being trained in seminary school, or Bible college. God may have trained someone up in the wilderness outside of man school in the school of the spirit. God often chooses a group that meets His criteria and starts a revival with them. This might not always meet the church's criteria, Isaiah 55:8. The revival grows because God has the liberty to do what He wants and how He wants without man's ideas of what God is to get in the way. God wants liberty to do what He wants, so He will choose a group based upon that. You know it's of revival caliber if the spirit of God is there, people are attracted to it, and it grows like a wildfire.

What the problem often is, is that when a revival comes and becomes well known. Then the leaders of the church come in and tell them they are not experienced enough to manage this revival, and that they should come and oversee it. What they don't realize is that God started it without their help; He doesn't need it now! Because they will not let Him move the way He wants to move. Otherwise, He would have started it in their church.

The misconception is that God goes by a certain set of rules. The church leaders have decided how God works and how He operates. They have put Him in a box. God is God, He chooses His rules, not man's. God is not predictable! He chose that group because they are humble and are willing to let God be who He is. God wants liberty to do what He wants, and it may be different every meeting. He comes according to what the need is and what He wants to accomplish.

The leaders that come in to change the established God structure are intruders! They think they have the authority to do this because they have been to Bible school and have years of experience. This is not what qualifies a person for ministry. What they should do is let God be God and just sit and enjoy God's work. Sometimes they're trying to position themselves so that they make a name for themselves too, which is of the flesh.

An example is, God started a revival with a certain man, and it grew. Then the leaders came in and convinced Him to let go and let the revival go on its own, let God continue it, so he listened to him and soon after the revival died (example paraphrased from a Rick Joyner book). God needs the person who started the revival to continue because God sanctioned that person. Also, God gave authority over the earth to mankind; God wants to honor the authority He gave us and work through us. Not just Him doing it by Himself.

God is able to train His own; if not, then how were all the prophets of old trained. Did they go to a seminary to even qualify for His use? No, God can train those He wants to use. It might be different from going to a Bible college, but He is able! Those who started the revival are the ones that should continue and keep it. Those leaders will tell them they're not qualified; if not, then God wouldn't have started with them in the first place.

The real truth is that those intruding leaders should step aside and let God continue what He started, untouched, unmodified! A revival should remain unorganized, because God wants to do what He wants and when He wants it. Often when it's organized, it's the wrong order; then God is grieved, and revival dies. The revival should remain as it is, and continue on the route that it was before those who came in to control it. Man's order in revival puts restraints on God when He wants liberty to do what He wants. So don't change the direction God has led you in. Stay in the direction that was started, and be led of His spirit.

Pastor, The stumbling block

I've seen many pastors in my travels; what they do and don't do. I've seen surprising behavior as well. Many pastors exhibit poor behavior or lack teaching on the more controversial matters. Things that need to be said to get rid of the sin in people's lives.

Many pastors are more concerned about their bottom line than keeping sin in check. Some pastors will not convict sin when it needs to be convicted. They are afraid of telling people of the issues that really matter, because they're afraid of losing tithe money or losing people to conviction. What a pastor should do is inform people of the sins he sees to better them spiritually. I'm not saying that it should be done in a harsh manner, just that it's talked about. Many sins in the church go unchecked. People stagnate in the Lord and stop at bare minimum salvation. Usually, they're just interested in preaching milk and not the meaty matters; keeping their flock in a constant baby state. Is your covering really covering you, or is this just in theory?

Where is the faith in God? Is there no faith? God is bigger than this! Matt 17:20. It seems more like a business of keeping people happy rather than checking sin. God is more concerned with keeping people out of sin rather than having full seats. If a person runs away from their problems and goes to the next church, that's on them. But if a pastor sees sin and does nothing about it, then it's the pastor's fault.

God is your provider, not man. God works in mysterious ways, don't look at the physical but the spiritual. You are doing that which is right by helping people out. What matters in this is life is what you become in the spirit and to help others around you. There are great rewards for helping others realize their full spiritual potential. What matters is you and me. The closer to God you become, the less sin there is to get in the way.

The church at large in its current state is a bunch of stalemated low-level Christians lacking any maturity. In Rick Joyner's final quest series, the church was three groups. The biggest group was a massive group that would float around like a flock of birds, random and chaotic. They were more interested in showing off what little equipment they did have. There were 2 other groups that led that 3rd army, each a bit better. The first was the best group, they were forerunners and created the way then the 2nd and 3rd group followed behind afterwords. When the 3rd group got to it, they wreaked havoc on the work, destroying it. Of course, the first army had moved on farther by that point. The biggest group in this vision is most of the modern church. The bulk of the church today is mostly stagnated in one way or another.

I went to a mega church in my youth; they were very good in a lot of ways, but I must point out one major issue. They wouldn't allow people to use their gifts in any official capacity unless they had been with the church for 20 years.

But then there is their son to be trained in becoming the pastor replacement. This is well and good, but do you have to be the pastor's son to get anywhere in God? What about everyone else's gifts? These people have to wait 20 years of being in the church before they will allow them to start using the gifts in front of the church. This should not be the case. Sure there will be a training time, but months not years, they need to let people learn their gifts right away and start training them, because even if they leave the church, you have built the kingdom of God in them, and maybe they will take what they learned, and build up the kingdom of God somewhere else, it's no loss. Even if they don't use it, our purpose here on earth is to help others. You have helped them grow, which really should be the goal of all churches!

These churches are thinking more narrowly. They are thinking how will this benefit their church and not the body at large. The phrase that comes to me is: are you building your kingdom or God's kingdom? Your kingdom is the overall church, but God's kingdom is the individual people. Who cares if they leave your church. You have either built them up to be stronger in their gifts or challenged them to become a deeper Christian. At least they had the proper opportunity to become deeper. The real purpose of this life is to grow as much as we can in God and help others do the same. So if we are putting leashes on them and limiting their growth, then we're doing God a disservice. It's one thing to preach to the whole church of basic matters, but the gifts should also be exercised. We should be more concerned about making all people as deep as they possibly can be, in all things. Because people are the reason for this whole existence, you will gain a greater reward if you further people in God.

Perhaps leaders of the church are concerned with people being wacky or disruptive. It's better to try and fail than to not try at all. In that failing they learn from it; trying to resolve the problems that arise but to let the training continue. Perhaps this can be done on a separate night that's specific to training, but also in the main service as well.

I also think if someone prophesies, and that prophecy fails to come forth, we shouldn't reject them for it. I think people should be allowed space to try and fail if necessary. That one has to be perfect is too much pressure for them to learn their gifts. Don't worry if they fail many times; it's just a matter of the prophet is subject to the prophet. People can see if they're not up to par. What I don't like is rejection of them if they fail; where is the grace to learn it? Why is it you have one chance and you're done? There really should be some breathing room to learn their gifts. I don't think there should be a limit, but take these fails as learning experiences and try again. There is forgiveness for everything else; why not this?

The point of this existence is to build the kingdom of God, not our own kingdoms. Now think about a pastor that thinks highly of how big his church and following is. The numbers of his church being his validation. This is completely irrelevant in heaven. What is relevant is how we build God's kingdom by building others; how we worked up their gifts in this life.

It's not about if they stay at your church, it's about them fulfilling their God calling. Between them and God, not between them and their church. It's not about being faithful to go to that church; it's about being faithful to fulfill whatever God is calling that person to be.

So the churches that are holding back people because they want to make sure their faithful first is inappropriate. They are snuffing out God's gifts in so many people. Instead, they should be openly training them and raising them up on a personal level, not on a church-wide level. They should have people who are proficient in their gift training others how to use theirs. The church should be more concerned about people learning all they can about their gift and exercising it into maturity.

We were starting worship meetings, and the local pastor decided that he should call everybody he knew and tell them to not come to these meetings. I don't know what his issue was; these were just worship meetings. He must have felt intimidated at losing the members of his church. It actually had the opposite effect; people wondered what was going on and came even from a long distance. This was improper for him to do this.

Some pastors might have the gifts of the spirit, but are afraid to preach them in fear of offending people; or on a very limited basis. What about offending the Holy Spirit? Why is man more important than God? We should really be interested in what God would have us do, even if people are scared off. So what if you lose tithe money; you have exchanged it for eternal heavenly rewards that last for eternity. Unlike tithe money that's here today and gone tomorrow.

Another dynamic is that the church will only be able to go as far as the pastor's spiritual level. If that's not very much, then you will hit a spiritual wall every time you try to go in deeper. Sometimes pastors feel they're at the pinnacle of understanding. That they know everything there is to know about

God, and nothing can change that; and they have all authority in their area. God seeks the humble, not those who feel they are wise men. It is the blind leading the blind if they feel they're at the top and know all things. God's river is always moving; you have to keep up with Him. Just like in Rick Joyner's Torch and sword book, if you don't keep up with Him, the torch will get too heavy to carry, and you will be forced to set it down.

I had a revelation once when sitting outside, and it was a sunny day. Then a small transparent cloud came over, and it became cold. This is what pastors are like; they're like that cloud that gets in between you and God. If they're between you and God, then you will not get the full effect. As soon as that cloud went away, the sun was nice and warm again. Don't look to a middleman; go to the source itself.

Modern-day Pharisee

A Pharisee in the Old Testament time was an example of how stiff-necked, religious, and stalemated religious people can be. So much so that God stood right in front of them, and they didn't believe Him. They became so intellectual that the spiritual completely eluded them. The spirit of religion did not end with the Pharisees, it still lives on today.

It's basically a demon that's assigned specifically to either derailing anything of God, or to make one go too far in their religiousness. Into a false version of the truth that seems like the truth but is a counterfeit instead. Because if the devil can't stop you, he will try to push you too far. Which has the same result as what the devil did with the Pharisees. This spirit is very active in the church to lesser and greater degrees. But let's not point the finger and say, yep, that certain pastor or denomination are totally modern-day Pharisees. Perhaps so, but let's not forget the lesser version of the religious spirit. Any religious spirit at all, in even a small amount, is not a good thing. This spirit is trying to have you miss God, whether that's small or great. The Pharisees completely missed God, having Him standing right in front of them, even to the point where they put Him to death. They were completely out of touch with God.

The devil is looking for any way whatsoever to get you to stop growing or backslide. So if he can do it with the spirit of religion, then he will. The devil is very active in the church today, because he fights against anything contrary to his kingdom of darkness. What you may not realize is the devil is active in all the earth; with every single person alive. He's constantly looking for ways to get in and ruin things. This doesn't mean people are possessed; it just means that the devil is very aggressive. (See Topic "The Devil's on the Outside" page 172). So people participate with him whether they realize it or not. The religious spirit will take those who are zealous for God, and speak to them to try to get them to go too far. So you may not even realize it, or in fact, think it's the Holy Spirit talking. The thing is, the devil's voice is so easy to hear; it's sometimes thought of as the Holy Spirit.

Now the voice of the Holy Spirit is very small and still; you have to be in a place of rest and peace in order to hear Him right. My dad had a vision once of juggling balls. The Holy Spirit was instructing him that the balls represented voices that speak to him. As he was juggling, the Holy Spirit said stop and quickly discern it; is it God's voice, your voice, or the devil's voice? Often people are completely unaware of this dynamic and just think all three of those are just thoughts that come to them.

Those who are too religious have been steered by either their thoughts or the enemy's nudging without even realizing. The devil can create a counterfeit of the real so that you think you're on the path, but it's a fake. One time I ran across a fake anointing; I knew what the real one felt like. This was very disturbing to me. If one didn't know better, they would think it's the anointing of God (See Topic "Pseudo anointing" page 63). I'm sure there are many counterfeits out there in many shapes and sizes.

Many people who have been duped by this religious spirit have been neutralized spiritually and pose no future threat to the devil. Because they have been steered off from the Lord to the counterfeit. The spirit of religion's job is to stalemate Christians, so that they're no longer a problem to the devil's kingdom. There is such a thing as being a Christian and being completely out of touch with God. This happened to the Pharisees. They were completely duped by the religious spirit. The result was, they didn't even know God.

I'm here to say that there are modern-day Pharisee Christians. Those who are so religious in their faith that they would miss God even if He walked right up to them. I'm not trying to shame them; I'm trying to wake them up! Trying to get them back on path and find the real power of God.

Do you think the devil stopped fooling religious people with the Pharisees?

The same religious spirit that fooled the Pharisees is still active in the modern-day church, in both small and big ways. The greater the religious spirit is, the lesser of God there is in the midst of it.

God doesn't like religiousness; it's like in Hosea 6:6 "For I desire mercy, and not sacrifice; and the knowledge of God more than burnt offerings." I think this is implying it isn't all about your sacrifices, it's about your relationship with Him. If one is stuck in his ways, then He will just let them be to themselves stalemated.

Now I will go one step further and say how the modern-day Pharisees persecute the real moves of God. The devil uses those people like puppets, and has tricked them to hear his voice so he can use them to come against the real. They think they're being used by God, where in fact, they have been unwittingly recruited into working for the enemy. Matt 23:24 "Ye blind guides, which strain at a gnat, and swallow a camel."

Now to lessen this blow, I need to remind you that the devil is everywhere, trying and trying to get in; it's a very common thing. Even I have to push demons back often. It's not that I'm a bad person; it's that the devil is aggressive and tries to get in any way he can! He's always pushing, talking, trying.

What you need to do is realize that the devil is very active everywhere with everyone. Even with the best of best Christians. He will start in a small way; once he gets some access, then he will try to grow his foothold into a person's life. This doesn't mean their demon possessed; it just means the devil is aggressive.

So with these religious people, the devil placed a seed of religiousness a long time ago. He gradually grew it until he can use them to persecute the real things of God. Trying to put the real works of God under that same religious spirit. The devil's guns are aimed at any life and power of God to destroy it. This is just one of the many ways he uses to destroy God's works; division is another example.

Yes, God always wins in the end, but the devil will do his best to stop the current work. I'm not trying to point the finger and say bad, bad. I'm trying to say wake up Christians! Realize that the same spirit of the Pharisees is able to guide you, and you need to get out of that spirit and find the real. You may end up fighting God instead of helping Him, just like the Pharisees did in the Bible. There are lesser and greater degrees of this; it's not all black or white.

It's many shades of grey in between. This religious spirit can affect any Christian whatsoever. I'm not talking just about leaders.

Often these Modern-day Pharisees are out there and have large followings. It's like the scripture blind leading the blind, Matt 15:14. Just because someone is a pastor, has a lot of doctorates, Bible school degrees, and decades of experience does not make them right. Even the Pharisees made God their life and continual quest. They were considered the Leaders and God's messengers.

These people have made God their lives, and they are in ever pursuit of God, but in fact, are modern-day Pharisees. This reminds me of one of Rick Joyner's final quest moments where there was a river, those protecting the river and the attacking army. Someone realized that they should offer this water to the invading army. When they were offered it, they were surprised by the offer and decided to try it. Once they tried it, they wanted more. They didn't realize how thirsty they truly were. Then they were converted and decided to help in offering the water to others. To the point where it became overwhelming, and they just had to invite them to come and get it for themselves. This river is the life of God; the invading army was Christians attacking the true. (See Topic "Worship is the only way to reach some" page 153)

The Pharisees rejected Jesus because they didn't even know the Father. If they had known Him, they would have never rejected Him John 8:19. They didn't know Him because their hearts were plugged up with their ideas of what God was.

God doesn't stay still; He's always moving like a river, never stagnating. He did something completely new when Jesus came to transition from old to new. Do you think God stops doing new things? If the modern-day Pharisees really knew Him, then they wouldn't be persecuting what He's doing now.

Do you really know Jesus and the Father, or do you know about Him; there is a difference. You need to have a personal relationship; that is walking and talking with Him in your everyday life, and He talks back in your spirit. But there is a counterfeit of this as well. (See Topic "Seeing in the Holy Spirit, and the leadings of the Holy Spirit" page 132)

The enemy is behind all this confusion. He doesn't want God to succeed, so he sets up traps of all sorts to get people off track. There are many more ways in which he can do this. Even bring a counterfeit of the real, where one thinks they're walking and talking with God, but in fact, are misled by the enemy. Luke 11:23, Mark 7:6

I write to you because you know it

1 John 2:21 "I have not written to you because you do not know the truth, but because you know it, and that no lie is of the truth."

I write to you because you already know it; you have already reached the pinnacle of your understanding, the height of your calling. You have attained all there is to attain. I am here to say not so. The river of God is always moving. I read the universe is always expanding and being created as we speak. The Lord is not one to sit around and stagnate; He is ever moving. You need to keep up with Him.

If you think you've arrived and stop growing, then you will simply sit still and stagnate. God doesn't want this; He wants someone He can mold as He pleases. If you feel you know it all and have reached the pinnacle, then you're missing out on what God has planned for you. You need to set this aside and seek the Lord in what your next step is. Be humble and trainable by the Lord because there is always more. But on the opposite side of the coin, the enemy can push you too far as well; there is a balance. There is such a thing as getting ahead of the Lord too. So you are either behind Him, walking right with Him, or ahead of Him.

Some feel they walk with the Lord and are always with what He's doing; but in fact, they are stagnated. This could be you; consider the possibility. You may know His name and know all about Him and His works, but do you really know Him? Knowing about someone and spending time with them are two entirely different things. You may know about Him and think you're close to Him where in fact, you really don't know Him at all. There are many Christians out there who think they're close to God, but in reality, are not. Because in order to know Him, you have to spend time with Him personally and be in contact with His Holy Spirit. People think that if they read about Him, and study Him, that they know Him. This can be good in some ways, but the more important part is to be in direct communication with Him. Be sensitive to Him, and hear His voice in your heart. But this is not to be confused with the enemy's voice, because he is trying all the time to trick us with a pseudo voice. So in order to know Him properly, you need to get in touch with the Holy Spirit and obey His leadings. Otherwise, we get into the blind leading the blind.

I ran across a situation where someone was told what God wanted them to do, but they immediately brushed it off. Saying that they were 100 percent sure of what they're supposed to do; disregarding the word that was presented to them, and feel they knew better. Often when God comes to someone and tells them what they need to do, they don't believe it and do it their way anyway, just like all the prophets of the Bible. They completely miss God and are stalemated. God is forced to just leave them stagnated. (See Topics "Seeing in the Holy Spirit, and the leadings of the Holy Spirit" page 132, and "Stay in touch with the Holy Spirit" Page 41)

The Price of the calling

The calling is more effective the more dead to self you are and obedient to His leading. That means a process of trimming your spiritual flesh over and over again. We shouldn't think that we have arrived and now we're done. God has a way of always finding something else to trim in your life. We are all sinners, so that means we sin. What God is trying to do is reduce that sin to minimal.

The price of the calling is you getting over yourself and being obedient to His leadings. It is getting rid of that which gets in the way. It is a painful process, but great is the reward. We all often want the reward, but don't realize the process to get to that point. Often when it comes to the point of discomfort is when people might stop and not progress any further, or slow down the process.

The more holiness God can instill into you, the more powerful and anointed you will be. Less of you and more of Him. When writing this, I was given the word instill but didn't know exactly what it meant. I looked it up, and this is what it means: Gradually Impart, or Drops (as in liquid). Which perfectly fits this topic God is trying to drop into you drops, and is working on you gradually.

Like if you were polishing something, you work on the worst part of it first. Then after that, you work on the smaller and smaller blemishes. He can't do this if you resist Him and His changes; you must be willing. Benny Hinn says: "quit trying and just surrender."

Now the price of the high calling is everything and obedience to His leadings. You must give Him all before He can give you His all. Like the song:

All of you, all that you have, and all that you ever hoped to be, for a life in Him. He's your source and provider, not you. He wants you to learn this because God is all about faith. He wants you to learn to trust Him in full faith without it making any sense sometimes; can you handle it! Gal 2:20, Philippians 3:14.

The 5 Ministries

Apostle, Prophet, Pastor, Teacher, Evangelist

All of these ministries are applicable to today.

    The Apostle is one to spark alive ministries in others. To start works, or to help others realize their gifts and plant the seeds. Many people think this ministry is retired and does not apply to the modern-day church, but it's still in fact active. It's just not acknowledged but persecuted.
    The Prophet is the one who sees visions, hears God, and is to relay this to His people. Like the watchmen of the city to warn the people before things happen, but there are scriptures that say that all should prophesy, 1Cor 14:31, Act 2:17. So we all have the ability to prophesy; that doesn't make us a prophet, it's just fulfilling our God given gifts.
    The Pastor is a confusing one, because most pastors in the modern-day church really are not pastors but in fact teachers instead. The ministry of a pastor is to encourage growth in people, and to personally help that person grow in their walk. It's like a garden, the apostle plants the seed, and the pastor waters that seed and takes care of it, nurturing its fruits. "Pastors" in the church today really are not pastors because they really don't get too involved in the lives of those they teach to.
    The teacher is one who teaches people to help them grow to deposit seeds of truth and teach and bring up to speed. To go into the depths of scripture and revelation.
    The Evangelist is one who witnesses to the lost that they might be saved through the belief that Jesus is the son of God. Or to plant a seed in the hearts of the unbelievers, that one day that seed may grow and they become believers.

1 Corinthians 12:28 "And God has placed in the church first of all apostles, second prophets, third teachers, then miracles, then gifts of healing, of helping, of guidance, and of different kinds of tongues." Ephesians 4:11-13, Ephesians 2:20

Women should be Free/Women Leaders

There seems to be some confusion with some people whether women are allowed to be leaders in the church or women have any power. But I'm here to say they should! We are all aware of those scriptures that Paul and others wrote about women, how they should act, and so forth. But this argument rests solely on those couple scriptures, and seems to neglect many more that point the opposite direction.

Now I did a little research, and people feel that these were the traditions in the Bible times. Certain towns were more sensitive to these matters, so perhaps these scriptures are rooted in those sensitive situations. But what about all the other things going on at the exact same time? Did you not know that there were women leaders that even Paul recognized and spoke of in Romans 16:7; Junia was an apostle. In Romans 16:1-2 Phoebe was a deacon, and Paul commends her and was saying to work with her. Acts 9:36 Tabitha was referred to as a disciple. She was always doing good and helping the poor. I am emphasizing Paul in these scriptures because of the couple of other scriptures that he wrote about women. It's believed that women at that time were not as learned as they are today. That was the particular situation in mind that those scriptures in question are referring to. Keep in mind that each of these books of the Bible was not intended to be read by everyone, but intended to be read by one particular group of people. In other letters, he is acknowledging women in leadership and asking people to work with them. Even as one of the top labels of the time, apostle. We can't just look at one scripture and base everything based on just that scripture. We need to weigh all scriptures and put them all in balance.

So if that wasn't convincing enough, let's continue. It is written in Galatians 3:26-29 "you are all sons of God through faith in Christ Jesus, for all of you who were baptized into Christ have clothed yourselves with Christ. There is neither Jew nor Greek, slave nor free, male <u>nor female</u>, for you are <u>all one in</u>

Christ Jesus. And if you belong to Christ, then you are Abraham's seed, and heirs according to the promise." There is no distinction; all are equal.

In Acts 21:9, there are four unmarried daughters who prophesied in Luke 2:36-38 there was a prophet Anna, in Acts 2:17-18 it says:"Your sons and daughters will prophesy…Even on my servants, both men and women, I will pour out my Spirit in those days, and they will prophesy"

In Luke 10:38-42, Mary asked Jesus for Elizabeth to come help, but Jesus says Mary has chosen what is better, and it will not be taken away from her. In John 20:14-18 and Matthew 28:1-10, Jesus appears to Mary Magdalene and she relays His being alive still to the others. Why wouldn't Jesus choose a man if it was such a big deal? That's because there's no difference according to Galatians 3:26-29 and Acts 2:17-18.

Now that we have talked about New Testament examples of women leaders and liberty. Here are Old Testament examples of women leaders and prophets.

In Judges 4:4-5, Deborah was the Judge and Prophet for Israel. That means that she spoke for God. The Israelites would go to her for counsel on what God would have them do. This was before Israel had kings; God was the king of Israel. The prophet/judge was His voice to the people. Not just anyone could fill this position; God had to choose them, and they had to have a solid relationship with God. Deborah was no dummy. She was a full prophet and judge, with God speaking into her ear for instructions to give to Israel.

2 Kings 22: 14-20 prophetess Huldah, who prophesied in verses 15-20 "And she said unto them, Thus saith the LORD God of Israel." In Nehemiah 6:14, prophet Noadiah. In Exd 15:20, Miriam Moses's sister was called a prophetess.

There's no difference between a man or a woman. Anything a man can do, a woman can also do; neither is better than the other. It's just simply a matter of Obedience, purity, their calling, and devotion to God which determines what they're to be doing and how effective they are in it. Just like anyone else. Jer 31:22
"How long will you go here and there, you backsliding daughter? For the Lord has created a new thing in the earth: a woman shall encompass a man."

Mantles

What a mantle is, is a commission. It's the authority and anointing to do something or have authority over something. The definition for mantle is role, responsibility, or authority. So there are a lot of different types of spiritual mantles; one for every God's purpose. A mantle is more than your personal spiritual gifts, because the gifts are without repentance. A mantle can be dropped out of disobedience, or negligence to the purpose. It's an anointing or a work that God is doing. Commissions are earned by obedience to His will. Once you have proven faithful, he will put you in a position that fits your giftings. Whether it's big or small, that is up to God. There's no small or big in the Lord; there is only obedience (See Topic "Accountable to what you have been given" Page 51). To continue in a mantle you have to be obedient to the purpose of it, and to His leadings. You can also lose that mantle if you veer off course from that mantles purpose, or make compromises in that mantles purpose.

You have to do what that mantle is for, otherwise it's a compromise. If in time you're still compromised; then that mantle will either drop to the ground and remain unused or be given to another to fulfill. God may allow the mantle to be used in a compromised condition for a while. But if you don't change things, then He will look for someone who will use it properly and give it to them. That person may be a nobody or the unexpected person. Just like David, the unlikely shepherd. 1 Samuel 16:7 "for the Lord seeth not as man seeth; for man looketh on the outward appearance, but the Lord looketh on the heart."

You do not have to be an ordained minister or go to Bible school to qualify for a mantle, or anything in God for that matter. Bible school is nice, but it isn't required by God; only man thinks this. What is required is sensitivity to God's will and obedience.

The devil will come in where a mantle is present and try to thwart God's purpose. To cause you to compromise the calling and veer you away from His purpose. Because the devil tries to compromise all God's works. If he's successful, then the mantle is dropped and will just sit there dormant until either the original person or group picks it back up. If an appropriate amount of time has passed to recover it. Then God will lead someone else to pick it up who will use it.

There are many mantles out there; they can be full ministries or an anointing like healing, speaking, prophet, or many other things.

Now another dynamic is sometimes "God gives pieces of mantles; so that they're required to work with others in order for them to work properly" (paraphrased from a book I read somewhere). God likes the corporate anointing, so it's not a one person show. One person does one type of thing, and another does a complimenting other thing. They are not all the same thing; they're different and work harmoniously with each other. Together they create a whole.

Humility

"He who is greatest among you will be your servant. Whoever exalts Himself will be humbled, and whoever humbles himself will be exalted." Matt. 23:11-12

Jesus is the son of God of the most high God, which is the Word of God in a person, the only one who is worthy of breaking the 7 seals, the Lamb of God, and part of the almighty Godhead. You would think if anyone had anything to boast about, it would be Him. But that would degrade His name and who He is.

He said: "For even the Son of Man did not come to be served, but to serve, and to give His life as a ransom for many." Jesus came very humbly, in a manger with animals. In today's terms, that would mean that Jesus was born in a smelly barn; unannounced to the world. Then He lived a humble life as a carpenter, He came to serve, and He was humble. Humble doesn't mean submissive; it means no pride. We should follow Jesus's example. Many times, when we have a gifting or anointing, we tend to sometimes think of our importance. Which reminds me of a heavenly experience book I read where in heaven they said that man over emphasizes his importance. God needs us, yes, but He will use another if we are too prideful or have vain glory. Thinking, God showed up because you were there. This may be true in a way, but don't get prideful about it. God showed up not for your sake but for the sake of His people. You just simply were His instrument to accomplish the task. He doesn't want us to get into pride because of the gift He gave us. But He also doesn't want us to have false humility and not use our gifts either. He gave us those gifts to use them, not to let them stagnate in the corner. Rick Joyner says the true test of humility is to listen to someone you think is lesser than you.

In Rick Joyner's final quest series, Rick was wearing shiny armor that represented His calling. Soon after, he was offered the cloak of humility. It was a cloak that covered up His shiny armor and was very plain and average. By looking at it, you wouldn't know what was under it. We should also put this cloak of humility on like he did. Being more concerned with getting the task done rather than our shiny armor showing.

God uses us, but we're simply His tool that He uses to come and do the work himself. If God didn't show up, do you think we of ourselves with our anointing and mantels could accomplish anything? God gave authority over the earth to mankind. He needs to use the authority He gave us to come with the anointing. He will not come unless we participate.

Jesus was showing us something about humility when He washed the disciple's feet. He was showing us love and humility; this is powerful if you think about it. The love and humility that comes out of Jesus is awesome. "God resists the proud, but gives grace to the humble." James 4:6.

Often you may be afraid that opportunities may pass you by, and you won't get to use your giftings. But God is big enough of a God where He will orchestrate the start and the end of all things. This is not to say that you should not use your giftings; just let God show you. Do not be concerned with getting the praises of people. God deserves all Glory; so don't try to take some of that glory unto yourself. You are a servant of God, and He should get all glory. I used to think when I walked into a special meeting that I hoped they would see my giftings, and recognize them. I thought about this and came up with the conclusion, let them see God, not me.

Also, we're working as a team, like in the final quest, where Paul asked are you trying to build your kingdom or God's kingdom? We need to realize in the body of Christ that we're all on the same team and work together to get to the spiritual goal. Not working against each other, or stumbling all over each other to try to get to the top first. This is of the flesh and not the spirit. You're trying to build your own kingdom, not God's. You are building God's kingdom when you work as a unit and not caring if you get any credit for it; it's God doing, not you. Think of it like this: God is our leader in the army of the Lord. He's orchestrating the game plan from above. He tells you to go do a portion and calls another to do another portion to complete the task at hand. Any of these people could say they did it and be jealous of the next person who claims the same. But you're not the one who did it. God orchestrated multiple people to do it, and He should get all glory. We should not take credit for something God is having us do. Yes, we have the giftings to do what He told us to do, but He also gave other's gifts as well. God will give you credit for your faithfulness and humility, and advance you in His army as you're humble and obedient to His will.

As you know, In the real world working together as a team works much better than every person for themselves. It's much more productive, and it gets done faster. God is the one who made us, gave us our gifts, the one who empowers our gifts, and where all things come from. He just simply wants to use us, not to stink up the room with our pride, because pride is a stench to God.

If we are unteachable, He will have to move on to someone else who is more humble and receptive. You might miss your high calling this way and have to settle for a more mediocre calling instead without even realizing it.

John 13:12-15 "So when He had washed their feet, taken His garments, and sat down again, He said to them, "Do you know what I have done to you? You call Me Teacher and Lord, and you say well, for so I am. If I then, your Lord and Teacher, have washed your feet, you also ought to wash one another's feet. For I have given you an example, that you should do as I have done to you."

Luke 14:11 "For everyone who exalts himself will be humbled, and whoever humbles himself will be exalted."

Luke 18:10-13 "Two men went up into the temple to pray; one was a Pharisee, and the other was a tax collector. The Pharisee stood and prayed to Himself like this: 'God, I thank you, that I am not like the rest of men, extortioners, unrighteous, adulterers, or even like this tax collector. I fast twice a week. I give tithes of all that I get. 'But the tax collector, standing far away, wouldn't even lift up His eyes to heaven, But beat His breast, saying, 'God, be merciful to me, a sinner! 'I tell you, this man went down to His house justified rather than the other; for everyone who exalts Himself will be humbled, But He who humbles Himself will be exalted."

Bow down low to receive the next level

God told me once through a prophecy if I ever get into pride that I've lost it.

I've been thinking about that for many years. It's easy when you get more power or position from God to get into pride; because of the abilities God has given you and what anointings you have. For me, it was a battle, because there's the tendency to think highly of yourself because of the anointing.

I read a book about someone having a vision of heaven; in that vision, someone said "man often over emphasizes his importance," or overrates his abilities and how God uses them. God wants to use you, but He wants a heart that's pure and without pride. "God resists the proud but gives grace to the humble" 1 Peter 5:5 (CSB).

He doesn't want you to have pride in your giftings or anointings because He alone should get the glory. He's the one that gave you those gifts. Do not try to take glory onto yourself. Any gifts that you or I have are because He gave them to you. He should get any and all glory. He wants to bless you with more anointings and gifts, but you must prove faithful with what you have. He will not give you more when you're full of pride; pride is a stench to Him. In one of Rick Joyner's final quest books, someone said: "you are known by your humility." But you are also measured by your obedience. In another final quest book, the old eagle said: it doesn't matter how many things you do for Him in this life. What matters is obedience to do His will and what He has called you to do; that is what we're measured by. God wants you to be humble, not puffed up with your gifts. He gives grace to the humble.

I often see people with anointings think they have hit the top, and perhaps God has brought them far, but God always wants to give more. If you're faithful with what He has given you and are humble, then He will give you more. He doesn't want you taking glory unto yourself; because if He gave you more, then it would become even a bigger mess. God is in the business of taming the flesh; He wants less of you and more of Him. He wants to keep trimming you and trimming you.

I consider dying to self a continual process, always moving, never stopping, more and more. It's the same with the anointing; if you will be faithful, then He will give you more. If God never showed up in a meeting, then it would be nothing and lifeless. He might not show for your sake but for the sake of the people. You are like an extension cord; God is only moving through you. You are not the power! Remain humble and give Him the glory in all things. James 4:10

Obedience vs. Works

We need to hear from God what He would have us do in our life and do it. But we need to be careful because we may invent our own calling without knowing better. Often we can get into the hype of doing things, or a zealousness for heavenly rewards, but is this what God told us to do.

Often we can get derailed from our actual calling in doing things that seem right to us. Not every opportunity is right. We need to weigh in our hearts if we are to do that opportunity. Listen to the Holy Spirit, is He grieving our heart, and pray about it. Our flesh could propel us toward that opportunity. We need to learn the difference between our flesh and the Holy Spirit's leadings. We could be completely derailed from what we were supposed to do! An example is: there was this person who was in a very public ministry position, but then they discovered that their higher calling was something else, something simpler than what they were doing. The greater opportunities are not always the right opportunities. Often we can get a good feeling from doing something good, and do it again to feel good. That good feeling doesn't mean that's what we're supposed to do it.

Ask God to reveal to you if what you're doing is what He would have you do; when He does, be willing to do whatever He tells you. Even if you have to bend around backwards to do it, or feel like you're losing your progress. God knows best. What may seem good to you may actually be bad in the spiritual sense.

What if you were in completely the wrong place? A place that you invented. But God had other plans for you. Even if your current position seems like a high position; in order to get right with Him, you have to do whatever He tells you to do. Even if that means giving up all power! In the spiritual sense, if you're not in the right position, then you really are not in power or position; it's man-made and powerless in God. It may seem well and good but really isn't.

Maybe God has something greater for you, but He has to train you in a more simple position first before He can advance you. If you choose to ignore His instructions, then He will leave you to your own devices, and you will be powerless spiritually, in rebellion.

If you're in the wrong position, God is doing you a favor. You really are not losing from this point, but gaining. Because true spiritual maturity is obtained in obedience and humility, not in the works that we accomplish in this life. You basically were off the right path, and God is getting back on the true path, because before you were on your own path. 1 Chron 16:11

True authority and maneuvering for position

There is a process that God uses to train and bring up those who are willing. And it can be different for every person. God knows when a person is ready and when they're not. He also knows what they need to work on and so forth. He may put them in a lower work to train things into them. When their ready, they will be promoted to a more fitting position. This may take more time than one may like. The lower position may or may not be desirable. This is God's process, and we must trust Him; He knows what He's doing. He's very aware of what we are capable of.

He often wants to work into us strength; hardening our abilities so that whatever the enemy may throw against us in the future will not deter or derail us 1 Peter 5:8. This is God's process, we must be patient with Him. But some want position faster, and try to make their own way into position. It may seem good that we would want to fulfill our full potential. But what you may not realize is, is that you may be choosing the lower road, one that may seem great to you, but is not in the spirit.

The path that God chooses for you may not be as glamorous at first, but He knows what He's doing! The position you have chosen may succeed for a while, but God is not in it. In the future, it will either stagnate or be dethroned. We can not get anything God has not given to us. It may appear that we have it, but in reality, we don't. Perhaps it is the proper position, but you're not mature enough yet, or the time isn't right.

God needs to work into you the stature that you need for your success in the position. He may see that you need to be stronger in one area; or work something out of you that would deter, weaken, or even pollute your calling. God sees your entire being, and He knows what things you will face in your calling. He will release you when you are fully ready. Not when you may falter or not be potent enough. You may be successful in the position, but He may want to work in you a higher standard; to make you more potent and effective in that position. So be patient and let Him show you when you're ready. You need to be faithful to what God is having you do. Then God would move you into a true position when it's the right time. Luke 16:10

More people doesn't always mean more anointing or authority. Lesser sometimes is more. God may choose to put you in a smaller, more potent situation as the final position. If that is what God is having you do, then that's the best place you can be. What appears to the eye to be more, may actually be less. Only God knows this, and you must let Him position you like only He can. This is true authority. True authority is where favor and the power of God are. Maneuvered authority is where He leaves you without power and favor; this is not a good place to be.

If you have taken a position or calling without His permission. You should pursue God to what He would have you do and listen and do what He says. Even if it's not very desirable, be open to it. That is what you need to do to get back into alignment with Him.

God is the source of power. No one can have the glory or anointing without Him. Some try to make it happen by themselves; if God has not authored it, it remains fruitless. He's the one who brings the anointing, and when you step outside of this, you potentially step outside of His anointing.

If you have been told what you need to do and don't do it. You will dry up in that position because you have been dethroned. We need to be in God's will, otherwise, He will not bless it, and it will dry up. Also, your reward in heaven will be compromised. So stop vying for position and just build the kingdom of God. In the end, God will get His way, whether you submit to it or not. It's better to listen to His corrections, then at least you have a chance of recovery of your calling. It may be undesirable, but if you're faithful to submit unto Him, He will see that and get you back on the path of true authority.

I must become lesser so He might become greater

Just like John the Baptist said: "He must increase, but I must decrease" John 3:30. For God to be in control of our lives, we must release our all to Him. We must get our flesh out of the way and surrender all.

You might think, okay God I surrender all, but do you know what that really means. The ultimate form of this is anything that would greave God, whatever that might be. There are many layers of this; He doesn't expect you to do it all at once, just as He shows you. God will continue to reveal things to you that need to be trimmed out of your life. There is the tendency to think that you've given all to God and are good. Yes, to a point probably, but there are still things that God might not have revealed to you yet. It might hurt, the things He would ask of you, you might say you've been there too. Don't dismiss it so easily. Consider that there's always something that God can show you next; just be open to it.

We must become lesser and lesser so that He might become greater in us. I read somewhere that the more that you die to self, the more liberty there is, not for the person but for God in the person.

It's like a horse that needs to be bridled. The horse at first is uncooperative, but in time, they become tempered and don't need that bridal anymore. How untamed are you? Does God have you tamed, or are you all willy-nilly with your will? Does God orchestrate your days, or does He only when you want Him to?

There are times when one has great experiences in His spirit. But in everyday life, we need to continue to hear and work with Him in even the small matters. He wants to do this so you learn to walk with Him. The sharper you are in His spirit, the more He can trust you with. He wants to lead you every day, because when you get good at it, He can use you greatly. The laborers are few, and the time is short. Are you willing to endure the cost?

The point of Saturation, and The Pain of Correction

In our walk with God, we progress toward His holiness and dying to self. God then wants to show us the next step in our growth; something that we need to work on. But this may or may not be comfortable, depending on how important the presented flaw is to us. We may very well like that flaw a lot and don't want to part with it because it would hurt to get rid of it. Sometimes it's easy and obvious that it needs to be gotten rid of, and other times not. Sometimes it just plain hurts what's presented to us to change. We may even deny it, which can often be the case. We deny it because it's too painful to face, or we like it and want to keep it. Sometimes God can use others to point our flaws, but often this can be rejected. What usually happens is when they're confronted about a serious matter, they get hurt, run away, and blame the person who told them about it. They couldn't handle the information being presented, whether it's directly from God or through another person. I like to call this the point of saturation. The point where it becomes too much to handle, where you don't believe it and want to quit. Kind of like a sponge, when it's full of water it can't accept anymore. It is over saturating that it's hard to handle. You have to squeeze some of you out, to put more of God in. I have gone through many of these points of saturations myself.

I'm just realizing that it's Him who decided to tell you through the other person. So don't look at the person who is helping you out of your issues; look at God. He's the one who did it. I have read many times in people's heavenly vision books, that He wants us to go through His fire (spiritual fire/dying to self). So that He can burn off the chaff and any extra nonsense that doesn't need to be there; this is a painful process.

But in reality, correction hurts, and it hurts a lot. You need to realize that it's a good thing; God is using this as a tool to help you grow into more maturity. You need to be humble and consider the things that were said and not just blow them off. Because if you blow them off, and you really have those issues, then the issue remains unresolved. God will just have to stall you, and you won't progress any further until you resolve it. But if you don't, then you will be stalemated at that spiritual level. God wants the most possible for you. So take the corrections that come your way seriously. Because God may actually be behind it, trying to speak to you.

Many at this point will say yes, I got that covered, but yet still have issues that remain unresolved. Doing everything I just described by running away from the problem, I've seen this many times. The key is to be humble and ask God are these things really true; consider and try to be fair. Step outside of yourself and view it. It hurts a lot, but don't respond out of this pain and reject it. Let the pain work the problem that was presented.

You need to consider if there is truth to what's being said, giving it a true chance; is any part of it true? Be humble and think about if there is anything that can be changed on your side. Be truthful and honest about it with yourself.

It is overwhelming, and it's hard at first. You need to just roll through the pain and just keep going. Considering it a possibility is a start. It takes a day or longer to heal the emotions on the matter. After a little time, the matter at hand will seem more manageable and not as painful. This can even be especially true when being rebuked; yes, it hurts a lot but turn into the pain and don't reject the message. Time will heal your pain, and in considering it, you will grow spiritually.

God says He reproves those He loves Rev 3:19. It's to get your attention. God doesn't remain angry at you if you have a teachable heart. If you don't change, then He could remain frustrated with you. When you consider change, God will see the change in you and bless you for it. A couple of phrases I like to say to myself are: put up with the changes or plow through it.

I am saying these things because I have had this process happen to me over and over again. But what I have found is that God is there with you, working through the pain. He sends me His presence while I'm working through it. He's the one who did the correction, so don't point the finger at the messenger. God is often the one thinking these things. He wasn't able to tell you because of your lack of hearing or stubbornness. So he had to send this messenger to you.

What you need to do is just put up with the correction even though it hurts, and digest it the best you can. It's a good thing in the long run. God knows what you need to work on, so trust His judgment. He knows what He's doing; He has done it time and time again in humans in all the history of humankind. Be humble, willing to change, and open to consider correction from anybody, even if you view them as lesser than you. Like the scripture says, He has hidden from the wise and prudent and has given it to babes, Matt 11:25, Luke 10:21. Often people see the errors in others, where that person doesn't see it at all. Humility is the key; consider what is being said, if any portion of it is accurate. Contemplate what you can change, and make that change.

Hebrews 12:5-11 "And ye have forgotten the exhortation which speaketh unto you as unto children, My son, despise not thou the chastening of the Lord, nor faint when thou art rebuked of Him: For whom the Lord loveth He chasteneth, and scourgeth every son whom He receiveth. If ye endure chastening, God dealeth with you as with sons; for what son is he whom the Father chasteneth not? But if ye be without chastisement, whereof all are partakers, then are ye bastards, and not sons. Furthermore we have had fathers of our flesh which corrected us, and we gave them reverence: shall we not much rather be in subjection unto the Father of spirits, and live? For they verily for a few days chastened us after their own pleasure; but He for our profit, that we might be partakers of His holiness. Now no chastening for the present seemeth to be joyous, but grievous: nevertheless afterward it yieldeth the peaceable fruit of righteousness unto them which are exercised thereby."

We are chastised because He loves us. Out of that chastisement, if we submit to it, we become closer to Him. Because the sin is being corrected; the less sin we have, the closer we can get to Him. Realizing this is half the battle.

Too Busy, Don't over plan and miss God

Some people are too busy on a day-to-day basis. They fill up their entire schedule to the point of overflowing. And if they ever have a let up of things, they think of something else to fill it.

One time I seen a ministry that had a side business that was related to their giftings. Even in the same building that they do ministry events. But the business was very demanding. They scheduled a meeting on a certain day and also scheduled another thing related to the business right after the meeting. The meeting went well, but the anointing wanted to go further. The event was scheduled, so they stopped the meeting and anointing. We need to give God space and be willing to change our schedules at a second's notice. Their ministry business was so demanding that the things that God wanted to do had to work around the business. God should be first!

People can also get wound up in doing things for God, that they will start things that sound noble and good to do, but can neglect what God wants them to do by making plans for God. The person is making plans for God in their own mind. Often forgetting to seek God in what He would have them do. Don't get ahead of God and plan for Him. Seek what He wants! Lamentations 3:25-26

Someone told me a parable that they were given because they asked Jesus to give them a parable like in the old times. Then one day, He sat down next to them and told them a parable (paraphrased). God owns a hardware store. He hired people to tend to the hardware store and had many employees. But many of the employees were more interested in working in and doing the work of the hardware store. They just did their own thing and were more interested in the works than in Him. They were caught up in what they wanted to do. But there were some who would spend time with Him.

Sometimes He just wanted to spend time with them. God wants us to seek Him rather than being more interested in doing His works. Rick Joyner says: It's more important who we become in the Lord, rather than many works accomplished in this life.

There is a hype and excitement to do things for God, but that can turn into making plans for Him. This process can even push Him out of your life without you even knowing it. This seems to happen a lot in the church world. Thinking that they're doing things for God, but are actually doing their own things for God. He might have something different for you to do that's of more importance to Him. You need to be sensitive to Him in what He wants. If He wants to change your schedule, let Him! Be spontaneous, because He doesn't always give you a schedule. He often likes to give you what you're supposed to at the last minute. We often get impatient and make something happen. Don't get ahead of Him!

Changing God's will out of convenience

God often imparts a vision or a direction in one's heart of doing a particular thing for Him. And they feel strongly impressed to do so, perhaps start doing it, and God blesses them in it. Sometimes hard times can come, or an opportunity comes that causes a person to reconsider what God told them. They might say maybe God has different plans. Maybe I should put what God told me to do before on the market (like in a land for God), and if it sells, maybe God has different plans. But actually, you may be selling off your high calling, and it could be lost if you did.

I am referring to a couple of situations in my mind as I write this, both a little different. One sold land that they said was set aside for God, and another was losing a house to foreclosure that was meant for God as well. They listed it on the market for a lesser price than full. Someone became interested and was going to put a statue of some god right where that person committed their life to doing His will. They didn't feel any peace listing or in selling it. They were almost to the end of the foreclosure process, but the fact was that they were not supposed to do it. It doesn't make any brain sense, but it made God sense to not do so. (proceed at your own risk)

God is able, and His ways are not our ways. Some will bend God's will around to what's convenient at the time. Basically, doing what they want to do, rather than what the heart of God is. Putting up fleeces like if it sells, then it's probably okay, is not always true! If you feel no peace about it, then that is your answer; follow after peace.

You may have peace about doing something contrary to what God told you to do. This may be due to you feel relieved to be done with the pressure, but this isn't necessarily God's peace. Or perhaps you're out of touch with God and feel your own peace.

Think back to what God told you originally and follow that. Even if it's totally inconvenient and hard, or even ridiculous. God is the God of what you think is ridiculous and undoable. What seems to be convenient is not necessarily what you should do. (See Topic "Faith" page 26).

Some people do whatever they feel like doing. They're afraid of difficulty, uncertainty, or insecurity. You need to take a step of faith and trust God. God sees you and your situation, and He also knows the future. So trust Him, He knows what He's doing.

The surety of it might seem to you as unsure, but God will meet you; you need to trust Him. God sees the whole picture; He even sees what's going to happen and knows it will be fine. "Now faith is the substance of things hoped for, the evidence of things not seen" Hebrews 11:1. It may come differently than you think; it may be unconventional or take time. Be flexible!

Think about Moses parting the red sea. Did they know what was going to happen as they were heading there? No, in fact, they were heading toward a military blunder in man's mind, closed off from escape, an easy target for the Egyptians. Especially when they heard the Egyptians were coming. It would seem they were done for, but God told them to wait there. Then when the time was right, He performed something they never dreamt of. God opened up the sea! If you think about it, this was pre-planned by God, and the best way to get rid of them. We think of this story as fact and don't think of what an amazing miracle this was; a creative miracle that we take for granted today. God is the same past, present, and future.

Spirit of Fear

The spirit of fear is an actual demon that specializes in fear and sending fear. This is his sole purpose and specialty. There is a demon for every single negative force in the world. He can push fear onto you; it's your job to learn to push it off of you. He can put this energy of fear on you without you doing that much to provoke it. If he knows he can get you to participate in this fear, then he will do it on a regular basis.

I watched a video about someone who used to be a warlock, and he was able to command demons at his whim, telling them what to do. Then he talked about a spirit called a waster spirit. That would work themselves into a person's life little by little, and in time it would push an extreme form of fear that would cause them to be fearful of everything there was to be afraid of. Even to being afraid of being alone, going out, and many other things. An all-consuming fear that would ruin that person. This man could tell this spirit to go to someone to ruin them.

I personally know the spirit of fear. Because I have had a big battle with it, and am just getting some victory over it. Fear over this or that, it just doesn't end in either small matters or big matters. He gets you to get fear over even small matters or non-matters. It's his job to keep you fearful; fear is the opposite of faith. I imagine that fear is one of the devil's greatest tools. It is even mentioned in 1 John 4:18 "There is no fear in love; but perfect love casteth out fear: because fear hath torment. He that feareth is not made perfect in love," and 2 Timothy 1:7 "For God has not given us the spirit of fear, but of power and of love and of a sound mind."

The devil tries to get you to stay away from faith by using fear. Because there is great power in faith, and the devil doesn't want this power wreaking havoc on his kingdom of darkness. The devil is empowered in fear because you're having faith in negative things. That is exactly where the devil wants you. So we need to replace fear with faith (belief in the positive and Gods abilities). See Topic "Devil's last stand and strong demon submission" page 178 on how to overcome this spirit, because it's a sticky one. The key is to not participate with it but to contradict it. Even though you're feeling the fear energy in your heart, that is the enemy pushing that energy on you. Matthew 6:34

Spiritual Suffocation

One of the devil's goals is to stagnate you spiritually. Where you're a lesser threat to Him and more manageable. There are many ways in which he can do this. If left unchecked, it can cause a person to get dry spiritually or completely numb. In some cases, a person's eyes will look void of much life of God. Matthew 6:22-23.

It can happen through various emotions that leak out life and dry you out, like sadness, worrying, anger, hate, etc.. These emotions can numb your spirit to the things of the spirit, like hearing the Holy Spirit, feeling His presence, or spiritual sensitivity (feeling demonic presence or oppression).

Another dynamic is the enemy tries to push negative energy on you. Often it's a tangible energy that you can feel in your heart. Sometimes there can be spiritual oppression on an entire neighborhood or town (See Topic "Know your spiritual boundaries, what you have authority over" page 180). The devil can develop a stronghold of a particular kind, depending on the situation, like a spirit of depression, lust, hatred, laziness, or just an oppression. It could be anything as long as the neighborhood, town, state, or country participates in it. Then the devil will try to push that feeling on you and try to get you to participate in it as well. But you need to wrestle with it and push it off.

There is even a demon specific to sucking out spiritual life out of people. Often people are unaware of these things. Whether you believe it or not, it is happening. People who are unaware or don't recognize it get sucked dry spiritually. What you need to do is recognize it's happening and push it out of your space; which isn't always easy. It is an icky feeling or a spiritual press. You need to pray through it and cast away demons involved out of your space (See Topic "Devil's last stand and strong demon submission" page 178)

Many people think this icky feeling is them having a bad emotion or day. This icky feeling is not coming from you, but being pushed on you from the outside by the demonic. The best way to rid of it is to pray in tongues and say: I bind this demonic spirit off of me. Be gone in the name of Jesus. Or if it's especially stubborn, then say:
"in the name of Jesus, the devil has to leave," over and over again, without fear in your heart. You have the right to kick these things off of you and out of your space! But be careful because you can't kick it out of someone else's space without their agreement. But if you've been given permission to be somewhere,

then you have authority over the space given to you. (See Topic "Know your spiritual boundaries, what you have authority over" page 180). If you're in your home and have these issues, then there are a few things that help with oppression. Like putting a worship cd on day and night to a level that's not audible, because the devil can still hear it. Or get a water fountain. Because falling and splashing water has all the frequencies of audio both high and low; which is peaceful, and the enemy hates. And spend time in personal worship with a cd/mp3 player and headphones, not just over a speaker. I believe there is something about headphones that makes worship more potent. I can tell if my spirit is dragging. So when I come to this point, I will worship to pick it back up. Try it, you may not realize just how thirsty and dry you really are until you do it.

Also, things that you allow in your home can affect your household as well. Bad movies, video games, sometimes objects can have bad energy. You need to keep your spiritual boundaries up and don't allow anything to contaminate your space.

Another thing I learned recently was I was growing a garden, and one type of bug was ruining one type of plant. With anger, I said I hate that bug. The next morning the Holy Spirit said to me that hatred spills His life. Spiritual suffocation can be subtle also. What you need to do is to recognize that it's happening and deal with it.

Everybody Speaks the Same Language

I consider dying to self as a continual process and that I haven't arrived or am there. I was in a semi-mountainous area of the United States and was high up and almost at the top of a mountain. We were staying there for some nights. I decided I wanted to go to the top of the mountain to see if I can see panoramically. (Caution: This can be dangerous, you could get lost; do not attempt this. Because one has a tendency of losing their direction, where everything looks the same. I was disorientated when I walked back.)

Before I started, I saw a top and figured that is the top, and it wouldn't take long. So I started and got there, then I saw another top. I said okay, just that much farther. So I got there, and still another. I kept going, and yet another, and another, and another. It ended up being 5-7 that I thought were the top, then finally I got there, and I was absolutely exhausted. And I discovered it was way, way farther than I ever imagined. I kept going because I thought each top was for sure the top. This is like our walk in God; there are many levels of maturity. Just like when Jesus refers to the greatest in heaven. That must indicate that we're rewarded according to our obedience and humility, 1 Peter 5:5. Yes, there are many levels of rewards in heaven. It is according to your obedience of how faithful you were to what you have been given. How far are you willing to go, and how much are you willing to sacrifice here on earth, so that God can have His way through you? But don't try to do it all in one step. Let God show you what you need to work on and be willing and pliable. Some people will limit how much they allow God to use them by their choices. I'm not referring to the works that you do for God. I'm referring to the level of holiness and obedience.

God calls us up His mountain. The farther we go up, the holier we become and the more of the flesh that has to be trimmed. How much control does God have over you? Who runs your life? The Holy Spirit or you, and to what degree? This doesn't mean you have to be perfect. It means that you're pursuing Him the best you know how; pursuing His will, not your own. You need to seek Him in what He would have you do and be willing to do it.

Now for those in ministry, this doesn't mean you're on top either. It's a continual process, like the mountain I climbed. There are many tops; you may see a top and view it as the top, but it probably isn't. The river of God is constantly moving! Not sitting and stagnating. You must continually pursue Him and His will. Like the river, He is not sitting still but moving forward. He doesn't always do the same thing every time; He may do different things each time.

The reason I wrote this topic is because I see many people all talk the exact same language or verbiage; yet be at completely different levels of maturity. Or even talk about something that in fact, they haven't fully attained yet, but speak of it as if they have. They feel that they have, but in fact, have more yet to go. It's a veil over their eyes, like the mountain hilltop that blocks the view of the higher levels. There may be many more levels of maturity for you to progress. It's hidden from our eyes; that's why I stress to keep walking, keep seeking, and hear His voice. He will instruct you on what to do or not do in order to grow.

He is the same yesterday, today, and forever. God will speak to anyone who seeks to hear His voice, but it's a still small voice. Calm your mind and sit and ask Him to speak to you. Be aware the enemy can imitate the Holy Spirit and speak to you. His voice is easier to hear than the Holy Spirit; you have to judge it by its fruits. If the devil can't stop you, he will try to push you too far, and that's just as bad. It's easier to hear Him right when you wake up because your mind is neutral, and your spirit is calm. You need to ask the Holy Spirit to teach you how to hear Him.

Everybody can have the same words and all be saying the exact same thing, yet all be on completely different levels of maturity and growth. There are various levels of God's presence as well. He will only pour out as much as one can handle. And that presence can be very touching to that person because that is what they needed. But in fact, there are more levels of outpouring as well. Keep pursuing Him, and you will feel His presence in greater and greater ways; I view this as endless.

There are many levels in God, and there are many levels in worship as well. Not everybody is at the same level, even though they speak the same language about it. You can have someone who is on a much more mature level say the exact same words, and they sound like they both had the same experience. Where in fact, they were drastically different. This is determined by how much each person can handle and the level of dying to self. If there's more self in the way, it's harder to reach a deeper level in Him.

The "Who's your covering" misconception

There is no scripture that talks about being under a covering of a man. Some scriptures may sound like it, but are in fact, twisted to conform to the who's your covering concept of today. It says forsake not the assembling of yourselves Hebrews 10:25. That doesn't mean a church building. It could be a simple home group of people that get together. This thing about having to be under some pastor as your covering is twisted scriptures, just because most people believe one way doesn't make it true. When contemplating this topic, I heard the Holy Spirit say "Tradition."

Because we have been taught one thing for so long, we have a resistance to any other concept. The problem with the who's your covering concept is the church officials and people use this as a tool to silence those who don't conform to their ideas on things. Using it to disqualify those who are not under a covering.

Were all the prophets of old under a covering, or were they accountable to God Himself? I'm thinking church officials are concerned about someone going off into the wacky zone. I'd like to redefine covering: the prophet is subject to the prophet (or to each other), and we only see in part, 1 Cor 13:9. So if we only have a part, we must be humble to receive the other part from others. Also, be willing to consider if the corrections of others are true.

Most pastors really are not your covering; they may say they are, but really are not. That would involve knowing each and every person personally and knowing their personal life. Enough to where they could help them with their downfalls personally. God does this in other ways, often by the people around them. I'm referring to a walk towards holiness, which can be subtle sins. Sure they can preach in front of the pulpit, hoping they hit the right topic, but that's complete hit or miss. To tell you the truth, people of Christianity really are walking sloppy grace lives. They often really don't pursue the path toward holiness. They might have a symbolism of it, but really one needs to work on it continually. There are many layers and levels toward holiness; sin is rampant in the church and left unchecked.

Perhaps you may not realize what level of holiness I'm referring to; the mainstream church of today overlooks most of it! I'm not talking about blatant sins; I'm talking about subtle sins that cloud our spirit and keep us at a basic level of Christianity. It's the pursuit of holiness that is lacking. Yes, we are all sinners, but we need to try to be better at it.

Sometimes Pastors are afraid to talk about these things because they don't want to scare off their tithe money. I'm not talking about doing it in a spirit of anger, but in a spirit of conviction and repentance. Like one thing is, you can contaminate your spirit with many forms of bad TV, games, or internet. Today's pastors are either blind to these dynamics, or don't bother to convey them to their churches.

The real covering is the Holy Spirit, Jesus, and each other. But don't deafen your ear to where you can't hear Him or to others He sent. Be subject unto each other, just like the prophet is subject to the prophet. Because we often can see the errors in others whereas that person doesn't see them at all.

Who is your pastor's covering? Who's that person's covering? And so on to nothing. It's like a warm day when a cloud gets between you and the sun you *feel cold. Pastors as "coverings" are that cloud between you and God. You should go directly to God yourself. Another dynamic is when you're under a man's covering, you are limited by their spiritual level in everything. When you approach their spiritual level, which may not be so great, you hit a spiritual wall and have to stop. Be accountable to one another in Christ, not to a covering.*

The understanding of coverings today is manmade and not true Christianity. But don't go making even this into a religion that has to be followed; like you have to belong to a home church. Sometimes people can have such a rich relationship with the Father that they're loners, but they should still be willing to receive potential correction from others and live a Godly life.

Arguing, Defense and Walls a better way

Something hurts someone, or an offense happens. Often what can happen is both sides in the argument might argue loudly, exchange insults, or strongly disagree. These are certainly things that can happen. What I realized is when you yell at someone, attack them, or they feel judged, they will put up a wall and close off their heart. They are less likely to hear your side to any real effective resolution; it often pushes them further away.

I discovered people are much more responsive if there's an open floor to just talk out the issue back and forth, hopefully calmly. One will say their offense, and they in turn say how they feel. Maybe it was a misunderstanding that would be cleared up with a small amount of communication.

It is my opinion that a healthy relationship is based upon communication; open and free, talking it out. But each person is different; you have to figure out how to communicate the best with that person. Leaving out judgments and insults also helps. Because you're only hurting the other person. They will put up walls in their heart, which disables effective communication and resolution. I know you're hurt too, but I feel this gets way further because both feel they can express how they feel in an open unhindered environment. Where both sides don't put up walls so much, making it easier to resolve things.

Another thing to consider is, often both sides have a fault in the matter, and both need to admit to their part of the fault (See Topic "Apology tool of great healing" page 104). But don't reserve your admitting to your fault only if they will.

I heard of a story about a man who went out and the sun and the clouds made a wager on who would get the man to remove his coat. First, the cloud blew, and blew, and blew harder, but the man clutched his coat tight and wouldn't take it off. Then the sun tried by beaming down its beams gently. Then the man took off his coat. There is some obvious illogic to this story, but the story is implying that people respond better to a calmer approach rather than a harsh one.

I'm not saying that you can't yell, just only as much as needed. I think the calmer, the better. That way, walls are not up, and misunderstandings can be cleared up. Things can get resolved easier, and it greatly reduces the hurt that happens in an argument, which often is half of the battle anyway. "A hot-tempered person stirs up conflict, but the one who is patient calms a quarrel." Proverbs 15:18 / Colossians 3:7-9

Another thing is relationships with friends. Often it's fun and a happy relationship. But if there is ever the rare exception of a disagreement, and it escalates into something further. People will often disconnect from the relationship altogether without much resolution. Just running away from the problem and possibly never talk to them again. This is very displeasing to me. Why can't people talk it out and work on it? Is there any resilience to stick it out in these relationships? Or is it one bump in the road and you're out? This goes into ministry relationships as well. If people would just stick in there for a little and try to work it out, I think things would probably be worked out. What we need is a resistance to separation and the ability to talk things out and work on it. I've seen many situations where the parties in question were separated for a long time, but all it took was just a little communication, and the relationship was mended. Why can't we do that upfront when it happens? I find it very frustrating when people just choose to run away from the problem and ignore it, thus ending the relationship. I think it's very immature, but yet so many people do it.

Relationship and communication

It is my opinion that the best relationship is based on communication. Even if it's a difficult thing to establish. Open communication on both sides to say how they feel, without being judged or belittled, and in turn, the other would talk about how they feel going back and forth, calmly if possible. Because there is less hurt and more openness in calm talk. At minimum, you at least conveyed to the other person how you feel, and they can think about it, even if they deny they will right then and there. Also, you can think about the things that they said too; an openness to change.

The Holy Spirit helped me understand that sometimes things take time, and you need to just ride it out. Think of these things in the long run; in time things will get better. The person may be completely unwilling to budge. Perhaps in time, with open communication being the key, you can understand each other and have a better working relationship.

It's not always a presto, everything is perfect, sometimes it takes time. The biggest thing I had to work on was the, what if. Taking something that someone does, and formulating in your mind that this is just the beginning of it. That it will only get worse and worse if you submit to it. Let your guard down, or apologies for your part, it's all in your mind (See Topic "Apology tool of great healing" Page 104). Or the, if I let them have their way here, they will keep going in it, wanting more and more, a fear of them controlling you. This is unfounded and a formulation of your mind.

Usually, your imagination has a way of formulating the worst possible situation, and usually, it ends up being way less or not at all. I had to work on stopping my imagination and just take the request for change at face value. You need to not be afraid of the, what if, or your imagination. Work with the issue as if that is all it is and will lead no further.

If it does, don't worry about it. Flex for what you can without the worrying of being controlled, even if they're not being as fair as you are. That comes in time and as trust is built. Leading by example is sometimes the way it has to be, but don't tell them that, or it will ruin it. Tell them you want to have open communication in the relationship with them, to where both sides can voice how they feel. To talk things out, because often misconceptions can be what's hindering the situation.

Maybe one is thinking the other is doing something for a certain reason, where they were not at all. Communication clears these things up very quickly, where otherwise you would have spent days agonizing over it. Sometimes misconceptions can cause unnecessary pain and hurt. Just to sit down and calmly talk without being afraid of the other person's response. Communication can bring great healing to both sides. Because sometimes, we will keep things unsaid because of fear of getting hurt by it. It's a freeing feeling to get things out and talk about hurts. Often things are misconceived, and you can manage to work them out.

But if they don't want an open relationship, you feel betrayed and horribly dreadful; thinking there is little hope for resolution. If this being the case, you have to try to be real in a different way. Don't give up hope for a healed relationship. The key to a healed relationship is learning to compromise or change. Both sides need to learn this, including you! What you should do is change what you can in yourself after each argument. Consider what's being said; is there any truth to it at all? If so, change that part of it. This might just jump start the process.

What you also need to do when given the opportunity is say how you feel about what's happening. Preferably calmly, even if the other is yelling, because sometimes yelling happens. But yelling things is often less received than if it were talked through calmly (See Topic "Arguing, Defense and walls a better way" page 99)

You need to try to not get bent out of shape if a change you talk about doesn't happen right away. Even if they outright deny your request. You have said your peace, be at peace that you said it, and let it go until next time.

What you're doing is planting a seed, whether it's received or not. They might think about it and maybe change in time. You are doing all that you can do. View it in the long run, it usually can get better. But consider how you can change part of your behavior. This might be a necessary ingredient to start the process, do it even if it's hard, and it makes you vulnerable. It might just reach them, and maybe they will do the same.

Also, pay attention to what they do, it might be different than what they say. There might be misconceptions, you're saying one thing, and they may be responding thinking you're talking about something else. Or maybe they said one thing, then thought about it and changed it without saying anything. If what they do is in the direction of what you're okay with, then there might be your healing there, or part of it.

Another thing is when you have worked something out with someone, repeat what the resolution is. Sometimes one might think one thing has been resolved, but the other is thinking something entirely different.

In more rough relationships, you need to choose your battles. Go after the bigger problems first, leaving the small ones alone. Yes, something is hurtful to you, but how big of a deal is it. Look at the one incident only and don't assume it's a trend to get worse. Do they do it often, or is this just a one-time thing? If it's a trend, then it's something that needs to be talked about. But in the small matters, think about it this way, a person can only handle so much change at once. If you overwhelm them, they might just throw off the bigger matters. It's a weighing and measuring process. Perhaps if it keeps happening in time, then it can be discussed.

Don't worry if you have to wait till next time to talk about it if it's a small matter. Consider what are the more weightier matters, and work on them first. Perhaps in time, when the more important matters have been healed, you can talk about the small matters. I say this because if there is a whole list of things that need to be corrected, you will just plain overwhelm them. Weigh which is more important to talk about, so they don't get burnt out with too much to change all at once. Choose your battles well!

Another thing is, don't make small things into big things. A thing they might do that is small you assume that it's only going to get worse. Or plug it into an equation where you think they're doing something worse or will in time. This is another one of these things I had to stop doing was projecting. I asked about it, and it wasn't what I thought it was. It was only a small thing, which wasn't a big deal anyway. What I imagined was worse, and it ended up not being true at all.

Another thing I thought was if I don't deal with this now, it will only get worse. There was the projected thinking, which wasn't even true anyways. I was afraid of being controlled. That was also my over projecting the small things. That's why calm communication can clear up so much. The devil uses this misconception and will feed you thoughts of worst-case scenarios; don't believe them. Stop your poison thinking, and ask if it's so bothersome; don't assume more than it is.

Learning all of this was one of the greatest things I have ever learned. I value it greatly, and it will help me with my future relationships as well. It's a process being in a relationship. It takes time, so be patient! Matthew 5:23-24

The Apology, the Tool of Great Healing

It takes great humility to say you're sorry or apologies, even if you lose ground in a discussion or argument. Even if they use it against you and will not admit to any fault themselves.

I have discovered that doing this is very powerful for healing in the long run. If you know you have done it partially, or even fully wrong during an argument, admit to what's true, and it will bring healing to the situation. You are doing what's right; humble yourself, for this is pleasing unto God. You may not get an immediate response from the other person, but in time, leading by example, they will get healed and may even start doing it themselves. Just don't tell them you're leading by example.

Someone's got to humble themselves first for healing to happen. But if they're stubborn, that's an entirely different matter. At least you're doing the right thing before God, and God will honor you for it.

It is my experience that saying you're sorry and admitting to what you feel is true is a wonderful tool of healing in a relationship. It clears up misunderstandings and heals the relationship. Someone needs to take the first step toward healing. It might as well be you!

Many people are afraid to take the first step and admit any fault or apologies. They feel vulnerable and that the other person will walk all over them, abusing the situation. In an argument, both are fighting, and both are legitimately hurt. It seems to happen over and over again, a stalemate sometimes. Try to think about the matter from their side; why they feel the way they feel or do what they do. Try to be understanding if you can. Often both can be at fault; so why not humble yourself and admit your half of the fault? Even if they don't. At least there is more of a chance for healing.

It is my opinion that the best relationship is based on communication. Talk things out no matter how hard. People will agonize over things the other person did for days sometimes. When a much shorter time of communication can relieve that pain in a matter of minutes. If the other person doesn't budge, just heal and wait it out; sometimes it takes time. Do the best you can do; you are trying. What else can you do? At least you're doing the right thing before God. Put Jesus in the middle of the relationship, and look to Him for healing when needed. Ask Him to be your counselor for the relationship and put it into His hands. Be patient with Him!

The fear of exposing yourself or being "walked all over" in an apology is often unfounded and untrue. But even if it isn't, at least you're taking the right steps toward a more healthy relationship and are doing the right thing. Talk out the rest after the sorry or apology; perhaps they're half at fault too. If necessary admit in even the small matters. But I am true to myself, I admit to my faults that I'm aware of. If I don't agree with the rest of it, I just admit to whatever is probably true, being humble and honest. But trying to resolve the rest that they may have done as well. And perhaps you need to come up with a compromise. Something that works or half works for both parties. Relationships are often about compromises. Just don't say, yeah they need to compromise; maybe so. But how about you? What do you need to compromise? It's a two-way street. You need to learn to change yourself in this process also. It's not all about them. This is something that I have had to do myself, so I'm speaking from that experience.

Another thing is, be careful with your Words and sharpness. Because one word can hurt someone deeply; choose your words carefully. Being sharp, even just for a moment when you're having a bad day or moment, can also be piercing and have lasting effects on someone. I am learning to try to tame this myself. I may not even be upset with someone, but if I had a bad moment and was ornery about other matters. Then someone comes along my path, and I snap at them out of that frustration. This rough manner can hurt their emotions. Even if it was one gruff remark and all went back to normal. Words have power and will affect people even if it was brief. These can have long-lasting effects on others, and they have to deal with the pain that you inflicted on them. Even if it's a word that was said calmly, the word itself can have power, so choose your words carefully. James 5:16, Matthew 5:23-24

Don't Stuff Your feelings in

There are some people that instead of working through their pains or feelings they just stuff it in and go on. The pain doesn't just go away. It remains there until you deal with it, or it will stay there continuing to hurt your heart. Pain and unresolved issues don't just disappear. It needs to be released by talking it out, crying, etc.. You may not realize it, but unresolved negative emotions poison your soul. They don't just go away because you ignore them; they stay there and affect you.

If it is done enough, your heart becomes callused to where you don't feel it anymore. At this point, your heart has so much pain in it, it's overloaded and becomes numb. But what you don't realize is that this affects you as a person. Your entire being is affected by unreleased pains. Your eyes begin to harden along with your heart. You as a person are completely affected, whether you know it or not. The heart is the very being of a person. It affects who you are, what you do, and how you do things. God designed us to have clean, healthy hearts, but He will not go against your will if you choose to hold things in and not heal. He will attempt to bring you to healing, but you must be willing.

We need to heal these hurts and pains. One of the main ways is to ask God to heal your heart and to cry out any pain as the opportunity presents itself. Take the hurt and the problems that you have, and imagine lifting them up to God with your hands. Imagine Him taking those problems and hurts into His hands and release them to Him.

If you are not willing to cry, then ask yourself why. Are you embarrassed to cry? It could be a form of pride. You need to set this aside, because crying is one of the biggest releases of pain. Which reminds me of when I was a teenager and was just turning back to the Lord; for some reason, I was unable to cry. I said to Him I want to cry. Why can't I? So I asked Him to help me to start. When I was finally able to, I was watching a movie, and a black person was wronged just for being black. Something let loose in me, and I just cried my eyes out. I don't remember the movie. I wasn't necessarily holding things in. For some reason, my crying ability was dried up. Even though I wanted to cry, I wasn't able to for some reason, but this is past now and healed. If this is you, you need to seek the Lord to heal this, because it's very important to cry.

If you don't get healing for this, then your heart will be plugged up. And this will limit your spiritual level; a form of hardness. It's important to have a clear and healed heart. It helps in your relationship with God; because your relationship is affected by your heart. If there are any hidden pains, then you will only be able to go so far with Him until your heart is healed.

He will start to restore your heart, but you may be unaware of it, forgotten pains. Sometimes God gives me dreams revealing hidden pains, and I cry them out. I have been surprised by some of the things He has shown me to heal. I have often forgotten about them or thought I was already healed of it.

But if you are unwilling to heal them, then He will not go against your will; there is nothing He can do at that point. You have to open yourself to the Lord and let Him see you and heal what needs to be healed. He wants to connect with your heart. In order for you to have the deepest relationship with Him. Your emotions need to be healed.

Another thing to heal pains and hurts is to talk to the person or situation in question. It is my belief that the best relationship is based on communication. Then going to God to heal your heart of any remaining pain. Sometimes a small amount of communication can go a long way (See Topics "Relationship and communication" page 101, and "Arguing, Defense and walls a better way" page 99).
There are those who are out there that are hardened. It has been integrated into their personality; so much so they don't even know. And it affects those who are around them. Whether it's pain, anger, negativity, depression, or whatever. These emotions permeate your very being. You become that negative energy, and it hardens your heart.

The enemy can push this energy on you as well. Because he can push negative energies on people to oppress them. It's okay to have some of these emotions for brief periods but not to dwell or live in them. What you may not realize is that negative emotions or hurts can emit a spiritual energy around you of negativity. And this affects the spiritual environment around you. The same is true of positive emotions; they create life around you. So be careful what types of emotions that you're dwelling on. You need to break those bad habits and find healing in other ways rather than using negative emotions as your release. You will be a much more whole person for it, and everyone around you will be affected as well. Seek the Lord to have Him custom tailor your healing, whatever that might be, and ask Him to heal your hidden pains. Luke 4:18

Manipulated out of the calling

I have come across many situations of people that are married. Where one understands the real calling, but the other is clueless or a stumbling block. I'm talking about where both are Christians, consider themselves close to God, and think they're on the right path. But one doesn't understand the higher calling of the other, and sometimes, believes it to be fictional. This role can be either man or woman; I have seen both. Now the degree to how much control one has over the other depends on the situation. Some will let their spouse pursue their calling unhindered. Yet others will manipulate and sometimes control the other person. Whether it's subtle or powering over them. In most situations I've seen, it's the man controlling the woman out of her calling. They say the woman must submit unto their husband. But let's say the husband is a subtle religious person who's stuck in their thinking and spiritually blind. If the wife is more spiritual and free in the spirit, obviously the man will not understand her. I feel in this situation that the woman should be diplomatic with her husband, but not allow him to control her out of her eternal destiny. I have also seen where the woman is controlling the man to not fulfill his calling. So I'm not stereotyping men as always bad. You are responsible for your own calling. In heaven, there is neither male nor female, so what's the difference down here. It would seem unfair just because a woman is born a woman, that they can't fulfill a high calling, even if their husband doesn't come along. (See Topic "Women Should be Free/Women Leaders" page 77) I view it that every single person has a calling, and it is not contingent if you're a man.

 You are responsible for your own calling. But it's more ideal to have both man and woman work together, marriage as one. God will have their giftings work together in harmony; the gifts will complete each other. I read in a Rick Joyner book, that sometimes someone will have part of a mantle, and another will have the other part 1 Co 13:9. When they work together, they complete that mantle, and the full power of that mantle is released.

 One can put a thousand to flight, but two can put 10 thousand to flight, a multiplication of 10! That's why the devil is behind division in marriage. He knows there is power in numbers, especially in marriage. So it's ideal to have the two work as a team, but that's not always possible. In such a situation, that person must pursue their calling the best they can. But I have seen a marriage where a man totally dominated the woman. She was a pushable personality, but he would threaten divorce or whatever else. That is called manipulation or control. To everybody else, he was a wonderful man, and you wouldn't know unless you were told. They may also slam their fist on the counter, yell, or just be temperamental. These are manipulation techniques used to control another.

So what does one do in an impossible situation? The decisions that you make here affect your eternal ruling and reigning in heaven. Your position is rewarded by how obedient you were here on earth to fulfill your callings. If not, then why would Jesus say the greatest in heaven, implying differences in position? I feel you should not allow another to control you out of your calling.

What I would do in such a situation, is whenever they were doing things that were manipulating like anger and threats; I would say: I'm sorry, I really need to listen to what I feel God is calling me to do. Please don't stand in my way. I need to listen to God and not man. If I listen to you, I will lose out on my eternal rewards. What you're doing is manipulation. I will not let you bully me out of my calling. If they threaten to do something, say I don't want that, but I need to listen to God and not man Acts 5:29. I need to fulfill my calling; this decision has eternal consequences, and I take those very seriously. I hope you understand why I have to do what I need to do. It's highly inappropriate for you to try to control me in this fashion; you're out of line. I would also say, I want you to come with me, but I can't let you stop me from fulfilling my calling. I am responsible to God; He is the boss.

They may try other forms of manipulation, like pitting others against you or doing the threat. This is a tough thing, but you have to stand up for your rights. Like I said before, it would be ideal to have them with you, because there is power in agreement, Ecclesiastes 4:12.

Now things don't have to be decided in the heat of the moment. Perhaps as things cool down, the real compromise can be had. Because when people are angry, they might say things they don't mean or make brash decisions. One should wait till there has been time to think about things and consider possible compromises.

I have seen a situation where both man and woman are heading generally in a good direction with God, but each had their faults. The man had anger spurts, and would be very controlling in situations. He was the dominant personality and would make decisions without her. Or even with her knowledge, make decisions she didn't agree with. The woman was embittered and would gossip to her friends about what he did. She did it so much that everybody around him would be poisoned with this information. It may be true, but this is gossip, and gossip is sin. Then the man had an experience with God, and he was changing for the better, but still had some traces of the past. God was advancing him, but she still insisted on slandering Him. After this experience, he was a changed man and is now on the right path with God. She was also pretty close to what her destiny is.

One can be right about something, but it's how you handle it. "Two wrongs don't make a right." Just because they wronged you doesn't mean you need to wrong them back. Pursue it in a Godly manner and let God be the judge. In my opinion, they both were wrong, and both were at fault. Do the right thing, it may hurt a little, but I found that leading by example does work; they do notice and maybe even change. But if they don't change, at least you're doing the right thing before God.

Consider your motives behind what you do; you may even do it without even thinking it's bad. Normally you are justifying it as venting or needing someone to talk to. The result of doing that is the friend is developing resentment or a different attitude toward your spouse. This is gossip. If you want to know if you are gossiping or not, here is the general result of gossip. The person being gossiped to changes their opinion based on what you're saying. They start thinking of that person in a negative sense. The character of the person being gossiped about is being degraded. They will either treat that person differently or think of them in a negative matter; even back off from them.

But on the other hand, a person might want an opinion on what to do or requires council. In a counseling situation, the atmosphere is to a solution. Not a session of degrading of the other person's character or you poor soul but toward a healthy solution. Some people say they are seeking counsel, but then go to all their friends and tell them. This is gossip, not counseling. If you need council, you should go to someone you trust. That is mature enough not to spread the info to others, and will not develop a negative attitude toward the person being talked about. You have unresolved pains that need to be dealt with but are dealing with them in the wrong ways (See Topics "Relationship and communication" page 101, and "Arguing, Defense and walls a better way" page 99). What would Jesus do? Do the most Godly thing you can do in the situation, even though the abuse may continue. So that you don't also sin. Ephesians 4:2-3,32

Boundary setting, why can't you say no!

I have run into many people who are afraid to say no or talk about something that offends them. They will just keep it to themselves and complain behind their backs. I have even seen someone give permission to do something and say they're happy about it. Maybe at first this was okay, but they changed their minds and didn't say anything to them.

This is not the person's problem with the permission; they think they're okay. It's your issue if you can't tell them about how you feel. Maybe you can set new boundaries telling them it was okay at first, but having a change of heart on the matter. That new boundary might be a modification of the current understanding; perhaps in some scenarios a stop altogether. It depends on the situation. Make a compromise that works for both of you. If it's a major change, then consider giving a grace period to enact the change.

People will often just let the offense carry on because they're afraid that it will offend them. But if you don't tell them, it's not their fault. You have that right to set your own personal boundaries. You can even relay it in a friendly way that will not offend. Just be real with them; let them know what's on your heart. Let them know your circumstance that it was fine at first, just that you need to modify it a little or set a reasonable stop date.

This happened to me. I found out later they were telling people near me about their complaint but didn't bother telling me. I finally was told the issue. It hurt more finding out indirectly from someone else rather than being told directly. Which in my mind, I would have completely understood and would have been fine with it. I had full permission from this person to do so. It's frustrating having to try to figure out if someone is getting secretly offended. If you're getting offended by something, it's better for both sides to talk about it, and much healing comes from it.

I know of a situation where someone needed to stay with someone for a while, and they were fine to do it. But the situation's dynamics made it longer. The person giving was getting weary of the situation. They were feeding them as well; it was really draining on their finances. But they didn't want to tell them that because they were afraid of offending them. But instead, they complained to everybody else about it.

What should have happened, is the person being wearied by the situation should consider what really are the biggest problems. Do you feel you need to entertain them all the time? Is it financial? Whatever it is, determine the issues and resolve them. Discuss a solution with them; let them be to themselves more than having to keep up with them all the time. If it's financial, then discuss with them any potential solutions. Whatever it might be, figure out the root of the matter, and resolve the issues that are at hand. If an exiting plan is needed, then discuss that possibility and how that might work. But if it's something that can be resolved by setting boundaries, then that is best. To some people, it seems like the solution is either all on or all off. Why not consider resolving whatever the issue is instead of ending it. But sometimes ending it is the proper action; each situation is different. All the possibilities need to be considered and weighed, and a decision needs to be made. Perhaps with them in the decision making process.

But if it's a truly abusive situation, then that needs to be considered as well. Perhaps you think it's abusive, but in fact, it's a lack of communication on the matter. Because sometimes, a small amount of communication goes a long way.

You need to learn to set boundaries to respect yourself, rather than complaining behind people's backs. It's so much better if you tell people the issues directly rather than them finding out what is being said behind their backs which is far more painful. (See Topic "Who me, a Gossiper? Yeah right! and Confidants" page 137)

You also need to set boundaries in your regular relationships as well. Otherwise, offenses are building under the surface where a conversation will reduce such offenses, or at least they can think about it. (See Topics "Relationship and communication" page 101, and "Arguing, Defense and walls a better way" page 99). Matthew 5:23-24, Leviticus 19:16

We need another one of you

I was watching a Bob Jones video, and he responded to someone saying something to him (I don't remember what it was, something about duplicating his anointing). He said, "We don't need another one of me; we need another one of you." That caught my attention. Everyone is trying to copy other people and their experiences and maturity levels, where the fruits of your calling and ministry may be completely different from someone else's.

Everyone's ministry is different; each one has a different result. Don't feel bad when you don't exhibit the same things another person does. Maybe you're called differently. What you need to do is seek the Lord in what He would have you do and pursue that. Don't feel envious or down because you see someone else have a greater experience; maybe you're different. Just pursue the Lord with sincerity, and what He would have you do, that is all that matters. Luke 12:7

You're better than me, I'm better than you

I used to think that because someone else did something that I haven't like have an open vision, see angels, or see in the Spirit, that I was not measuring up or missed God somewhere. What I discovered was that each person has their own unique gifting, and they often will not be the same. People will compare each other based on the information that they know or what they've done. Determining if they're on a higher level or deeper walk than others. If the person reveals something that changes that perception, like someone doing something for God that they haven't. The person that considered themselves more mature will get jealous in their heart that they haven't thought of that or done that. This is all unsaid and not blatant thinking, just a minor mental process that one will use within themselves to make themselves feel good about what they have accomplished in God. A long time ago, I was walking into a new situation, and I thought people might notice how advanced I was. At that moment, I said to myself: no, they shouldn't be noticing me; God should get the glory. Come in and be as a nobody, let God have the glory; don't try to take any glory that belongs to God unto yourself. That would be building your kingdom rather than God's.

Some may consider themselves on a more mature level in God because they had a certain experience. Like the Idea that everyone has certain experiences based on their maturity level. Like A - B - C - D, once you reach a certain spiritual level in God that you will have certain experiences, like God speaking audibly. At a further level, another type of experience like having an open vision, or God taking a person into a heavenly experience. This is all a misconception. Just because someone has a heavenly experience does not mean that they're at the top of their game and fully matured. They could still have a long way to go. It's not God's stamp of approval that says they're at the top spiritually. God just simply wants to use them and did. God does not do the same thing with every person. It is an assumption that we all can do the exact same things. God made each of us different; we each have our strengths and weaknesses.

God created our gifts like pieces of a puzzle. You have to put the pieces together to get the full picture. God has made every snowflake, bird, fish, and land animal uniquely different. God has made us all uniquely different in looks, personality, and giftings. Giving one type of gift to one person, and another type to another; each uniquely different from the other 1 Peter 4:10-11.

I had a dream years ago where symbolism was used. There were many different musical instruments used. The instruments in the dream represented the gifts of each person, how God has called them. One person started playing their instrument, and I saw a piece of a puzzle laid down called A. Then soon another person started playing complimenting the music and I saw piece B put into place that fitted with A. These were not what you think of puzzle pieces, but odd shapes that fit together. Then it continued one by one. People started playing their instruments, and I saw more and more letters of the puzzle put into place of different shapes and sizes. It was almost like it had an order in which people would go, who should start first, and so on. Then it came to someone who had a small piece; they didn't think their piece was important, so they didn't participate. So they were skipped over, and the next in the order joined in, but it was missing that person's portion. The music was distinctly missing a piece now! It was obvious, and not nearly as effective. I saw the puzzle and a small piece missing out of the middle of it.

Everyone has a piece; each is different and have to be used together. If some are missing, you notice it 1 Corinthians 12:25-27, 1 Peter 4:10-11. We won't all have the same-looking piece. Ours may look completely different from the others, and the experiences that we have may be different from others.

Each gift has a different function. So just because you're not experiencing the same things doesn't mean that you are failing. It just means that you have a different gift that does something else unique and wonderful. If an eye is seeing something, why should the ear feel sad that it is not seeing it? Or why should the eye be sad, if it's not hearing? Each person is part of the Spiritual body, and each has their own unique function. They all work together in unity to complete a purpose that one part could not do without the other, 1Co 13:9.

So experiences are not a measure of maturity. It may simply be a part of that person's calling, and the other person is not called to have that type of experience. So don't measure yourself against others based on your experiences. Maybe the Lord is putting that person through a wilderness at that time, so He may not be giving them much for a season.

Often God will at some point take us to our spiritual desert to train us. This happens in worship as well. To the young, He will give wonderful experiences in worship. This is to encourage them into spiritual growth. But God starts weaning after time to strengthen them. It's not permanent, just a strengthening period which we often don't like. Of course, it's also possible to be spiritually stagnated in worship as well; not to be confused with that.

Another dynamic is when we work on things in ourselves. One will be more successful in one area, and another person in another area. So we each have our strengths and our weaknesses. Not all of us see our weaknesses and are often blind to them. It's our job to try to help each other with those weaknesses if we can. Because often, my strengths are your weaknesses, and your strengths are my weaknesses. When one is healed or delivered in an area, they're given the key to help others in that same area.

Don't try to make yourself feel better by measuring yourself against another. Why would you feel better anyway if someone has not progressed as far as they can? If they have done something wonderful that you haven't, be happy. Hope that all will attain the most that they can. Give them what you have, even if that makes them go higher yet. This is our purpose in this life; to help each other grow in God.

Let it go, let others benefit from your experiences. Think about how God views you and not how you're viewed by others. God views helping others at your own expense, a very wonderful thing and will bless you for it. The measure that you bless others, will be the same measure by which you will be blessed, pressed down, shaken together, and running over! Luke 6:38

Christian vs. Christian

It's the mentality of many Christians to view other Christians of different denominations as lower, or maybe even as an enemy. God never intended for such a division to be in the church. He said to love one another, John 13:34, that includes fellow Christians, not just people we're trying to save. Jesus said to love one another. Do you think God views Christians by denomination? No, He sees them by their heart.

There have been many situations where I have seen people in denominations that you wouldn't think would be in touch with God, but in fact, they are. God looks at the heart of the person and goes by that. I have seen many Christians from different denominations, and many have a relationship with God regardless of their denomination.

God doesn't go on what's in your brain, but what's in your heart. I've seen Catholics that hear from God and are full of His spirit. I've seen Baptists that have His spirit and work with the gifts of the spirit. I've seen a Methodist that was full of love and knew that we should love one another regardless of the denomination. The Amish, Hutterite, Mennonite groups have small groups that are being touched by the Holy Spirit, speaking in tongues, and coming out of those communities.

God knows no boundaries. He looks through the entire earth looking for a receptive heart, no matter what or where it is. He's looking for where He will be let in. God shows up at churches all over the place because He loves them. No matter what the denomination, if there is true worship and sincerity, He will be there.

But many churches deny His gifts and who He is, so He has to leave. Then He can't do anything; because He will not come against our will.

We shouldn't treat different denominations indifferently. It's better to love them; at least there's a chance to reach them. Even if it's in a small way. I have read many books about heaven. There are no denominations in heaven, we are all one there.

Jesus says, love one another as I have loved you. Many distrust or even attack other Christians with scriptures. It's not what's in your brain, it's what's in your heart. It's not your understanding of God that counts; it's your openness to His spirit. A real relationship with Him of obedience and holiness. Even if they were your enemy, Jesus said to love your enemy. You have no excuse to act this way. Some Christians treat other Christians despitefully; you are not using God's power against them, but the enemy's.

Another thing that I had to deal with was my prejudice toward pastors because of how they held people back, hurt them, squelch the Holy Spirit, and

limit the works of God. Whenever I came across a pastor, I would be resistant and put my assumptions on them, but I needed to stop this. It's possible they might be what I'm thinking, but it's never good to assume and expect it. Instead, I wonder if they are, but give them a chance without resisting them. Perhaps you have similar prejudices, maybe not like mine, but one that you have developed toward certain types of people.
Each situation is different, so you can't assume that someone is one way or another way. You need to drop prejudices and just treat each situation as a new one. Sure you can have your reservations about them, but don't assume it; give them a chance. They might surprise you! Even if they live up to your concerns, you still need to love one another anyway. Ephesians 4:2

Don't squish what little one has

Some people are just simply where they are spiritually. God has cultivated in them what He can and is working at their level of Christianity. They might not be to the full par of what's possible. But this is just simply where they're at. You might come along and see this and might not think much of it. Whatever you do, don't make their situation worse by judging or ruining what little they do have. This might discourage them, possibly cause them to lose their progress, or stop their growth.

It is not our job to tear down what little they have. The Lord may have revealed to you something about someone, but it may or may not be the right time to tell them. We should be in touch with the Holy Spirit so that He will guide us in what to say or not say. But if you're supposed to tell them, then do so in the spirit of Love if possible. It's also possible that you're only supposed to pray for their situation. You need to have the Holy Spirit guide you to which is the proper approach.

Rick Joyner, in one of his final quest books; came across a tree that he felt was bad (representing a negative spiritual growth), and he decided to cut it down. The result after was way worse than it was originally. Perhaps the tree shouldn't have been cut down yet; it may not have been its time to do so. We need to know God's right timing in everything. Only God knows best in what to do or how to approach situations. We need to seek His guidance.

You will be held accountable if they fail because of what you say or do to them. Don't squish what little they do have. God is working with them where they're at. But sometimes, God will ask us to say something to them, point something out, or bring correction in an area. This is a part of God's process, and needs to be done if we are told to do so. The purpose of correction is to help us draw closer to God. Sometimes people can be stubborn, so God might have to be more firm with them, but there is hope in it for them to get back on the right path. Sometimes they are growing properly, and are just simply where they're at. We might see them where they are and think they're not where they could be. This might be true, but maybe they are just in the process at the moment.

This is not to negate when God needs to bring correction to a person; this is equally as important. We just need to find the balance in it by seeking God in what needs to be done in any particular situation. Romans 14:1,4, Ephesians 4:29

Hidden pains of the past that affect who we are today

Sometimes things happen in one's life. Perhaps in childhood, maybe adulthood; the principle is the same. If a trauma happens to a child; how does a child know how to respond to such pains or evils? All they know is the trauma, pain, or being wronged and forced to deal with it. Often what happens is they cover it up and bury it deep in themselves, unresolved. Now, these traumas are varying in what they are, depending upon the situation.

That trauma doesn't just go away; it stays there if not resolved. The child doesn't know this, so it remains there into adulthood. As teens or adults, they still have this buried trauma in their heart. Their entire person is bent around this trauma without even knowing it. They are often unaware of the effects of these emotions or traumas. They are unaware that it's shaping who they are today.

It's like a cut; if you choose to ignore it, it will get dirty, infected, and will throb and hurt. Some people have these buried pasts just like the cut, you can't ignore it. The pain is still there. It doesn't go away just because you choose to ignore it. Maybe you're unaware of that pain because you have lived with it your whole life. You are just used to that being in your spirit, and it has become hidden to you. Maybe it's completely hidden in you until it's touched, and that pain surfaces again. Maybe you have something that affected you so young that you don't even know better what it's like to live a healed life. Maybe that's all you know, and you just simply don't know better. There are greater and lesser degrees of this as well. You may act a certain way because of previous hurts in your life. You need to properly heal this pain by acknowledging it, facing it, crying if you have to, possibly seeking counseling to fully resolve it, and ask the Lord to bring these pains to the surface and heal them.

Without this healing, it's shaping who you are and how you act. Each person is different in what this means. Perhaps you are fearful, a rough person, do things that fill the void in your heart, or have trigger points that bring back the pain. These are some of the symptoms of this.

I think that most hardened criminals are the result of having terrible childhoods. They have terrible pain in them, which is why they are so hard because of this pain. They shut off their emotions and do the things they do. This is an extreme example of this, but it helps you understand better what I'm talking about. These experiences have molded who they are and have caused them to become hardened.

People with inner pains have often gone on with life and consider themselves just fine, or even consider themselves healed. But in fact, there are more subtle amounts of this pain still lingering, still affecting their person, in subtle ways that are not thought about. So it's possible for one to have only half healing.

I'd like for you to take a moment and think about all the traumas in your life; starting from the beginning to now. Do any spark emotions? Perhaps you didn't have an emotional response. Think about those situations. Do you feel that any of those traumas affect who you are today in even in the smallest of ways? If so, then there are unresolved issues in you, and you need to seek the Lord to heal those pains, perhaps counseling.

Now I'd like to give you a subtle example. I know of someone who likes the good feeling they get from helping people out, and they do it all the time as a lifestyle. This is of course is a good thing, but this person gets satisfaction from it that eases her subtle pain that she's unaware of. She seeks to find the next fix per se. There was a trauma that she experienced when she was young, and to get away from this hidden pain, she seeks these fixes to make herself feel better. Doing good things for people has a good feeling associated with it, but you can get addicted to it. It's her way of dealing with this long forgotten trauma. The symptoms can be big or small; you need to determine if there is something that you do to ease or avoid these buried traumas.

When I was young, I was picked on in school, and I shut myself down emotionally. Later in life, I found that my emotions sparked if I saw someone speaking into another person's ear near me while looking at me. Even though it truly wasn't anything; this is a subtle example of this. Another thing is God has given me dreams a few times of smaller matters that I needed to work out of me. I needed to heal those previous things that I even forgot about or didn't think were a big deal. After having those dreams, I exercised those emotions and got them out, and I was healed of the matters. But these are small examples of what small things that can be buried in one's person. The bigger matters may take more to heal. Doctor Jesus knows exactly what you need and will prescribe it for you. You just need to let Him.

This is not per se limited to childhood, it can be any trauma in life. Your homemade solution to covering your hidden pains can vary from person to person; it can be just about anything. You need to stop your own solution and seek true healing from Jesus for this heart pain. Often good heart felt worship is a good start (not church, but uninterrupted personal worship off of worship CDs and headphones, not just speakers. Where you feel an anointing touching your heart). Have a conversation with Jesus, tell Him about it, and ask Him to heal you fully, and in time, you will heal.

Matt 11:28-29 "Come unto me, all ye that labor and are heavy laden, and I will give you rest. Take my yoke upon you, and learn of me; for I am meek and lowly in heart: and ye shall find rest unto your souls."
(This psychiatry concept, was originally developed by Carl Jung.)

Actions speak louder than thoughts

Sometimes a thought will come to you that's completely off the wall, sometimes very bad. You wonder, why would I think such a thing? Maybe even feel bad about it. What you may not realize is that the enemy sent you that thought. It's not your making; the enemy can send images and thoughts. These thoughts and images are not your fault or making. You need to realize what's going on, rebuke that thought or image, and tell the devil to go and to never return in the name of Jesus. The devil will always try to tempt us to participate with that thought. You need to recognize it and cancel it.

It's also possible to have a bad moment, think bad thoughts, or have bad actions. Then to think upon it, be repentant, and return to do the right thing. Matt 21:28-31 (paraphrased) which is better one who says they'll do it, then doesn't, or one who says no but then thinks upon it and later does it. The better is he who actually does the right thing, so actions speak louder.

Don't Worry

Something that I had to strongly deal with in my life was worrying about things and fear. Sometimes even in small matters. Jesus says:
"Therefore I say to you, do not worry about your life, what you will eat; nor about the body, what you will put on. Life is more than food, and the body is more than clothing. Consider the ravens, for they neither sow nor reap, which have neither storehouse nor barn; and God feeds them. Of how much more value are you than the birds? And which of you by worrying can add one cubit to his stature? If you then are not able to do the least, why are you anxious for the rest? Consider the lilies, how they grow: they neither toil nor spin; and yet I say to you, even Solomon in all his glory was not arrayed like one of these." "Seek the kingdom of God, and all these things shall be added to you. Do not fear, little flock, for it is your Father's good pleasure to give you the kingdom. Sell what you have and give alms; provide yourselves money bags which do not grow old, a treasure in the heavens that does not fail, where no thief approaches nor moth destroys. For where your treasure is, there your heart will be also." Luke 12:22-27,31-34

Who, by worrying about a situation or things, can add any benefit to that situation? It will only cause you pain. To what benefit is that? You neither add nor subtract from the situation; put your trust in God. If you're worried about a person that you made stumble in their walk. Then repent and do what you can to correct the situation peaceably, then give God the rest.

My mind has a way of thinking of all the possibilities that could happen. Sometimes I will imagine a high-pitched sound in my mind to clear all the worrying thoughts. All you can do is do what you know to do in the situation, then not worry about it. Another thing I do to get a situation out of my mind is to do something that will take my mind off the subject (Out of sight out of mind). Even if that means going out and doing something. You are only hurting your heart by worrying, and you don't benefit any. So try to walk in peace and trust in God to take care of you.

Stuff happens in life

Things happen in life. Often you have a situation where you do something, and it backfires on you. Like you lose money, time, or make a mistake that you can't reverse. You wish you could go back and change it. In one situation, I was having strong emotions that were depressing me. I heard Jesus say to me: "detach from this world."

"Come to me, all you who labor and are heavy laden, and I will give you rest," Matt 11:28, "And which of you by being anxious can add one cubit to his stature?" Luke 12:25.

These things happen; all you can do is just do the best you can. What I do with these emotions is I try to keep them neutral and try to not participate with them. You have to realize that God will take care of you.

I have paid attention to the pattern of what happens with big situations. The first day is often the worst, but you will feel some better at the end of the day. Then the next morning when you wake up, often you feel a big rush of bad emotions. Then once you get up and do your day, you feel some better. On the third day, it's still there but less. Then days after that, most of the pain is gone, and it's better.

You also need to do all you can to remedy the situation the best you can. Take the steps you can. If the situation is uncooperative and won't change; then you need to change your expectations of it. Change them to conform to the current result. Accept the result and go on, you may not like the result, but this is life. Like the phrase: "Some things in this life are out of your control." You may think of the loss from time to time and are disappointed, but the pain of it is gone.

Often when you make some sort of mistake, you have to wait and see the result. Usually, it turns out to be not as bad as you think it would be. My mind has a way of churning the worst possible scenarios. Usually, it often isn't even close to what I thought I might be. These are also painful, but you need to just hang in there and try to keep your thoughts in check. I usually say to myself it probably is not going to turn out that bad, so calm down.

God doesn't want you to feel these horrible feelings. You need to master your thought process and stop these emotions before they start. Because your emotions are linked to your thoughts; stopping negative thoughts helps stop those emotions. Sometimes I just have to pretend I have a high-pitched sound in my mind, replacing these thoughts and empty my mind.

I feel to stress that if you need to cry, do it. It helps release pain and is very healthy for your spirit. I also like to write a list of all the positives in my life and weigh them against the situation. They often far outweigh the negative. Praying in tongues under your breath also helps.

You sometimes have to wrestle with these emotions. I read somewhere where a woman was describing these emotions as thoughts. And she said that she sometimes has to spend hours cornering those thoughts and eliminating them one by one. Because often you can forget even why you're feeling those emotions, and have to try to remember how that emotion started.

What also helps is to get away from the problem; do something to distract yourself, like having fun. It can help you forget about it for a while and ease your pain. You also need to envision putting the problem into God's hands; because God is able to help your situation, whatever it might be. Ask Him to heal your pain, because He's the healer. 2 Corinthians 1:3-4

Emotional Pain

Emotional pain is the worst kind of pain because it's difficult to heal. Something's in life are out of our control. We need to let it go and give it to God. We often go into emotional pain over things that are out of our ability to fix. This is life, you can only do so much. Beyond that, it's in God's hands. You need to put your trust in God's abilities to take care of you; He is mysteriously able to help you. I know from personal experience that He is able to help in unique ways. He works in the invisible, and His hand is not too short to help you if you ask Him Num 11:23. Matt 11:28 "Come to me, all you who labor and are heavy laden, and I will give you rest."

When I have gotten in emotional pain, I tried just stopping the pain saying:

okay I'm done, and get off from it. But that doesn't work; the pain still remains. Emotional pain is very sticky; it takes a bit of time for it to subside when you get your mind off of it. But the second you start thinking about the situation again, the pain instantly comes back. So the pain is directly linked with your thoughts.

What you should do, is pray to God that He would work in your situation. Then to do the best you can do to remedy the situation and get your mind off of it. These thoughts often keep turning and turning in an endless cycle. You need to shut down the thought as soon as it starts.

Also, doing other things and getting your mind off the matter also helps break it up (See Topic "Stuff happens in life" page 122). What you need to do is change your expectations of the situation. Change what you're expecting out of it. The situation has changed; you need to change along with it. If you have done everything you know to do, and there is nothing more you can do. Change what you expect to happen in your mind. If Life gives you lemons, make lemonade; make the best of the situation that you can. This is all you can do besides asking God to help. Emotional pain takes time to heal. It will get better in time as you get more acclimated to the situation. Some people swear when they feel emotional pain, but you shouldn't do this because you're cursing and using the enemy's power. You need to find better ways of venting your frustrations. If you look at this deeper, you will see hurt and pain behind those actions at the root of it. You may be acting out of this pain without even realizing it, a gut response. Your heart is hurt, but you're not recognizing it and acting out of these hidden pains. They're not really hidden, because you're feeling the effects without realizing it. It's important to recognize what's going on and address these deeply rooted emotions. This goes for pain in others as well. There often is a reason and a root to the matter why they act the way they act. Recognizing that root is half of the battle.

Some people have hidden things in their hearts from their childhood that they have buried so deep that this pain has become accustomed to them without them even knowing it. Perhaps it's not pain per se, but a condition in you that has been fostered by this early life trauma. It has become so buried that you as a person are revolving around this early trauma without even knowing it. So find the root of your issues and heal them. Find peaceful solutions to remedy the situation, and learn to vent that pain in a more appropriate manner. (See Topic "Relationship and communication" page 101, and "Hidden pains of the past that affect who we are today" page 118)

Follow After Peace

The Lord has given each Christian the ability to know right from wrong. He also has given the Holy Spirit to guide each and every one of us. It took me a little while to learn this one; once I did, I got in less and less trouble. In one situation, I was with a group of friends at a backyard barbecue; at the end, they wanted to all go rollerblading. I wanted to do more with them, so I went. I have roller skated many times but only once have I rollerbladed and only in a roller rink. When they started talking about it, I felt a check or a heaviness in my heart, but I ignored it and proceeded. My friends said, let's go downtown metro and skate around. I thought, wow, that would be fun. (Warning: my accident described) So I went with them with a borrowed pair of skates and basically ended up with a foot cast for over a month because I had to stop for a traffic light too fast.

From that point on, I realized that the Holy Spirit was trying to pre warn me about things, and it would have saved me from one month of being in a cast, and at work, they put me on some monotonous sit down work everybody avoided. So from that point on, I tried with trial and error to learn how to go with the Holy Spirit's leadings.

What He will do is put a heavy feeling on my heart. Follow after peace; if you don't feel peace when doing something, then don't do it. Weigh each option, and go with the option you feel peace with, Proverbs 3:5, but make sure it's not your flesh made peace, because you can come up with a peace that is manmade.

Don't just go with the flow because the Lord can see into the future to see the outcome. It might not make sense to you why; you have to trust the Lord that He knows best. You may never know why, because God sees a potential future and is having you avoid it. One time, a group of friends were going on a ski trip, and I really wanted to go, but the Holy Spirit revealed that I shouldn't go. I did not want to hear this, and didn't go. Not so much later, I got laid off and found that I could not have afforded it. I have seen people go against their peace before, which is why I feel compelled to write this. Follow after peace.

Don't Intellectualize, but Spiritualize

There are many Christians who rely more heavily on their intellect than on the Holy Spirit. The Holy Spirit is 100 times smarter than us; He can see things we can't. People view the word and God from an intellectual standpoint; this is flesh-based, of the soulish realm, and bears no life.

God's works are like a river, always moving, never stopping. If it were to stop, it would stagnate. This is what using your intellect is like; it's using your power to understand things of God. God is Spirit, He is not intellect. He can put things in your spirit like show you pictures or speak to you.

He speaks in many ways; it isn't always in English. There is spiritual death in intellectualism. You may not realize it, but your spirit becomes dry and parched; this is because you're using your power to do things. With God, there is life, and life abundantly. You may feel Him in your local church, but this doesn't mean that you have obtained His perfect will. He's coming and touching you because He loves you; this usually happens during worship. This doesn't mean He's putting His stamp of approval on you and saying all is well.

Many Christians use the word as a weapon, but on each other, because they feel they know it better. Love one another, don't forget that. We often forget the simplest things that Jesus said for us to do, yet they are the most important.

Our intellect is spiritual death if overused, you end up slowly drying up spiritually. If we use our intellects to figure out the things of God, we will end up spinning in circles, chasing our tails, and stagnating. We are nothing compared to God's wisdom, Isaiah 55:9, so we need to lean on Him. You may say you're leaning on Him and learning things, but this may still be your intellect.

I have also seen where people hear their own voice, and not hear the voice or the leadings of the Holy Spirit. If we're too much into our heads, it will be difficult to hear Him, because our intellect pushes Him out.

I had a vision when I was a younger Christian of sheep in a sheep pen and a massive field of lush green grass with a river running through it. Inside of the very small pen was trampled dried brown grass. Jesus was calling to them to come to the lush grass outside of the pen, but the sheep would say no, that's not Jesus, and would ignore Him. There were a few that listened and went with Jesus. He took them and washed them in the river.

This pen was mainly referring to the church and its current condition. That pen is like the confines of intellectualism, and the massive field is what they're missing. Don't confine your spiritual maturity to just a small pen. Tap into God's ability to think for you. The wisdom of the wisest man that has ever existed is foolishness before the wisdom of God. So, our wisdom is foolishness. We need God's wisdom through His spirit, not through our intellect.

If you are one who heavily uses your intellect as the way to learn God. You need to consider getting into good worship, because this is where God touches the dry spots in your heart and heals and changes you. There are many forms of worship out there; most are dry and listless, so it's hard for me to refer you to any specific worship. Here are a few examples of good worship. The best one is the song called: hosanna by Scott Brenner on the CD paradise is waiting (do an internet search to listen). Another is called Majesty by Hillsong United, on Aug 29, 2011, another is the song Oceans (Where Feet May Fail) by Hillsong United May 31, 2013, (I wrote the specific dates on purpose because these are the best versions of these songs (do an internet search to listen)). Or do an internet search for Hillsong United or Hillsong videos till you find something you like, because Hillsong seems to have anointed songs often enough.

(See Topics "I want your Heart, not your religiousness" page 187, "I write to you because you know it" page 74, "Worship" page 145, "Worship is slow, less is more" page 147, "Surface Worship/Heart Worship" page 150, "Worship in Spirit and In Truth" page 151, "Worship is the only way to reach some" page 153, "Seeing in the Holy Spirit, and the leadings of the Holy Spirit" page 132, "Doctrines" page 45, "Modern-day Pharisee" page 70, and "God doesn't fit in a box" next topic)

God doesn't fit in a box

There are many Christians and pastors today who feel they have studied much and have figured all there is to figure out in Christendom. Even went to Bible College and earned degrees and doctorates in faith.

Consider for a moment the most seasoned Christian in the faith. Perhaps a pastor who has been a pastor all their life. Who is renowned and has studied much, and has years and years of experience. If this pastor is not in touch with the Holy Spirit or doesn't have a real relationship with him; where the Holy Spirit talks to them daily, and guides them even in the smallest of matters. Then all that he has accomplished and learned is more than likely stale.

God is like a moving river; He is active and does new things all the time. Often Christians think they have figured out God. What He will do and what He won't do, how He works. Even down to having a narrow interpretation to all scriptures; they only have a portion of the truth. The greater portion is with the Holy Spirit and His leadings.

Just because we believe a certain way doesn't mean that it will happen that way. God's going to do it whatever way He wants to do it anyway, whether we believe it or not. We don't need to know all things perfectly. It's a journey with the Holy Spirit; let Him show you.

Many today sit around intellectualizing the scriptures very detailed, every jot and tittle. Analyzing and reanalyzing, and after many years of contemplation, they feel they know all about God and put Him in a box on how He works.

The Bible is basically a compilation of letters that were written to various communities in the Bible times. To help them out with various issues that need to be worked on as they came up. They never intended it to become the only source in the future in which to glean from. It's a foundation, not a stop. Yes, the new things will not contradict the Bible. People today can get fresh words from the Father that are just as valid. Like for instance, Rick Joyner's final quest series and Anna Rountree's books are fresh visions and instructions for today's world. As well as many other fresh heavenly visions and words from the anybodies and nobodies!

I do Not presume the following. But as an example, for a moment, consider this book I am writing. If I lived back in the Bible times would my book become part of the Bible? I write in a very similar method, trying to talk to people about their issues that need to be attended to. I'm only human; what if I make a mistake? What if someone micro interprets what I said when I meant something completely different?

This is how it is today. People are micro interpreting the Bible down to every tiny word. You should look at that basic principle and not micro interpret them. In one of Rick Joyner's final quest series, he was in heaven and was introduced to Paul himself. Which, if you didn't notice, he wrote most of the New Testament. At one point, Paul said that we should not put him as the foundation of the church, but Jesus. What if he worded something slightly wrong, and it was misinterpreted?

When Jesus was about to leave this earth; He said there are many things which He wanted to tell them, but it would overwhelm them. So there was more to learn! This was for the Holy Spirit and the Father to show us in later lessons after Jesus's ascension. If there was more, then why would there not be more now? But whatever new revelation there is, it should coincide with the Bible, not contradict it.

I read in a book of a vision of heaven where Jesus was saying: my word is always moving, never stopping or stagnating like a river. Just like I created the universe to be ever expanding. God is dynamic (constant change, activity, or progress), not static (lacking in movement, action, or change). He is always moving forward.

God can't be put in a box! He's too big for that. That box probably fits on the tip of His pinkie finger. This is what we think God is and what He isn't. Many Christians have put God in a box, and have a certain set of rules of what He is and isn't. Anything outside of that box is rejected. Think of the Pharisees; they did this and missed God altogether. When the truth was staring them in the face. Why don't you think it would be any different today? Like the Pharisees, people have become blind because of their narrow beliefs. These were the top leaders of the faith, yet they completely missed God and even killed Him.

If Jesus were to meet you today and you didn't know it, told you things that contradicted what you think, the religious person would probably brush Him off. The pastor would dismiss or even persecute Him. This is happening today. Jesus and the Holy Spirit are being brushed off, and the pastors are dismissing them. So He leaves them to their beliefs, stalemated.

God is always speaking new things to His church. He's always doing a new thing. He hasn't stopped at the Bible. Jesus said that the Holy Spirit would come and teach us more John 16:12-15 "He will guide you into all truth." This means that there was more to learn. Jesus also said in this scripture that He had much more to say, but they could not bear it. By this time, Jesus was out of time and was shortly after crucified. This job was then left to the hands of the Holy Spirit.

The time for getting more from Him in Christianity did not end when Jesus died, it only began; He just planted the seed. God always has more to teach us, even to add to Christianity. It's like painting a picture; more can always be added, but it will all work together. It won't contradict the Bible; it will add to it.

God is going to move on with or without you and leave you in the dust stalemated. It's like the book the torch and the sword by Rick Joyner. Rick was given a torch, but when Jesus walked away a little, the torch got heavier. If He got too far away, then that torch would become too heavy, and one would be forced to put it down. If you don't keep up with the Lord, then you will be forced to put the torch down (ministry or God purpose).

He still loves you, but you will be stalemated and left behind spiritually. I'm not referring to salvation, but to spiritual works and purposes of what God is doing. You can't ever say in truth that you know all there is to know. I understand from someone's visit to heaven that we will spend eternities learning the things of God. We don't stop after we go to heaven; it keeps going even there. The only way you can keep up is to have a real relationship with the Holy Spirit and hear from Him. Many say they do, but in reality, don't.

Old words, new words

There are those who say only the Bible has relevant words from God, and we should only use them. Yes, the Bible is good and the words of old, but God did not stop speaking just because a few hundred years had passed. God has never stopped speaking to us. The thing we need to understand is that it's all from the same source.

Jesus said in John 16:12-15: "I have yet many things to tell you, but you can't bear them now. However, when He, the Spirit of truth, has come, He will guide you into all truth." Which means He was going to tell them later, after He was gone through the Holy Spirit. Some don't believe when people say they have visited heaven and talked with Jesus. These things are not contradicting the Bible, because it's all from the same source. If you have many reporters reporting the same story, each one might get a little different detail, but it's all still painting the same picture. There are some or a lot of details left out originally, but God is giving us more and more in time, growing it. It's like painting a picture. More can always be painted on later.

Jesus said He still had more to tell us but decided to tell us later after His death in visions, dreams, and heavenly visits. The Bible was made by humans like you and me. They certainly were not perfect. But we treat it like it's the final word God will ever speak. Why can't we get more words today? For example, Rick Joyner's final quest series and Anna Rountree's vision books. These books are pure heavenly visits, verbatim. They are like new Bible material. They were meant to be gentle nudges in the right direction. But I don't feel that we should treat it religiously and treat it like we treat the Bible.

For example, how do we treat prophecies? They are fresh words directly from God. Do we write them down and make them a new Bible? No, we take and absorb the words and apply them to our lives. But they are just as important as the Bible because they're fresh words and visions from God. The reason the Bible is important is because its instructions from the founding fathers of the church. They were only humans, so they're not perfect; only Jesus was perfect. So we listen to them and their words and the heart of it, just not microscopically so, dissecting every tiny word for a meaning. Just like in Rick Joyner's final quest book, he visited Paul, and Paul said to him at one point that we should not put him as the foundation of the church, but Jesus.

The Bible basically is documenting the coming and teachings of Jesus and letters to help certain church groups correct their problems. In 3 John 1:13-14, it talks about coming to speak face to face many things, so what were those things.

Also, were the letters of the Bible of more basic matters, and the more advanced matters like being led by the Holy Spirit left out and taught to each other directly as needed? Were all these advanced teachings lost in time because it was on a person-by-person basis? There is no proof of this, but I suspect it.

We often learn things in the moment, and by spending time with others who have experience. It isn't necessarily documented. Sometimes people learn things little by little as they grow or ask questions. I do not presume this, but for example's sake. What if I lived in the Bible days and my writings made it into the Bible? Things that are written could be perceived one way or another if the causal writings that I only took moments to write were dissected to the microscopic detail. Would interpretations come out of it that I never intended? We are only human; only God can be perfect. He weighs every word to completion.

Of course, there are those out there that get counterfeit revelations that aren't necessarily true, not to be confused with that. The problem with that is church officials go overboard, being scared of the misinformation that they throw the baby out with the bathwater. There just needs to be some discernment is all.

Many say the Bible is so simple that a child can read and understand it. Why don't we approach it as a child and not as an intellectual? If there is revelation to be had, let the Holy Spirit be the brains. He will enlighten what needs to be enlightened.

This topic is about getting fresh words from God today, to where they can influence, change and challenge our Christian walk. Rick Joyner said once that God is often not as religious as we are.

Seeing in the Holy Spirit, and the leadings of the Holy Spirit

These are visions and words that the Holy Spirit can impart to you to show you dynamics that are going on and what He wants you to do. The Holy Spirit wants to tune you into His channel, because He wants to use you the way He wants. He can use you provided you share or act on what He's implying you to do. The Holy Spirit often likes to impart this way, maybe because it's faster. A picture speaks a thousand words. But you have to be sensitive to hear and see the pictures He shows you. You need to turn off your loudspeaker your brain so that the still small voice can be heard, 1 Kings 19:11-13.

The Holy Spirit may sometimes speak, and other times, just show pictures. To see His pictures or mini visions, you have to relax, turn your mind off, and have no fear, anxiety, or any negative feelings, but peace, and wait for Him to either speak to you or give you picture flashes. The pictures are often quick and brief. If you're not paying attention, you wouldn't think anything of it. You would think it was your imagination. But the Holy Spirit doesn't always speak. You have to be sensitive to when He is speaking or showing you pictures; which may be at an unexpected time.

I have often found that people are already seeing in the spirit but are not realizing it. The Holy Spirit is already giving them pictures they just think it's them because it's such a quick flash, and they think nothing of it. Now, some of the things seen may seem silly to you, but when presented to a prophetic group, it might make sense to others. You need to share it, no matter how silly it may seem. Often people are intimidated to share what they think they've been given, because they feel awkward speaking up in a meeting. You need to get over that and go ahead and feel silly and say it. I was told prophetically that I need to give what I have been given, and when I'm faithful in that, I will be given more. That I will scare myself with the things I will do. You need to be faithful with what you've been given.

When you're faithful, the Holy Spirit will give you more and more. I was told one time by the Holy Spirit when I had fear in my heart because of something He told me to do in a meeting; "fear is half of the battle, and once you lose that fear, you are halfway there." I am more of an apprentice at the time I write this, but I have shared what I know.

The Holy Spirit will also speak through feelings and drawings of your heart. But this may be tricky because our flesh can drive our feelings toward something also. We need to learn the 3 voices which are: your voice, the devil's voice, and God's voice in you (See Topic "False Voices, that Mislead" page 62).

One way I seek the Holy Spirit in what I'm supposed to do is, in my heart, go between the two or more options. Go through each option and pause a while and see if you feel a resistance to it or not. If the decision is based on several locations, you can use a map and consider each location in your heart. Now, this can be tricky because your emotions can dominate this because of how you feel on the matter, whether positive or negative. You need to try to sort this out because the answer is not related to how you feel about it, its how does the Holy Spirit feel about it. Emotions can cloud this type of hearing. You need to be completely neutral in it and see what positive or resistance feeling you feel. It's kind of a tricky thing to figure out at first. The Holy Spirit might speak and give visions all at the same time. He has many ways of speaking to us, we just need to recognize it, be sensitive to Him, and obey.

You also need to be aware of the Holy Spirit's leading in your day as well. He can give you what's called a check in your heart. Which is a sign to you He may not want you to do something, be alert, or pray. He may be trying to alert you of something that is going to happen that's not good, and to avoid it, follow after peace. So be aware of this and be sensitive to it. The Holy Spirit is more than willing to lead you in even the smallest of matters. That's why He's called the helper.

Born in the Spirit with gifts already operating

I don't know when it occurs. Whether it's at birth, or whether it's when you receive the gift of the Holy Spirit, Luke 1:15. The Holy Spirit gives you your giftings whatever they might be; it can even happen at a young age. Every Christian has at least one gifting and the spiritual equipment that it requires. Romans 11:29 says the gifts and calling are without repentance. The Holy Spirit gives you your gifting whether you know how to use it or not. These are gifts of the Spirit that I'm referring to, not talents. The gifting sometimes can be related to a talent, but not always.

People often don't know that this is going on. They often use their gifts without even knowing it. The gift is in them and in operation at all times; it has become a part of them. So much so that they are unaware that it's a gifting they're using. People think it's their imagination, or that everybody has this ability they are naturally using.

What you need to do is realize what is happening in yourself. The Holy Spirit has given you your gift, and it's fully operational the second He gives it to you. Our job is to recognize it and learn how to use it. Often it's present even in your childhood. You just grew up with it and have gotten used to it, assuming that everybody experiences these things. It's unique to you; not everybody has the same gifts.

There are two common things given to most Christians. The first is sense; you feel things in your spirit or sensitivity in the spirit. It's a feeling in your center chest area, whether positive or negative. You're sensing the spiritual atmosphere around you; either God's energy (Anointing, peace, etc.) or the devil's (suffocation, death, unclean spirit, etc.). You feel a feeling in your heart, which people often think is their emotions, but it's the spiritual dynamic around them, whether it's positive or negative. This feeling can be either an area at large, a building, or a person.

The appropriate response to a negative feeling is to pray in tongues and ask the Holy Spirit for guidance on what to do. (See Topics: "The Devil's on the Outside" page 172, "Devil's last stand and strong demon submission" page 178, and "Know your spiritual boundaries, what you have authority over" page 180) If it's positive, maybe God wants to say or do something with you.

The second main thing is seeing in the spirit, or seeing in your heart. You would think it's your imagination if you didn't know better, but the Holy

Spirit is trying to get you to recognize quick picture flashes that He puts into your imagination. The devil can do this too, so learn to recognize the difference! Often you're already receiving the pictures but haven't recognized them as the Holy Spirit. More than likely, you think it's your imagination or your thoughts. The pictures put into your heart are so quick that if you're not paying attention, you'd miss them. A picture speaks a thousand words; so what better way for the Holy Spirit to convey things to you.

What you need to do is to calm your spirit, turn your brain off, and get fear out of your heart or any other negative emotion. Because overbearing emotions will clog your hearing of the Holy Spirit. The Holy Spirit said to me once in a meeting that fear is half of the battle; fear of saying what you got. Often you will hear words or pictures; pictures can often have symbolism or be straight forward. It's the Holy Spirit giving you what He wants you to either do or say, especially when you're in a meeting of people pursuing Him. The pictures are so quick that you have to believe what you saw; then say or do it, even if you feel silly. It will make sense to others in the room.

Sometimes the Holy Spirit can use pictures if you're laying hands on someone for what needs to be done. You need to present what you've seen, even if you feel scared saying or doing it. But beware, the enemy can also give pictures and lead.

For example, I seen a picture of a waterfall covering the earth (His anointing). I see Jesus on His white horse doing various things, or I'll see a picture of what I'm supposed to do. I will see silly things that don't make any sense until it's told to the group. Sometimes I see demons and instructions if there's something that needs to be done. Sometimes it's just for aware sake. You may not be given the authority to get rid of them in that situation. It may just be so that you avoid them. (See Topics "The Devil's on the Outside" page 172, and "Know your spiritual boundaries, what you have authority over" page 180). There are many different types of giftings; these are the two main ingredients included with most gifts. Ask the Holy Spirit to show you what your gifting is.

The thing that sparked me to write this topic was two separate people we spent time with in ministry. In one situation, we were in Utah, and this city was predominately Mormon. We were in her kitchen helping her cook, and it was Sunday. An icky feeling was covering the entire town, and it was spiritually choking. But she didn't recognize what was happening; she was becoming sad or down and didn't know why. The reason was not her, but the spiritual suffocation that was going on that day that felt like negative emotions. (See Topic "Spiritual Suffocation" page 94).

The second situation was we were with someone on their land, and we were seeing and doing prophetic things in the anointing. She wanted to know how we saw and heard so much and how she could do it. I explained how I got the things, and she realized that she was already seeing and just had to realize and apply it.

Prayer is a Powerful tool do not retaliate

The power of life and death are in the tongue. It's your choice how you will use it. In Matt 5:44 it says, "But I say unto you, Love your enemies, bless them that curse you, do good to them that hate you, and pray for them which despitefully use you, and persecute you." Love is more powerful than retaliation. This person has pain in their heart; hurting them further will not help them, but only push them further into pain. I think this is why Jesus said this.

The next time someone persecutes you, pray that the Lord will heal them of the pain that causes them to do this. Do not retaliate; let the Lord do the work for you. Don't pray a curse on them or an affliction, but pray and love instead.

"Two wrongs do not make a right." Just because they're sinning by doing something against you doesn't mean that you must also do the same and retaliate. The Lord has put at your command angels that can do the work of the kingdom, but you must choose to use them. Don't hinder them by praying negativity or curses; angels know not of it. That's the devil's work! If you're participating in such works, you are helping his efforts.

Love, do not hate, forgive and release. For the Lord delights when you're loving and forgiving. Do good and not evil against them, and watch the hand of the Lord in your situation.

You need to give the situation to God and let Him deal with it as He deems necessary. Perhaps He will dethrone them, but that's His business, not yours. You must stand back and let Him do it because human efforts are fruitless and in vain. Let the higher power take care of it, and you will be all the much better for it.

Who me, a Gossiper? Yeah right! and Confidants

There are many people out there in the Christian world today who gossip and don't even know they are. Will even talk about gossiping as a bad thing and talk about people who do. There seems to be a blinder on their eyes. The typical excuse for it is that they just need someone to talk to. There's a hairline between council and gossip. The funny thing is that it's very apparent to everyone around them. Sometimes they're told that they gossip, but they don't believe them because of their many excuses. Maybe you need someone to talk to, but it's the manner and quantity in which you do it, which is gossip. You need to limit it to a person who is mature and can handle your hurts in an objective and positive matter. Not degrading a person's character with another complaint session, no.

Me personally, I haven't needed someone to confide in. I do all I want with the Lord. I can tell Him anything and everything I want, and ask Him to fix it His way and heal my heart. If you talk to someone about it, it shouldn't be on a casual basis, but towards finding a solution and being responsible in the matter. If a person seems unmovable and hopeless, perhaps you have misjudged the situation. Yes, you live with it all the time, and it seems unsolvable. But sometimes, you have to take the first step to make it better and step toward healing (See Topic "Arguing, Defense and walls a better way" page 99).

The bottom line of gossiping is you need to look for a solution, not just sit around degrading a person's character by telling everyone about it. I have known many people who go around to everyone they can and tell them about what their spouse has done. Even to complete strangers that didn't even ask about it. They will go from person to person telling them all of their troubles or woes. Going to the next and the next practically telling everyone; this is full-on gossip. God does not want us tearing down people in other people's minds behind their backs.

People often don't think what they're doing is gossip, and will probably resist being told that. They have all their excuses why they think it's okay. Most gossipers are this way; they're blinded to what they are doing, but this is highly inappropriate. I think what needs to be looked at is the root of it. The root is often pain, trying to find a way to vent that pain and frustration, but this is not the way to do it.

You need to seek Jesus and His healing for your pain. This often can be found in personal worship and crying. If you need counseling, isolate the counsel to just one person preferably; someone you can trust that's wise and discrete. Preferably someone who is not related to the situation. Who can be objective and seek a solution. Someone who would not think less of the person after the communication.

I'm not talking about your best friend, who sits there and says, oh you poor thing. You are totally right, and they are completely wrong. Then create division off of it, start treating the other person in a negative matter, and spread the gossip. No, this is no solution at all; it's just making things worse. Division is one of the enemy's tactics. He loves gossip because it works greatly towards division; you are destroying that person's character.

You need someone who will keep it to themselves and give you council to a solution. Who presents a realistic solution. So if your friend is not good at counseling, but good at division making, then don't tell them. You shouldn't be looking for someone to vent all your frustrations on anyway. God should be your comforter, not your friends. You may have an excuse why it's an okay thing to do, but if you do this, you are gossiping. There are no excuses that will change that. This is not Godly manners; it's not everyone's business.

Sometimes things are just misunderstandings, where a little communication will clear it up. You might think they are doing one thing, where in fact, they're doing something completely different. Sometimes what you thought was going on wasn't even going on at all. A complete misunderstanding. I believe that the best relationship is based upon open communication, working through things (See Topic "Apology tool of great healing" Page 104). Sometimes a little communication goes a long way.

There are many Christians out there that do this; you need to stop this. God does not favor gossip or division. So go to God for your healing, try to work things out with the person (See Topics "Relationship and communication" page 101, and "Arguing, Defense and Walls a better way" page 99). This business is between the two of you, not everybody else.

Someone told me once it's the ear that's the worst, rather than the person speaking it. There can also be the person who wants to hear about things and seeks them out. This is just as bad because it's encouragement for the gossiper to continue. What needs to happen, is if it's not working toward a solution rather than idle chatter, the listener should stop it before it goes any further.

What is the spirit behind it? Is it negative, or towards a solution? Because sometimes people won't go to the person to resolve it at all. This can also happen in other situations; people gossiping about people they don't like or disagree with. Some people are afraid to talk to the person, and their solution is to gossip about it.

Sometimes people will project what they are thinking is happening and tell people that rumor, but it may or may not be true; this is also inappropriate. You may be spreading false information around that's damaging to that person. (See Topic "Boundary setting, why can't you say no!" page 111 may relate to the situation)

Bottom line is to talk to whomever and clear it up directly; instead of talking to everyone else and creating all sorts of division. The enemy does his work very well in misconceptions.

If you do any of these, you need to realize it for what it is and change; wake up! The scripture says if you have something against your brother, then go and resolve it. Matt 5:23-24. You need to go to the person and talk to them about whatever it may be, which more than likely is a misunderstanding anyway. What are you afraid of? (See Topics "Relationship and communication" page 101, and "Arguing, Defense and Walls a better way" page 99)

Ephesians 4:29 (ESV) "Let no corrupting talk come out of your mouths, but only such as is good for building up, as fits the occasion, that it may give grace to those who hear."
Proverbs 26:20 (ESV) "For lack of wood the fire goes out, and where there is no whisperer, quarreling ceases."
Proverbs 16:28 (ESV) "A whisperer separates close friends."
Proverbs 20:19 (ESV) "Whoever goes about slandering reveals secrets; therefore do not associate with a simple babbler."
Psalm 101:5 "Whoso privily slandereth his neighbor, him will I cut off"
James 1:26, 1 Timothy 5:13, Leviticus 19:16, Exodus 20:16, 2 Corinthians 12:20, Romans 1:29-30

Revival is Coming

There is a revival that is coming that no man can contain or tame. It will not be in one building or one location; it will be literally all over the world. God is going to pour out His Spirit unlike any time in history. Millions upon billions of people will be touched in a way that will be deep and personal. People will be challenged to be holy, to consecrate their lives. To set down their desires for the desires of the Lord. It will be a Holy revolution that no one can control. It has been prophesied as the great harvest, where people will find the river of life and will then show others. It will be worship like you have never known before. The end of the age has come; the harvest is ripe for the picking. Now is the time for the harvest.

It's a challenge for more in Him; to set aside our Laodicean ways. Lukewarm one day a week Christian. Showing God lip service; living their life as half-baked Christians. Looking good on the outside, but full of unfinished maturing. God doesn't want us to be barely saved. Being saved is just the start! He wants you to mature in Him as much as possible. There are those who consider themselves mature but really are half-baked. This is because the church is mostly baby milk level Christians. They may appear to be above average, but in reality, there is much more in the Lord.

Revival is often a wake-up call, not just a time to feel good and get goose bumps. God is calling you to more! The journey is just starting; keep walking, growing, maturing yourself, and growing in greater and greater amounts of holiness. John 4:35

Teachable Spirit/Unteachable Spirit

We don't know all things perfectly, nor will we! It says the meek shall inherit the earth, and whoever humbles Himself will be exalted, Matt 5:5, Luke 14:11. To be teachable is to be humble. It says in James 4:6: "God resists the proud, but gives grace to the humble." The more teachable you are, the more God can trust you with True authority, and the more responsibility He can entrust to you. The Lord is continually trying to grow your spirit and to work out things that get between you and Him. If you are not willing to learn, then you will not advance spiritually. You will have to stay where you currently are until you do learn it.

The path that the Lord is leading you on is the path of dying to self. The reason that He's doing this is to bring you closer to Him, that He might entrust you with more. But He can't trust you with more if you have an unteachable spirit.

The next time that you're confronted by someone, take some time to think about it, be teachable. Could they be right? Is there anything that can be done different next time on your part? Consider what you can change, even if the other person is partially at fault. That's their deal; do what you can do to be right before God. Just because they do it doesn't mean that you must also do it, and both be wrong.

You need to be teachable and not point the finger at others. What I do is I'm open to the possibility of change by considering if even a small part of what they're saying is right. To be teachable is the path of dying to self. Without it, you will remain motionless and stalemated.

Generous with the gift of the Holy Spirit

In a Rick Joyner final quest book, Jesus was talking about eagles as maturing Christians and the different levels. There were white, gold, and bald eagle in that order, white being the most mature. Jesus said there are many eagles because I am generous with the gift of the Holy Spirit.

In this topic, I will be writing about the bald eagle. One who gets things from the Holy Spirit to relay to others that are accurate, or giftings in Him. They gain confidence that God has anointed them and consider that they have reached the goal and are mostly matured and become unteachable (See Topics "Levels of Maturity and Obedience" page 53, and "Bow down low to receive the next level" page 82). They may even become rough with a lack of love. They still have accurate words or power in their gifts because the gifts are without repentance Rom 11:29. But it says in the scripture: "If I speak with the tongues of men and of angels, but have not love, I have become sounding brass, or a clanging cymbal. And if I have the gift of prophecy, and know all mysteries and all knowledge; and if I have all faith, so as to remove mountains, but have not love, I am nothing" 1 Corinthians 13:1-3.

What they may not realize is that this is a progressive path we walk. They have started the path, but the enemy has stopped them from progressing any further; because they feel there's not much room for improvement.

Sometimes God gives a vision or a word for someone so they can pray that it won't happen. Don't get me wrong, God sometimes has to be firm; He may even rebuke a person or a group because of their faithlessness. "But there should be a hope or a path out" (quotations: paraphrased Rick Joyner). This is a form of Love; God chastises those whom He loves Prov 3:11-12, Heb 12:5-7. Prophecy doesn't always have to sound loving or dovey, but some prophets will go around with a lack of love in all things. It affects their countenance and how they act and treat people. I just heard the Holy Spirit say: "I am the Lion, but I am also the Lamb." Know when He wants to come as the Lion, and when He wants to come as the Lamb.

I am referring to an individual who I ran across that would walk around without hardly a smile or much from their heart. They wouldn't go around frowning, but they seemed very stiff. You could hardly get them to laugh by making a joke. What you are on the inside will show on the outside. What they don't realize is that they are only a bald eagle; there still is more! There are also the Gold Eagle and the White Eagle. You become the greater eagle as you continue to mature in Him. Know when to come as the Lamb and when to come as the Lion by the Holy Spirit. But they have taken up all Lion and know not much of the Lamb; they need to learn the balance. We have never reached the top and should always progress the path towards holiness.

Don't justify yourself and your actions just because God gives you accurate words or power in the anointing. Another person I know gets lots of words and visions from God that are unique and wonderful. But they're a gossiper and division maker that holds a grudge in their heart. Unfortunately, they are blind to this sin in their life. When confronted about it, they turned everybody against the confronter and kicked them out. The confronter did it in a subtle and loving manner, but that didn't matter.

Just because God uses you doesn't mean he puts his stamp of approval on your everything. God is Generous with His gift of the Holy Spirit. Don't justify yourself off of it. Jesus gives us grace so that we can continue in Him. That's why those with poor manners still get valid things from God. That doesn't make it right! They will have to account for their poor actions in their life review and relive them from the victim's perspective. Realize this and correct these sins in your life, and in the process, your gifting will become more potent. In heaven, you are known by your humility and love!

The Purpose of this Life

It is God's purpose to have someone come to Him in spirit and in truth. God created the angels to praise Him night and day. Because they have seen His glory, it's easy for them to know that He is God. If anyone were to see God, they would instantly become believers.

In a book about someone's experience in heaven, I read that if someone has not been prepared to see God they would be so dazzled and amazed that they would become unconscious; because it's more than they can handle. God is so wonderful and powerful that when you see Him one day, your automatic response will be to worship Him. He is so awesome that you will be overwhelmed with awe. In 1Cor. 13:12 it says that we see through a glass, darkly.

This way, we don't see His full glory in all its splendor, thus creating the atmosphere to produce true servants. God took a risk giving man the ability to choose. But it is worth the risk because those who choose Him, choose Him truly. Not because of His glory, but because they love Him. They are worth more than anything. It's like a rich man that conceals his wealth and looks for a mate that will love him for who he is; not because he is rich. God is extremely rich in glory in power that He has concealed it so that His people will Love Him for who He is, not just an automatic servant because of His amazing glory.

A Phrase I read once is: "Love commanded is not Love at all." If God wanted someone to just say the words I love you, He could have created robots or a computer program for that. But that has no heart, would be unfulfilling, and empty. He wants people to come to Him because they Love who He is. If someone saw Him now in His splendor, they would become instant servants, but they would not be true servants. It's like one who is forced to serve Him because they have no choice. God gave us the ability to choose, and this life is a test to see how we will choose. What we choose here will reflect what our position is in eternity. How can the Lord trust someone with great responsibility who hasn't been faithful? Those who choose to come to Him now are true servants. When you're faithful with what you have, more will be *given to you.*

Use your worldly resources to benefit others

This world is but a vapor, but the things of God are forever. If you think about it, all the work that you do to gain money over a lifetime is mostly used to just maintain and entertain yourself. So once you're off this earth, to what benefit is that to you? Why not invest in eternal things that will give you an eternal reward?

"But seek the kingdom of God, and all these things shall be added to you. Do not fear, little flock, for it is your Father's good pleasure to give you the kingdom. Sell what you have and give alms; provide yourselves money bags which do not grow old, a treasure in the heavens that does not fail, where no thief approaches nor moth destroys. For where your treasure is, there your heart will be also." Luke 12:31-34

Use your worldly resources to benefit others, to help them mature spiritually, and your reward will be many times greater in heaven. If you're into the things of this earth, then your resources will be invested in the world. But if your heart is in the things of the spirit, then your resources will be invested in the Spirit.

To what benefit is it for the rich to gain all wealth, to tend to their comforts, but to neglect the things that are forever, and gain nothing in the afterlife. All will be for nothing because this life is a wisp, but heaven is forever. Does it not make sense to invest in that which will be forever, rather than this life that is for a moment?

You will think yourself foolish when you get there if you used your resources for personal comforts instead of investing in treasures in heaven, which will be forever. This life is like building a sandcastle on the beach. It will mean nothing but a moment's pleasure, then all is swept away; just like Anna Rountree's vision of building sandcastles on her webpage.

"While we look not at the things which are seen, but at the things which are not seen; for the things which are seen are temporal, but the things which are not seen are eternal," 2 Corinthians 4:18.

Worship

God made our inner person to need Him; without Him, we are empty. Worship is one of the easiest ways to fill our spirit with life. There are many out there who are spiritually parched and don't even know it. They strongly need to get into spirit-filled worship to heal their hearts. When He touches you, it feels like an undescribable healing of your inner person, like He's healing your emotions and hurts. What happens to me often is my eyes will water and slowly tear. It's a wonderful feeling. You feel you are slowly but gradually being healed. Your inner person is being filled with His love and life.

When you worship, you should not just sing the words to just sing them; you need to do it with your heart. It is not the words that God hears; it is your heart that He hears. Worship in Spirit and in Truth.

Sometimes, a church will have a good song, but then either move on the next or go into the sermon. Often more concerned with getting the sermon started, rather than what the Holy Spirit wants them to do. More like satisfying the minimum requirement of worship, then halting it with teaching. Often worship CDs will have some good songs, then jump into a hyper disruptive song. I'm not saying hyper songs are bad. But they need to be at the beginning and progress into the more intimate songs.

If you're looking for deep healing worship, do it in your personal time with a worship CD that ministers to you. Preferably with headphones, because with headphones, it's more saturating. What I will often do, is if a song ministers to me more, I will repeat it many times, then move on. He can meet you in your own home; He's more than willing to do this.

What needs to happen is that the church or worshipers need to become sensitive to the Spirit, and sense if the worship needs to continue. This is very much lacked today, unfortunately. I have had more of a touch of the Holy Spirit on my couch than in a church service!

Another thing is, worship is a corporate thing. All the people in the room are as one. If there's someone in the room who is lacking spiritually. The Holy Spirit will work with that person first, and only come with as much presence as that person can handle. Because if His presence went too high, that person would be overwhelmed. The Holy Spirit will use the others to intercede for those people. I say this because not all worship services are equal; you will only be able to go as high as the lowest link. This is not to discourage those from coming; by all means, please get your healing! If one truly wanted to soar in worship, select a smaller group of worshipers that are mature at a separate time.

Have you ever been in a worship service where you felt a heavy burden feeling in your heart, like a yucky feeling? I used to think it was me, that there was something that I did that made me feel this way. But I have discovered that feeling is actually a prayer burden or intercession. This is referred to as plowing in the Spirit. The worship leader has to break through this; it's hard work sometimes and may take a while. But once you break through, you will feel it and are released from the prayer burden. The Lord may put this burden on those who are healed and healthy spiritually because He may want you to help in the work of it. But if you have a small group of fully healed people, then there are no restrictions, and you can truly soar.

There are greater levels of worship as you progress more and more into Him. As you become less, He becomes more in your life. The less sin we have, the closer we can draw unto Him, chastening of our flesh.

Sometimes when the Holy Spirit is moving and touching people in unique ways, I used to think; why am I not feeling this? I felt bad and thought; what is wrong with me that I don't feel what they're feeling? The Lord is healing them; maybe He wants to touch you differently.

Another thing that I have found useful is that if I'm worshipping with others, and the song doesn't minister to me, I will sing the song in tongues, then it ministers to me. I feel some songs are too wordy and cumbersome, having to use your mind too much to worship. The songs that are easy to catch on to are usually more effective. Songs that talk about the Lord or what He has done, I don't think are very effective. I think they should be more directed at Him, not about or around Him. Of course, there are anointed songs that have more than just a few words. There is just a balance between too many words and just right. Like to Him who sits on the throne, and more Love more power are really good songs. There is also what is called a new song that you sing right out of your heart whatever you feel to sing. This does not apply to this. This can be anything and everything because you're connecting with the song and worshiping Him. Psalm 63:1

Worship is slow, less is more

Less is more, and slower more potent in worship. For some reason, everything is backwards these days. Many want to start slow in a song then go faster. Or have a slow song first, then a fast song after. It should be the exact opposite of this! Faster songs can be nice if it's an anointed song, but they're to help you enter worship; going progressively deeper and deeper. Sometimes these songs are needed because we often have our hearts cluttered with various things on our minds, hurts, or need to settle down. It's a process of preparing your heart and tenderizing it for deep worship. It's okay to have a slightly faster song at first, but as you progress, it should get slower and slower.

The closer you get to the throne room, the softer, slower, and more heartfelt it becomes. The slower worship is, the more potent it is, even down to ridiculously slow. I feel instrument playing should be more simple and basic the closer you get to the throne. Less is more! Fewer notes played, less quickness, softer, simpler! Like on the guitar, the most intimate would be a pluck every 5 seconds or so, letting the sound resonate. But this is when you're really in deep and have worked up to it.

Some people think the quicker and more beautifully you play, the more anointed. I have seen piano, violin, and guitar players alike, playing up a faster and faster storm of notes, feeling it's more anointed, sounding like a professional orchestra player maybe. Sure, this sounds great in the professional world, but it doesn't work for deep worship.

The Deeper you get, the more simple the playing is, and the much slower it is. When trying to convey that slower is better, people often will not think slow enough. So think slower, then go half what you think is slow; even to ridiculously slow. Maybe even slower than 5 seconds if the situation calls for it!

I like playing chords myself, with a flowy sound on a keyboard that just keeps playing and playing when you hold the key down so I can play very simply. I will play one chord at a time and go as slow as I can possibly go in a song. Also, in worship, you might feel compelled to make up your own words to the song, or make up a new chord progression spontaneously, on the spur of the moment, a new song. The new song is often more powerful because its words coming right out of your heart. It doesn't have to be anything complicated, it can be something simple, Psalm 40:3. Sometimes it's just simply changing the words to the song you're singing. Maybe not like the Ihop model (International House of Prayer), but perhaps similar (at least at this current time). I view Ihop as a great starting point for the young, but it's not the top of the top. What they may not realize is they are doing the same pattern or style over and over. This is great for training, and I'm glad for what they're doing. I feel that the songs that Ihop often sing are way too wordy. They are nice songs though, not to discourage anyone. If they would make the songs more simple and slower, it would be more ideal. I'm glad they're there, because at least they are doing something rather than nothing.

The song choice should be fairly simple and easy to catch on, not so many words that you have to use your brain more than your heart. I have heard of a minister in the past that went around showing people songs as simple as singing hallelujah over and over. This is getting pretty close to the principle and often will have a big anointing. You need to sing it as if God was right there in the room, singing the song directly to Him or at His feet. Some people use their brains a little too much, trying to imagine everything they're singing in their mind to Him. This is nice, but you need to turn your brain off when worshiping and express it from your heart instead. It's about singing from your heart and emotions. The brain is earthbound, but your heart is where the spirit of God is.

There are also many levels of worship, depending on a person's level of healing and maturity. Sometimes it's necessary for God to do spiritual heart surgery on your heart; it can even be deeply rooted heart conditions. People feel God touching them, they think it's very deep, but there may be deeper. These are levels of worship. Like if two people were in a worship room; to one, it would feel like deep worship, but to another, it would be average. This goes into the levels of healing and maturity.

Your level of maturity can affect how deeply you can go into Him. Yes, He touches you, and it feels like deep anointing; this doesn't mean that it is the deepest. To one, it will be a glass full; to another, a glass half full. That's because the other has progressed farther into worship. It's your capacity in which you are limited.

The less there is between you and God, the deeper you can go in Him. These may be sins you're unaware of at this time. It could be how healed your emotions are, if there are pains or hidden pains. Don't get me wrong, this all is covered under the blood. God touches everyone who's open to Him. It all feels wonderful and powerful, but what I'm referring to is as we grow in Him, our capacity to receive deeper levels of worship increases. As you progress deeper into worship, what once seemed deep will now seem like less. One may consider themselves to be deep where they are, but not see the levels ahead of them; this is very common. (See Topic "Everybody Speaks the Same Language" page 95). Matt 6:23 "If therefore the light that is in thee be darkness, how great is that darkness!"

    Another thing that can limit worship is spiritual atmosphere blocks. This dynamic is active in whatever area you choose to worship in. Whatever demonic influence is allowed in that area by whomsoever. Whether that is small or great depends on the area. This dynamic can be affected by neighborhood, city, county, state, or country, depending on those who own the land you're on. Things that are participated in that area or leadership over larger areas. These things will have to be wrestled with to get anywhere in Worship Eph 6:12. It's like a block in the heavens that will only allow you to go so far in worship until it's wrestled out of the way. This can be accomplished by either intercession or worship intersession. But beware, when you fight the enemy's territory, he likes to fight back. Make sure you're supposed to or not. You can, however, plow through in worship, even if it takes many times to accomplish. If you don't know it's there or don't know how to get past it, you will be limited by this dynamic and only be able to go so far. Be aware that you only have so much authority. Like you can't go into the middle of New York City and say, okay, all demons be gone! Because you don't have that spiritual authority and would receive a big backlash from trying to do that. This goes for all scales of this also.

    Another thing to try is to change your location where you worship; because spiritual climates are different depending on where you go. Like for instance, trying to worship in a religious church building may have limits because of all the religious blocks in the room. There are many dynamics to spiritual blocks, and they're not necessarily related to the area; they can be the local building or land also. Who has authority over that situation and whatever spiritual blocks they put on it will limit the spiritual ceiling, but if they give you authority to be there, then you have the right to push things back. It may not be a simple fix. You may have to fight your way through it spiritually, and if they're also in that same space at other times, then that spiritual ceiling will be reset every time.

    Also, when you bring life and light into an area, the enemy sees this and paints a target on it and tries to smother and attack it. Because the enemy doesn't want people to make progress, so he will do anything he can to stop it!

    When you worship, you get life, but when you go home and live your life, this life fades. Often the enemy can be trying to get us out of that life any way he can. You have to keep your guard up spiritually to keep that life in you. Things in this life drain that life off. We need to keep going to the Lord for our life. It often can be a battle too, because the enemy wants to snuff out any light he sees and fight against it.

(See Topics "Know your spiritual boundaries, what you have authority over" page 180, and "Intercessors" page 185)

Surface Worship/Heart Worship

    Surface worship is just singing the words to sing them, or to sing to impress other people Matthew 15:8. I have a decent voice. I used to sometimes without realizing it, sing to impress people. But one day, I was telling someone it's not what comes out of the mouth, it's what comes out of the heart. Then I heard the Holy Spirit say to me, "Tell yourself that." Some people may not even realize that they are not singing out of their heart. Maybe you're not singing to impress people, but still singing surfacy. Relax your heart and breathe out; sing from your heart. I'm not saying that you can't sing fancifully, just let it come out of the heart. Sometimes when you're really getting into the Spirit, then it may really come out. Let it come from the heart, sing to God, not to man.

    God sees your heart in worship. If you have pride, then that gets in the way of true worship; sing in Spirit and in Truth. We have made worship more complicated than it needs to be with so many words in our songs. Songs are really an instrument in which we use to bring us to the place of worship.

    Like in a relationship between a husband and wife. You can say the words just to say them without meaning, or be genuine with them. There is a difference between just singing a song and singing a song with your heart.

Worship in Spirit and In Truth

This means to live the life. To be holy unto Him and strive for holiness. Not to just sing and mean it, but to cleanse your soul and spirit of that which is polluting it. When you worship, you're presenting your heart and being before God. It is true that He accepts you as you are, but the closeness that you can attain is limited by your level of purity. There are deeper and deeper levels in Him. When you're worshiping, it may seem like you're getting in deep, but in fact, there may be deeper levels than you are aware of!

There are three courts in worship, just like the temple that God told David to build, the outer court, the inner court, and the holy of holies. In order to progress from the outer court into the inner court, you have to prepare yourself by making your life right before Him. Then, when going from the inner court to the holy of holies, you must prepare yourself further. The cleaner your spirit is, the closer and more intimate you can be with Him. God desires for us to be holy unto Him and live a life of seeking holiness. Holiness makes worship more effective because you're presenting a sacrificed life before Him.

This is especially necessary for those who lead worship. They are the instrument that God is using to minister unto the people. This is not to discourage worshipers from worshiping; we all fall short. Trying to be better is what counts. If one is not trying to work on their issues, then the issue will remain. God can come into a room with a compromised vessel, yes, but this can limit the anointing to their level. God wants to use them and there's grace in this because He loves us and wants us to learn our gifts. You certainly can't be perfect, but you need to pursue being holy and ask God to cover what may not be perfect. That you are trying and pursuing it is what matters, so don't stop ministering. God can cover you with His forgiveness if your heart is pursuing it. But if you're participating in something that you shouldn't, this is what is in question. John 4:23

New Song

In worship, there comes a point where you feel high in His presence that you can't help but make a dynamic new song on the spot. It may or may not be simple; it's a true expression of your heart. It's not to make a new song that you will remember from now on. It's a tool to get closer to God in that moment; because if done right, you may reach higher places in worship. It's worship in its purest form because it's coming directly from your heart. Sometimes I will just simply make up new words for the current song that I'm singing. Don't try to think of words to sing. Let it flow out of you naturally. Psalm 40:3

Layers and Levels of Spiritual sensitivity

We are on an endless journey that the ultimate shouldn't ever be considered fully attained; sought more and more. The closer we get to Him, the less of us there is to get in the way.

Spiritual sensitivity is where you can hear from the Holy Spirit better, sense God's presence, the enemy's presence, and the conviction of things that pollute your spirit. Many things in this life will detract from this; there are many considerations in what builds our spiritual sensitivity. What do we do in our personal lives? Do we do things that would grieve God? Do you feel spiritually suffocated after participating in certain things? It's possible you could be numbed to its effects if you participate in it often. You need to determine if there's something in your life that's hindering your spiritual sensitivity. Negative emotions, excessive anger, negativity, oppression, depression, fear, etc.., can affect a person's sensitivity.

Another dynamic is where you live; what type of spiritual atmosphere is there. If not guarded against, demonic pressures in an area can affect a person as well. For example, an entire neighborhood could have the spirit of oppression/depression over it. If you don't keep your spiritual walls up, then it will try to sneak in on you and affect you (See Topic "Know your spiritual boundaries, what you have authority over" page 180).

Do you have spiritual life or peace of God in your heart? If not, then you should do personal worship to sensitize your spirit (See Topic "Worship" page 145); this is important to keep His life in your heart. There are different levels and layers of sensitivity in worship as well, depending on the person. To one, a worship experience will be absolutely mind blowing; to another, the same amount would be average. This is because that other person has progressed *further into worship.*

Also, who you hang around can affect you. If they do things that are not Godly, this can affect you negatively. God loves us all, of course. But they're giving access to the enemy to come in; if you're with them, then you will be affected also.

I learned when traveling around the nation there are different spiritual atmospheres (demonic influence). This negative influence will sting my heart, and I need to define my boundaries and push it away. But if I participate with it, like get sad (oppression), or I sin, I don't feel that sting anymore because my spirit has been numbed to its effects. So I have to push it off of me or ask for forgiveness and pray in tongues to get my spiritual sensitivity back up.

If one doesn't know this dynamic, they may remain numbed and won't have as high of spiritual sensitivity, getting swept right into it. This spiritual pressure feels like certain emotions sometimes, and you may not know that it's demonic in nature. Demonic pressure tries to push on you and even numb you so that you don't even know it exists anymore, or you think it's your emotions.

It's a constant process; you need to keep your guard up and be aware of this. It can be anything negative or sinful. Like it could be the spirit of depression, anger, religion, lust, or anything negative. It's often things that are participated with in that area by others living there. 2 Cor 6:17, Rom 12:2, Eph. 4:22-24

Worship is the only way to reach some

In the final quest series by Rick Joyner, there was a small group of people surrounded by the enemy by a river of life of God. The more the river was used, the bigger it became, but if it wasn't used, it would dry up. They were determined to keep their ground because there were only a few places left to be by the river. The enemy had seized control of all other places. The enemy was determined to stop this and closed in more and more. A person in the protection group suggested that someone fill up water from the river and offer it to the enemy. As they did, they discovered the enemy were Christians, all wretched and dried up spiritually. When they offered them a drink, they were shocked and stood motionless for a moment, not knowing what to do but to take the offer of water. When they did, they realized their real thirst and wanted more. There were many people offering them water. Soon the demand became so much that they could not keep up with it but simply point them to the river. So they did and were converted, having their countenances changed. Soon they were helping the effort to convert their friends, and those they knew in the enemy army. I believe the river is worship and life in the spirit.

The only way to reach some Christians out there that are dry, listless, backward and stubborn is through worship. Not through their brain, but through their heart in real worship. I'm not talking about singing out of hymnals, but life filled worship.

Unfortunately, there really isn't much life in worship in the church today. It lacks power and usually goes only so far and stops. Yes, you may feel the presence of God, but it's but a small portion of what's possible. I'm talking about deep true worship that has not been seen much in today's church. Probably has been experienced to some measure sometimes or in revivals. I'm referring to real deep worship that's rarely experienced.

True Spirit-filled worship is the only way to reach certain people. Even to non-Christians or other twisted faiths because it goes into their heart.

In another heavenly book I read, Jesus said that God designed us to need His life, and on a continual basis, so we need worship and God's life. It touches a part of people that they didn't know they needed. Because they have gone without it for so long, it touches their heart and heals them where they can't deny it. The enemy army didn't know they were so thirsty until they took a drink of life and wanted more. Psalm 63:1.

Don't neglect Worship

Worship is important. Most of us are actually starving ourselves spiritually. I'm not just talking about reading your Bible; you need to keep up your spiritual life as well. Just think, if you were to only eat food, and not drink, you would become dry and thirsty. That is what we're doing when we ignore worship Psalm 63:1. This is above and beyond church worship, because it's more personal and tailored to your needs in personal worship (headphones preferred). While worshiping, I will skip to songs that minister to me and sing them a few times, then move onto the next song that is ministering. I can feel if I'm getting too dry spiritually, and I can't stand it. I then take a large amount of time to come to full anointing in worship, where my spirit is filled, and I feel life in my heart. Another thing I do is if I don't feel up to par in my heart, I will say "I pray for peace" and pray in tongues until I feel at peace. Sometimes that might even mean hours of praying in tongues quietly while I go about my day.

Musician's battle with Pride

When I became a piano worshiper, I never thought I would battle with pride in my life, but there it was. I was shocked that it was possible; I understand it's a very common thing. I feel to write about how I came against this kind of pride.

It doesn't matter how good you sound or how wonderful it may be; if God doesn't show up, it won't mean anything. Because God is who they're looking at, not you. You need to learn to let go of your pride and put humility on instead. Because this creates a heart condition in you of holiness, rather than self-absorbed glory, you are trying to have the glory, where God deserves all glory. Often what happens is a look at how good I am, and a pride can come out of that. If unchecked, it could create an assumption that you can bring God's presence because you're so good at it.

God may show up anyway, but He's showing up for the people. Once when I was playing, I didn't feel so great in my heart, but the spirit of God came anyway. I was saying to myself, these people are bringing the spirit of God down, and they are lifting me up and carrying me. It's true God needs us and our gifts, but he wants humility. Later, I was thinking about the angels and how they worship. They have the most beautiful voices: but they don't look at themselves and say, my voice is so beautiful, look at me. They are more concerned about being pure and giving God all glory, not trying to take any unto themselves.

So what is it all really about? It's all about what's in the heart. The more pure the heart, the more powerful and effective you can be. God resists the proud, 1 Peter 5:5. God told me through a prophecy that if I ever get into pride that I've lost it! If you become too prideful, keep in mind that He can find another that is more pure in heart somewhere else.

You may even keep your position, but it will lack life and power. He will leave you where you're at and move on. He wants to use you because the laborers are few, but you are too compromised to be effective. When you lead worship, try to keep your mind on worshiping Him; forget about the audience. Be solely concentrating on worshiping Him rather than trying to impress people.

Another thing is musicians often feel that there is one perfect way of worshiping, but in a book I read of a heavenly experience, some people in heaven were playing with washboards (old-fashioned laundry). There is no set in stone way to worship Him; it's all relative to the heart in worship. So don't judge or think less of people if they're not conforming to what you think is the best way of worshiping Him. Maybe that is how they do it or the only way they know how. Granted, there are better ways of worshiping, but still, for them, that's what works. So don't judge a book by its cover. Only God knows the hearts behind the worship.

Equip others

God is in the multiplication business, because it's by far more effective if one teaches and equips others than for that person to hold to themself their gift. Equip others to do their ministries, and the result will be twice as effective as if there was only one. God asks you to climb His mountain, but once you have attained it, He asks you to go back down and teach others to get there also. God rejoices over the one lost sheep, more than the 99, Matthew 18:12-13. He wants us to equip others and teach them to come up the mountain of God. God has blessed you with some experience that others might not have. We all are one and can learn from each other's experiences.

We all have a piece. We just need to have the humility to put our pieces together, to learn from each other. God will give one piece to one and another to someone else; we only know in part, 1 Corinthians 13:9. We must realize that we're a part of the bigger puzzle. No one person or ministry will have the complete piece. God did this on purpose so that we would learn to work together in unity. It is better if one person specializes in this and another in that. Because if one person has spent their life doing just one thing, then they would have much more expertise in that area than someone who does it all. Like when you build a house, one set of people do the dirt work, someone the foundation, another does carpentry, one does the electric, another plumbing, so on and so forth. We as Christians must realize this, and work with one another, each with our own area of giftings.

The Lord works into each individual their own unique gift, and it works as a functioning part of the greater whole. So we should build each other up in our anointings so that everyone will function to their full capacity. It's better if many are functioning rather than just one. 2 Timothy 2:2, Colossians 3:16

Physical healing

Something's are out of our control in life; they happen, and we can't change them except through Jesus's healing. You wish you could go back in time and change what happened and do something different and be whole again. This is life, some things you just simply can't change. What you need to do is get emotional healing and cry it out if you have to. This is important. Have an honest conversation with God about the matter. Let Him hear your heart and tears and all that you feel. He already knows it, but it will bring you emotional healing on the matter. Ask the Holy Spirit how to cope with any issues or pains you may have. He can come up with something that maybe even the doctors may not have even thought of, like often they ignore herbal remedies.

It's an emotionally painful time; you just want to be better. But you are stuck in a hole, and only God can get you out of it. If you think of this deep hole theoretically, you have zero means to help yourself out of it. You would have to call for help to get out of it and trust in them to find a way. This is the way it is with getting help from God. We don't see the solution until it's time to receive it. God may come up with a way to heal you that you didn't expect. You need to just keep believing, no matter what the situation may be. It's God's promise that you will be healed, and He does not fail in His promises. I read all you have to do is "only Believe."

Someone had a vision where they saw an angel bringing healing that was prayed for, but at that last minute, they doubted it, saying maybe it's not the right time. So that angel was forced to take that healing back to heaven. He was standing right there and ready to implement it.

To be healed requires faith in order to receive it. You may be standing in the way of your healing by your doubts about it. God may want to heal you in a different way than what you're thinking. He may do it in a unique way. Sometimes He may heal you slowly in time, but it's also possible that He would heal you fast like in the Bible.

Maybe people think it's all or nothing, but you need to keep your faith alive, because, like the vision of the angel, you need to keep your faith to the last second. This person was right on top of receiving their healing and lost it because of unbelief.

Having faith is a lifestyle. You live in faith of receiving it. It doesn't falter because of any circumstances. Just keep believing in it and stay there no matter what. Because it is also possible when you are prayed for that the pain can get stronger at that moment. In this situation, it might be a demonic spirit that has control over the illness and can increase the pain when there's a hope of being healed to try to discourage faith (See next topic Physical Ailment of a demonic nature page 159). Often, people will get discouraged and lose faith at this moment. That's what the enemy is hoping for.

Your only job in receiving the healing is "only Believe." In a book about someone visiting heaven, the topic of healing came up, and they said your only job is to "only believe." It is easier for one to have faith for financial needs than for healing. And the People in heaven couldn't understand why we doubted it because it was God's promise that we would be healed.

Keep believing, keep pushing, keep knocking, and you will receive it because it's God's promise 1 Pet 2:24. Whenever Jesus was healing someone, He would say, "According to your faith be it done to you." So it wasn't up to Jesus, it was up to the person being healed, according to their faith Matt 9:29.

Now let's talk about those who are standing in the Gap to heal people. Again, all you have to do is "only believe." You're using your God given authority over the earth to bring forth healing for this person. Jesus needs us to stand in the gap. He needs to work through us because He gave the authority over the earth to all people. So He needs us to give it back to Him so He can do things on this earth (See Topic "Dominion, and Good and Evil" page 169). You are like an extension cord that is plugged into the power and extending it to where it needs to go. You need to understand that God is the one who is doing the healing and that you are the extension of Him. So realize that Jesus is right there doing it for you. You need to stand in faith and let

God do it. Not to get into fear, because fear is the opposite of faith.

The other person could be lacking faith. It's a team effort both the healed and the healer need to be believing and not doubting. This is probably why Jesus said to the person, according to your faith. It was up to the person's faith to be healed.

There is also a fear that if someone doesn't get healed that you will be thought of less of as a healer. This is something that you should not be afraid of, because this will hinder you and discourage you. It might not be you; it might be them lacking some faith. You need to just have faith. It's better if you do it and fail than not do it at all.

Physical Ailment of a demonic nature

Sometimes physical problems or ailments can be caused by the enemy. It doesn't mean that it was sinful. It could be someone who was spiritually unprotected for a period of time, or someone who received the physical injury and after went into negative emotions. Those negative emotions can be an access point for the enemy; if left unchecked, he will keep harassing. Or someone who made themselves a visible target to the enemy by coming against his kingdom and didn't have authorization from the Holy Spirit to do that (See Topics "The Devil's on the Outside" page 172, "Know your spiritual boundaries, what you have authority over" page 180, and "Devil's last stand and strong demon submission" page 178)

Have you ever heard of someone getting healed in a prayer line then when they get back to their lives, the ailment comes back? This could be that the enemy got kicked off in the meeting but found a way back in. I'm not saying people have demons in them; they're on the outside of you pushing ailments. But this is not all situations.

When you get healed, you need to hold your ground and keep your faith, no matter what. Because the enemy might try to discourage you, whether it's by words or pushing ailments on you. One of the major keys is to not get into fear or any other negative emotion. Sometimes the enemy can push an emotion on you, but it's not yours but the enemy's. The enemy tries to get you entrapped in these emotions to gain access into your life 1 Pet 5:8. What you have to do is put your heart in neutral, put thoughts of faith in your mind, and resist any such emotions. Pray in tongues, and pray, I bind anything that might be coming against me in the name of Jesus. If you know it's the devil, and he's being especially difficult, then say: "in the name of Jesus, the devil has to leave," over and over again. When you're coming against him, he will probably try to increase his energy to double or more to try to discourage you from ousting him. When this happens, this is when you know you're defeating him. I often get encouraged because I know he's close to having to leave.

He's trying to discourage you, just keep going, keep your faith up, and have no fear or unbelief. Make sure you push in through to 100% peace, not 90%, because he still has a foot in the door. This is another tactic, when you're truly defeating him, he will stop and hide hoping you will stop with his foot still in the door. You feel a definite improvement and almost at peace, but a very subtle yuck feeling. I often say get out 100% you're not hidden, leave! Then he will often give one last stand. When you truly defeat him, and he is gone, you often will feel a very satisfying peace, not a partial peace. You need to be patient with this process because it may take hours sometimes. But it needs to be done, don't accept a partial victory because it's no victory; otherwise, you're wasting your effort. Often, if I have to go to sleep, I will just pray in tongues, coming against it solidly. Often in that process, I will fall asleep and wake up later with peace, as long as I was trying to fight it. How long it takes may vary from situation to situation; it may take longer or shorter. Be sensitive to what you feel in your heart and be willing to finish what you started. Just know that it's worth the effort.

When I was first learning this, it took me a while to figure this out. It took me a year of hard learning to fully defeat this hard pressing harassment. What he did with me was a buzzy-like feeling on my skin in my stomach area. I was so harassed by this; I didn't know how to come against him. It was so much so that I dreaded it and didn't know when it would happen next. It came to the point where I expected this feeling, and if it didn't happen, I wondered when it would. When one gets abused over and over again, they get used to it and are expectant of it.

Sometimes you have to keep weakening the enemy over a long period. Yes, you push him out, but maybe he will come back to try again. You just have to keep standing against him the best you can and keep weakening him (days, weeks, months). Until he doesn't want to come back anymore because he keeps getting beat up and knows that he can't pull this on you anymore. You have to prove to the enemy that you are victorious in this area, and you will be as you keep standing against him. You're weakening him little by little; learn what works and go with it in the power of Christ. In the end, what worked for my harassment was to put my hand on the area he was buzzing and use my newly learned tactics against him. This way, I didn't feel the buzzy feeling as much because of my touch (See Topic "Physical healing" 157).

Sticky Emotions and Demonic Pressure

Have you ever noticed that sometimes when you have emotions like fear, sadness, depression, or are troubled about something, that feeling will just not go away? If you have ever tried to shake the feeling, it stubbornly stays. I noticed this especially one day when I tried turning off that emotion and being neutral, but the feeling remained. It would simply not go away, even though I decided to detach from the situation. There are a couple of possible factors to this. It could be just you having that emotion, and it takes several minutes of keeping your mind truly off of it. Or it could be a demonic influence pushing that emotion on you, and you're thinking that it's yours.

The demon can be on the outside of you, trying to push in on you. This doesn't mean it's in you. Demons are constantly trying to find ways to get past your defense. So they push energies like depression, anger, fear, laziness, lust, or whatever works to see if they can get access. Sometimes they can send powerful oppression.

It says in the Bible that we wrestle with principalities and powers, Ephesians 6:12. If you feel a negative emotion, or are impressed to do something that is a negative action; don't give in to it! If you do, then the enemy has the right to stick around. Then he has been given access and will continue to push that on you and intensify it. Even grow it and cultivate negative emotions or actions into greater amounts as far as you are willing to participate with it, days, months, or years. It doesn't always work right away when you tell the devil to leave; you sometimes have to wrestle with them. It depends on the situation, which determines how long you have to wrestle with them.

Like if you live in a neighborhood, there could be demonic oppression over the entire neighborhood. This depends on the type of people that live there and what they do. Do they get sad, depressed, angry, or violent a lot? This could feed the demonic oppression in the area and press in on you. Several neighbors could be depressed, and that spirit would try to sneak in on you and try to get you depressed. Sometimes it can come from within the house, like your kids or your spouse getting depressed. In such a situation, you need to recognize that it's going on and help them the best you can, lay hands on them, and agree with them for a release from possible demonic influences. We need to not participate with it and kick it out, repel him 100%, otherwise he could still have his foot in the door.

If they don't know how to master their emotions, then you could pray for them daily. Try to encourage them. Maybe visit their room and pray for anything that might be pushing emotions on them to leave in the name of Jesus.

Have you ever had thoughts you wouldn't normally have? Wondering, why would I think that at all? Like murderous, perverse, or abnormal. The enemy could be pushing these thoughts on you. Other people in your area are participating with those thoughts, or watching bad TV, movies, video games, or internet. The demons of those perversions are strengthened and look for new people to try to participate with their energies. The enemy can project thoughts or ideas into your mind. The enemy is constantly trying. I'm not saying you have a problem in that area. The demon is trying to see if he can get you to have participating thoughts on that matter. It's not your fault; just rebuke the devil and throw that thought out. As long as you don't agree or participate with that thought, that's all that matters. It's not your thought, it's the enemy's thought.

What you need to do is keep your guard up and push any of it off and away from your property. It's also possible that someone in your household is participating with these things, which allows access to your home. Like Bad: Movies, TV, video games, Internet, or anything that's of the devil's kingdom. The demonic spirit behind it will be allowed access because of the participation in it. This is the key; if something is allowed, then the enemy will gain access and stay. Which brings a lack of peace or a putrid feeling till he is purposely removed. But keep in mind that you only have authority over your property. You can't go over to your neighbors and rebuke their demons because you don't have rights to their property, and you could get attacked by the enemy. But like in the instance of your children participating in anything. You own the home and can set rules that don't allow certain things; that's your authority. But if you allow it to continue, then these things are allowed access. When I was young, I was limited to what games I could play or anything bad.

If you have participated in anything, then repent and ask God to release you of whatever you have done and correct it. But you will have to keep kicking them out because they're stubborn and will keep trying to test you. But they will stop when they get beat up enough and know you have victory in that area.

But there are exceptions to this. If your neighbor agrees with you on the removal of their demons, then you have been given the right through their agreement. Or if you're visiting a hotel, you have been given rights to be in that room, so you can kick any demons out of that room (which may be a wrestling match if it's a bad hotel), and so on and so forth. Another exception is that God has directed someone to go take care of a situation or even over an entire town or region, but this is only when they know God has told them to do this, but not if He hasn't!

I know about this because I can feel these things in my heart. It's like an icky feeling you get in the chest area when around it. I travel a lot, and when I was staying somewhere near a lot of people. I noticed on sunny days the feeling was light and not much, but on rainy or cloudy days I felt spiritual oppression because they may be getting sad and down. Also, on Halloween, I often feel icky feelings, because this is the cult's high holidays. Sure, they made it cute, but none the less everyone is participating with it trying to be scary. These are a few of the many possibilities.

What I often do to push these things back is to imagine that I have a sword and use it. Or imagine the enemy in an aggressive fire or shoot at him fire lightning (long burst). The devil doesn't like fire because that's his eternal punishment. But don't try too hard, or you can get metal burnout. It's a simple belief that the devil is defeated that counts. Hover on the feeling lightly; that is all that's needed. It's by faith that the devil is defeated. I read somewhere that the angels are empowered or disarmed by the amount of faith that you have. They cannot go against a person's will, and if that person is not believing or having a lack of faith, they can't contradict that. Don't let the enemy weaken your stance, because he will try to test your resolve. If you falter, then he will have victory. But don't use negative emotions against the enemy like excessive anger. Sometimes you only need to whisper the command, and he has to listen. Other times you need to yell it; depending on the severity of the situation. Sometimes it's quick, but more often it's a long battle. I often am very stern with him and have a mild anger in my heart toward him. (See Topics "The Devil's on the Outside" page 172, "Know your spiritual boundaries, what you have authority over" page 180, and "Devil's last stand and strong demon submission" page 178).

Anger, emotion hidden within an emotion

This can probably be described in other emotions also but, I was actually angry at God about something. This is an area that God is working out of me, being angry in general. My type of anger is at myself more rather than at people. Mad for various reasons, mistakes I make, things that would happen while working on projects, and so on. If you knew me, you really wouldn't know this because I keep it to myself. I'm careful with how I treat people because in a heavenly experience that someone had, Jesus demonstrated to them that we're accountable for how we treat people and hurting them. Even to literally experiencing and reenacting the hurt person's feelings. How you made them feel when you hurt them in your life review.

So I was angry at God about something, and I was holding it for a period of time. After a while, I discovered something that was beneath the anger, a root and the reason for it. That root was emotional pain and hurt. I was hurt that God was doing something to me.

I have been trimming unnecessary anger out of my life. But I'm not saying you can't get angry; just watch the intensity and longevity of it, Ephesians 4:26. Usually, when I get angry at people, which takes a lot. I will say my mind to them calmly and in a direct and brief form, then I will let it go. My anger is in talking form. But as far as my anger against myself and problem projects, I have been trimming that.

What I have discovered in the process is that there is a demonic spirit of anger that can push a person and suggest things. I discovered this when I got angry at a wheelbarrow tipping over and dumping everything all over the place. I had a picture flash in my head of throwing the wheelbarrow as hard as I could, and I agreed with that thought and did it. The Lord then showed me that I just participated with the demonic spirit of anger. That this spirit put that picture in my head, and I agreed and did it. I don't normally do such things, but this time I did. This is what the devil does. He temps us to do something by making suggestions in word or picture form in your mind. Or in an energy form, he will push an angry energy upon you. It's your choice whether to participate with it or not. If you're an angry person, this demon can be regularly suggesting or pushing you. Each demon has a specialty, and this one is anger. I immediately repented and was determined not to participate again. I told that devil that he was exposed and that he had to leave in the name of Jesus.

Power playing argumenter

I have run across a few people in my life where it seems that they must remain right in a discussion or an argument. Where they will even use manipulation in the argument as well. Like take a benefit that's happening and threaten to revoke it. It's a tactic to manipulate and keep power in an argument; I'm here to say this is inappropriate and immature.

Let the argument be at face value; don't power play to keep control. When one does, there is a shock that happens to its victim; this is abusive control. These people need to keep in control by any means necessary and will use anything and everything to keep it. It reminds me of when I was a child. If another kid had a toy that we played with and we got into a disagreement, they would say, it's my toy, you can't play with it anymore.

They keep controlling the situation by any means necessary. This is manipulation and control. Using control and shame, or whatever they can use to remain in control. If they have a benefit that they're providing, they will use that benefit as leverage. I have even seen a married man control his wife by threatening divorce because she was trying to fulfill her God purpose that he didn't agree with. She unfortunately submitted and is losing out on her destiny in God, that God has called her to do!

Another thing they may do if you don't submit to their controls is go into a martyr syndrome where woe is me; everyone picks on me. I'm just trying to be a good old boy/girl. They need to realize that it's not all about them, it's about others also, and the right balance needs to be found between them. So find that balance and healing can be had.

What one should do if they're in such a situation is to be careful of the benefits that are provided, but not allow the manipulation to continue. They are controlling, manipulating, and shaming you, and this needs to come to a stop. No one should use situations and items to control others. This is wrong, yet there are many out there that do this. I don't run across a lot of them, but I have seen people under this before.

What you need to do is try to get them to stop. Tell them they are power playing and manipulating you with anything and everything; that it's not appreciated and would like it to stop. They will kick and scream and throw their arsenal of word weapons, manipulations, and power plays against you to keep in control. You need to find the balance and not allow the control to continue (See Topic "Relationship and communication" page 101). Each situation is different, figure out a way to stop the abuse in a peaceful way. These people are fast on their feet with words to manipulate you, but you need to figure out what they really want and does it contradict your needs and rights, try to come to a solution, don't just throw the baby out with the bathwater. Figure it out and come to a solution that works for both of you.

But don't get me wrong, there are situations where people or leaders have legitimate authority, not to be confused with that. They have the right to exercise authority over their matters. So in those situations, you will have to listen to their rules because they are the authority. I'm talking about where both are neutral, and both have the same rights in the matter.

Some may say I'm the head of the household; they need to listen to me. Being the head of the household doesn't mean that you become a dictator. I think it has more to do with spiritual protection, not control. A married couple should have equal say in matters; no one should power over another. Another situation would be parents having the right to put rules on their children. It's also possible that someone might have authority over something, but they're overstepping their authority; going too far is also inappropriate. I'm aware that this topic could be bent out of shape to mean something that I'm not intending it to. There are many variables; I can't predict them all Matt 5:9.

Rejection Syndrome

I have run across a few people who have rejection issues. One of them was associated with a group that we knew, and they were suspicious that the others were rejecting them quite often, and would end up getting rejected because of their actions and words. It's an unfortunate cycle; they think they're being rejected, but are causing their own rejection by their actions. There must have been a past experience that caused this rejection to be in them. And they have the pain of that rejection still remaining in them.

When I was young, I was picked on and rejected by most of my classmates because I didn't conform to their mold of what it was to be cool. So I understand rejection and how it feels. What you need to do is seek the Lord in healing that hidden pain in your heart. You also need to recognize that it's there. It may be buried from many years in the past, but only the Lord can heal this. Also, try not to get hurt if you're not included in things. Be confident in who you are and don't try to be something that you are not.

Which reminds me, some people put on personalities that they think everyone else will accept, but that action gets them rejected, because people can see if you're being yourself or not. You need to accept who you are as a person and not try to be something you are not. People can also detect fake personalities and reject you based on that. So again, you're back to creating your own rejection. The person in the first place wants to be accepted, so they take an action that they think will get them to be accepted. But that action causes them to be rejected again.

Only the Lord can heal you; you need to heal those deeply rooted wounds of rejection. This is often done in worship. Ask Him specifically to heal your heart of the pains of past rejections. You also need to become self-confident in who you are; don't worry about what others think of you. Don't be hurt if you're not included in everything, or not close to those you hope to be close to. Be content in all things, Philippians 4:11, be confident and healed, and don't let that pain of rejection sneak back in.

The very actions you're taking to not get rejected are the very things you are getting rejected for! You need to seek the Lord for your needs rather than from others. If you're not invited or not given the opportunities you want, don't let it hurt you. Be okay with it and move on. People respond better to being neutral more than being overly needy. What you can do is lightly ask if you can participate, but don't apply pressure.

This is kind of a poor example, but it's what comes to my mind. I don't like it when dogs run up to me and push themselves on me and lick me. I like it when they stay their distance and let me approach them and pet them. I am forced to deal with their need for attention. I find my heart appreciating an animal that respects my space and lets me decide what I want to do with them. I think in a way this can be what people are like. They want to have the space to decide for themselves what they want to do. And if they don't respond as you would like them to, let them be then. Seek the Lord for your needs, and get the heart healing you need for your past bad experiences.

Exaggeration

I know someone who does this, so I feel to briefly write about it. Whatever anyone did that was good, they had to either match it or be better in just about everything. If you bring up a topic, they would talk about how they had done it before. Perhaps they have done some of these things. But it seemed that they had to be the greatest at everything. It wasn't boisterous or anything. They were not challenging you or anything, just the fact that they had done almost everything, were super at it, and had better things.

None of this is necessary. Just be honest, you don't have to top everyone or have done everything. Even if you have, let the person talking have their moment, be humble. Unless you have something legitimate to add to the situation. People are not expecting you to be the best at everything. If you try to be the best at everything, it's annoying to people. It's okay in moderation, but not all the time.

Really, what I think is happening is the exaggeratory person may have had something happen to them in their life where they felt less. So they felt to over compensate to make themselves feel good. Maybe negativity was projected towards them, and they felt they had to compensate for it.

What this person needs is emotional healing from their past. It's okay to be better in a few areas, but don't try to outdo everyone! People can see right through this, and they may end up rejecting you based on your exaggeratory nature. Which adds to the hidden pain that causes this in the first place, creating the cycle all over again. You are trying to be acknowledged but instead are being rejected again and are creating your own rejection and getting more hurt, an endless cycle.

I was watching a TV show of people that were constantly challenging each other over silly things. Saying they're the best at it, or they can do better and would have constant competition over simple things. It's not our job on this earth to outdo everyone; it's our job to build up and help one another. We need to be humble and realize we're not going to be better at everything. This really is a form of pride. It's okay to have friendly competition, but not, I can do that better than you attitude; if one loses, they rub it in. There are many factors in competition; it can go either way sometimes. Perhaps you both think you're better; so what. Does it really matter? 1Pet 5:5, Luke 14:11.

Mocking Spirit

This is something I have had to deal with myself. It's not an obvious thing, but more subtle. I was made aware of it when someone had a prophetic word for me. I didn't even know it myself until it was pointed out. I thought it was funny to make fun of things in my mind. Nothing major, just minor stuff. The word I was given was mocking spirit. It was done in a light way, and I had to think about it later to realize what it meant. Realizing what it was, was the first step in overcoming it. In time, I tried to stop making fun of things in my mind, but it was in fact, a spirit that was pushing me to do so. This is another example of how the enemy will try to find any access point to get in. He will find your weakness and exploit it no matter what it might be, but that is another topic. It's not that he's inside of me; he's on the outside influencing. Recognizing it is the first step Proverbs 1:22.

Dominion, and Good and Evil

God gave dominion over the earth to man (men and women) from the garden. That means full authority over every aspect, including the spiritual, to all mankind. Not just Christians or Jews! God is not in control of the earth, because he gave it unto man until he comes back to claim it.

All mankind has authority over the earth. If they choose to use their authority for bad, then bad will be allowed access. If used for good, then good is present. It's mixed soup spiritually. It depends on the people present in an area that will determine its spiritual condition. God can not intervene unless He has been given authority back by us. This is why prayer is so powerful. Matt 21:33-41.

    Why is there evil in the earth? Why are bad things allowed to happen? It's because God can't intervene unless given authority back in that situation. Man allows it to happen by not involving God. God can not intervene unless someone prays and uses their authority on the earth to counteract that evil. Satan has been allowed in and has to be seriously fought back and taken proper authority over. If there are many people involved, then they all play a part in the earth authority equation. If they're not in unison, then it will have mixed results. This can be overcome through legitimate prayer and time in waiting for God's unique solution; because God's ways are not our ways. The solution might be something you don't expect. It's very complicated because humankind is at the steering wheel of this life. Now with both good and bad people both involved in the same situation; both having rights in the earth will have mixed results. It's a war in the spirit; evil is not a pushover Ephesians 6:12.

    Someone asked me once, "Why is a girl allowed to have cancer and die, and a bad man in prison allowed to live to a ripe old age?" God would heal that little girl if someone were to ask Him to. But both healer and the person afflicted would have to have the full appropriate faith; taking their God given authority and ask for that healing. Otherwise, God is powerless to help. Because He has given the authority to mankind, and can't intervene unless someone were to take their authority and hand it back to God for Him to intervene. But if no one does that, then He can't intervene. God wants to heal everyone if He was given the authority and faith in His abilities by those involved. The bad man in prison is allowed to live because it's been allowed by man. Now personally, I think it's a good thing that these bad men have a chance to find Jesus before they die; otherwise, they would be lost forever. At least they have a chance to find Him. If that bad man in prison were to find Jesus, then it would have all been worth it because he will go to heaven for eternity. If you take issue with this, Jesus told us to forgive, and you need to learn forgiveness Matthew 6:14-15. It's like the parable of the hired laborers. Even the worker that worked only one hour was paid the same as those who worked 12 hours Matt 20:1-16. God will give this man eternal life if he's faithful to repent of his sins and turn to God. Even if he was a bad man before, he is now a good man. The reason this man is bad is probably because of pains in his heart, a bad childhood, or bad experiences. He is acting out of those pains. What this man needs is to turn to Jesus to heal those deep and hidden pains. God doesn't look at your past, but your repentance and your belief in Jesus, Ezekiel 18:25-32 "if a wicked person turns away from the wickedness they have committed and does what is just and right, they will save their life."

I apologize if this explanation offended you. This was not my intention. I'm just trying to explain why bad things happen to good people, why this life is the way it is. Man is in control, not God! God has to be invited in to affect change. The same goes for the enemy! So you see, it's complicated. When healing someone, it takes an unwavering amount of faith in both the person praying for and the recipient. If either wavers, it could prevent it from happening. God's ways are not our ways, so it may also come in a different way than you expect.

Witches and warlocks have power because they're allowing the devil to have access to the earth through their authority. Authority has been given to all humankind, period. Without this permission, the devil would be like a barking dog with no bite. Unfortunately, he has been given authority, whether knowingly or unknowingly, by humankind through their actions. So if they participate with the spirit of depression, then it will be allowed access; if lust, then lust, if gossip, then gossip. Participation with any evil will allow access to the demon behind it. But those who allow God to work through them are giving God access to work here on earth. God will not go around the authority He has given to us. So we have a mixed soup of spiritual climate throughout the world. Every single person and whatever they participate in, the spirit behind that will be allowed access. Anything contrary to the things of God has a negative or demonic presence to it. If someone participates in sinful things, then that yucky energy will be allowed access and will choke out the things of God. It's just that simple. People are inviting spiritual energies all around the world without even knowing it. The devil is legalistic; if you participate in it, then he will consider that an open door and come into your living space and stay there. If you seriously participate in it, he will live in your spirit as well. Psalms 115:16

The Devil's on the Outside

The reason I'm writing this topic is because of the misunderstanding and offense that happens when someone is told they have demonic harassment affecting them. We live in a spiritual world, whether we realize it or not. There's the physical realm, and the spiritual realm. The spiritual realm is where both angels and demons exist. This is invisible. Otherwise, we would see our angels and demons with our eyes all the time. Why do we have guardian angels? Because we need to be guarded! The devil and demons are real; they have been cast to this earth and put into the invisible realm of the spiritual. They are still there! Not all in hell. The devil is constantly trying to find your weaknesses; once he finds them, he picks at it. If you participate with that weakness, then he's strengthened in his abilities to harass you in it 1 Peter 5:8. A few examples would be fear, confusion, depression, unforgiveness, gossip, pride, religiousness, poverty, negativity, lust, hate, murder, mockery, or anything bad or negative.

Non-Christians can also be influenced by demons. The devil looks for any participation, whatever it may be. Once the devil has found something that you will participate in, he is let in the door and is strengthened to do more, putting his roots in. It can be something innocent, like fear. He exploits it; he will even try to magnify it in you.

The devil is more rampant than you think; he is doing this to everyone. Every single person alive, whether good or bad, has the demonic trying to push and gain access. Now, if one is aware of it, they can tell the devil to leave. The devil can push negative emotions or thoughts on us without our permission. Even if we are innocent of those thoughts or emotions. To try to tempt us to participate with them. These are not your thoughts or emotions but the enemy's. You don't have to participate in it. You can resist it and tell the enemy to leave.

If left unchecked, the devil can influence us on a regular basis. He knows your weaknesses and how to exploit them, because he has been allowed access through continued participation. If you go somewhere where there is an evil spirit, like an establishment that participates with it. One of those spirits could follow you home and try to harass you with thoughts or temptations. A few examples are: a bar, a pagan rock concert, a gossip group, or any evil or negative environment. If a spirit is participated with in any sort of way, that spirit can affect the entire building and everyone in it. The devil can project energy over a large area if more are participating with it; then the strength of that energy increases.

Why does the devil do all these things? For many reasons, one to try to drag you down trying to get you to fail. Another is when God created the earth and the garden, He gave authority over the earth to mankind. The devil has no power or authority in himself. So he tries to get man to sin and is allowed access to this authority because of the participation.

If everyone on earth repented and kicked the devil out of their lives, the earth would be pure again. All have fallen short; there is no way to fully accomplish this but to keep repenting and cleaning your environment. It's like dirty laundry. If you wash your clothes, then you're clean again, but if you wear dirty clothes, you won't be. The devil is then kicked out of his previously gained access and powerless again. There are various degrees of what type of access the devil can achieve. He can just simply come and be present after gaining access, or sometimes, go into a person. This all depends on the situation.

There are many types of demons, each having their own specialty. When the enemy finds a weakness in you, he will assign a demon associated with that energy. What you may not realize is that emotions, intentions are seen in the spirit. The enemy can see negative or positive things in the spirit and act accordingly. I don't know what it looks like to him, but he sees it as physical and tangible, possibly smell. When the enemy sees this, he tries to push it. He can push energy on you like depression, stress, hyperness, depression, sadness, anger, and lust. Often you react to it without knowing that it's the devil pushing this energy on you, thinking it's you having that emotion.

This is often a hard thing to tell people. They get offended that they might be influenced by a demon. But this is way more common than everybody realizes. The devil does this all the time. We need to realize that this is a reality and don't get offended. Everyone can be affected by demons, whether big or small. It doesn't matter how holy you are; the devil is still going to try to trip you up. This can even be in small areas. This doesn't mean that he's inside of you. He's often on the outside affecting you. Pushing energy on you, and you unknowingly participate. A few examples could be anger, stress, hype, sadness, depression, worry, fear, or a lot of other things. These things can happen without a demon, but if it's consistent, consider if it's the enemy, pray against it, and don't participate in it.

    I have experienced this many times. Recognize it for what it is and kick it out, don't participate, and bind this demonic spirit away from you in the name of Jesus. I say it this way because if you're in public and others are participating with it, then you can't tell it to leave if others give it the right to be there. It can be on you rather than in you. Like for instance, a spiritual snake around you, strangulating you, or a demon riding on your back. This spiritual snake could be an overwhelming emotion trying to choke you out of your spiritual life. The devil is harassing you the most he possibly can; just know that the devil is very aggressive. So don't be offended at this; it's just reality. Even the slightest participation is all the devil needs to have access. He's aggressive and smart, but you have all authority in Christ Jesus. You need to not participate and kick Him out. Sometimes this means you have to wrestle with Him.

    Eph 6:12 "For we wrestle not against flesh and blood, but against principalities, against powers, against the rulers of the darkness of this world, against spiritual wickedness in high places."

    Don't get all worked up about this, and be scared of it. Jesus is all-powerful; He will not allow you to be completely defeated. He will only allow what you can handle. He uses this sometimes to train you to be stronger and allows it depending on your spiritual maturity. He's always there to never let it go beyond the threshold of what you can handle.

    I went through a period of this; He was training and hardening me in the spirit. I had a phrase that I developed when I was going through this "you can't put a good man down." No matter how far the devil may push down on you, you can always go to God and rebuild your strength again and get stronger in the process. It doesn't matter what the devil does; even if it affects you, it's recoverable with the proper deliverance. I'm not saying you're invisible; he can affect you physically if you cross the wrong lines (See Topic "Know your spiritual boundaries, what you have authority over" page 180).

    Sometimes the devil has been there a while and is more rooted. He knows how to gain access because he has been with the person longer. Even being prayed for doesn't always solve the problem. The person needs to change and pull out all the deeply embedded roots. If they have the demon cast off but still do the same things, then it can come right back again. Because the devil gets permission again to come back. The key is change. You have all power and authority in Christ Jesus. So don't be afraid of it because fear is the opposite of faith; Jesus is there every step of the way to help. But sometimes it's not just as easy as telling Him to go; sometimes you have to wrestle with Him! Eph 6:12

Now it's also possible that he can go inside a person if he has established himself in a person's life and they strongly participate with him. This doesn't mean they're a bad person; they just need deliverance. (See Next Topic "Devil's last stand and strong demon submission")

Now I'd like to take it one step further and explain how I have seen demons affect people in ministry and ministry leaders. This doesn't mean major things; it could be stress, over busyness, oppression, suffocation, sadness, overburdening, lack of knowledge, or any negative emotion. Demons can attack and press in often unchecked.

These people are not necessarily bad or out of God's will. They are just unaware of the enemy attacking and do nothing about it. The enemy needs to be constantly pushed back and resisted. If he isn't, then it will be a spiritual mess. People don't realize the reality of demons and just how aggressive they are. They may feel the effects of it but don't know what they're feeling; thinking it's them feeling stress, having a bad day, or bad emotions.

It is an unfortunate reality, so please don't be offended at this. If you don't think it exists and that you can just snap your fingers and the devil has to leave, then you're basically ignoring him. He can just sit around doing his nasty business unchecked. You have to realize what you're feeling in your heart and not put up with it; come to peace.

There are many types of pressures that demons can use; it depends on what works. In the following, I give some examples of demonic harassment. I'm not trying to say that these are bad people. But in fact, they are all very good people and do good works. They are just ignorant of the attacks against them. I'm not trying to point the finger and say shame on you. I'm trying to bring light to what's going on so that we will keep our guard up and not let it happen.

1. One ministry was super hyper had a business and ministry in one building. They were often missing God because of their business; the spirit of hype and confusion were present.
2. Someone who lives in a Mormon city feels a yucky feeling on Sundays. They thought it was them feeling sad and didn't associate it with Mormons having

their services on that day.

3. A ministry retreat that had a past history in ministry use was full of demons and oppressions, but they were unaware of it. Because demons, once they've been given access to something, they won't leave until they're kicked out. They thought kicking the devil out was a simple few-second prayer.

4. Someone lived in a super oppressed town and tried to do ministry in that town. They had to contend with all the demonic of that town. But if one were unaware or ignored it, then their ministry would be overrun by these pressures.

5. I briefly visited a room that a Lutheran church rented, and there was an extreme suffocating feel in there. I also visited a church of the latter day saints which had a troubling subtle suffocating feel to it.

6. A ministry leader in a really great intercessor group had 2 python demons wrapped around them, suffocating them. Their office had extreme suffocation, but nowhere else in the building, just their office. They're recognized as a big part of the local area in a very big and nice building with a lot of people coming. The demonic must have noticed their works of coming against his kingdom and set out to attack them and found a weakness and full out attacked. They didn't know how to recognize or deal with this oppression on them. They more than likely were aware of the feelings, but unaware that it was a demonic attack against them! This is a wonderful person, and they do great works! They just don't realize this is going on.

7. We went to a ministry couple in their 60s and visited their home. The second we drove into their driveway, we felt a big yucky feeling. It seemed they were oblivious to this going on. As the meeting went on, it was an extreme oppression in the room. I think they might have ignored this oppression, mostly thinking that they have full authority over them. It's true that you have all authority. What people don't realize is that it's a wrestling match sometimes, not patty cake! You need to keep your guard up and keep pushing things out. They had their adult son temporarily living downstairs, and they lived in a housing development, which may be some of the attributing factors. I've seen an intercessor that lived in a large compact city, yet it was peaceful in their home.

8. I met this woman who had a sleeping disorder that could barely sleep. She described waking up in a fright. As soon as she mentioned the fright, I knew it was probably the spirit of fear that was harassing her, and she needed to take

a lot of time and kick that thing out of her life and be willing to wrestle it out and keep it out. (See Next Topic "Devil's last stand and strong demon submission")

This sounds extreme. But if you don't realize how aggressive the devil is, then he will walk all over you. He especially notices those who are tearing down his kingdom. It's like a war; if the devil's kingdom is attacked, he will attack back. If that person doesn't know they're being attacked, then the devil will keep at it and stay. This doesn't mean these people are possessed by demons; it means the devil is attacking from the outside, harassing.

What should happen is 1. The people should be told what is going on, perhaps have them read this topic. 2. Don't be offended by being told this. Consider the possibility that this might be true and review what they have been feeling in their hearts. Reevaluate the emotions they feel in their ministries and consider that it might be the enemy pushing them. 3. Be delivered of it 4. Not think less of them because this happened 5. For them to continue with their ministries now delivered of that attack, 6. Keep their guard up and be aware of the possible same or new attack.

These people are often on the front line of the fight against the devil. So they are bound to have more attack than the average person. Because they're being noticed by the enemy and are in direct conflict against the kingdom of darkness.

The church suffers for a lack of knowledge. So, for this lack of knowledge, they're being attacked and suffocated by the enemy unchallenged. The enemy is very tricky! He will do whatever works in tearing you down; it doesn't matter what it is (See Topic "Know your spiritual boundaries, what you have authority over" page 180). It is telling the devil he has to get out and not participate with it anymore. Often, this process takes a little time to push him out, but just keep at it until your heart is filled with complete peace. A partial victory will not do! The devil is very legalistic; he's either all in or all out. If you stop with his foot still in the door, he will come right back in. Full peace must be accomplished! If you try to push him out, then know that the devil gives one last stand before he comes out, he increases his energy to double or more to try to get you to give up, but that's when you know you got him, you have to be just as stubborn and throw him out till you achieve complete 100 percent peace.

These dynamics are more common than you think. Even I have to struggle with these energies, every person in the world has to; it's commonplace. It's better for this to be brought into the light where one can be aware of it rather than be swept under the rug and ignored. If it's ignored, then the devil can walk all over you.

Devil's last stand and strong demon submission

When the enemy has found a weakness or an access point and is allowed to exploit it, he has gained ground like on a battlefield. The devil's main goal is to try to thwart us in any way he can, 1 Peter 5:8. Once he gains this ground, he will do anything to keep it! What I have discovered when defeating the enemy in various areas of my life; is that when you get close to kicking him out, he will intensify his attack to try to discourage you from expelling him. It's often very effective if not recognized. It took me a little while to figure this out. I would lose confidence that it would have to leave and had thoughts of discouragement, even burnout. Once I realized this dynamic was going on, I called it his last stand. I just have to stand my ground that he has to go. But don't try too hard, or you'll get mental burnout. It's just a simple belief in your heart that he is defeated and has to leave. Stand in that belief with no fear or negative emotion. I also tried to tell him to go over and over again, but that wore me out as well. I then came up with the thought I am his authority; he has to go if I say go. It's not an instantaneous response on his behalf. Often you have to wrestle with him! Like the scripture that says we wrestle with principalities and powers Eph 6:12. It's not always right away; it depends on the severity of the situation and the dynamics involved.

If it's an extreme attack and you are in your rights of authority, which is your land and what you have authority over (See Next Topic "Know your spiritual boundaries, what you have authority over"). Then what has worked for me is to say: in the name of Jesus, the devil has to leave; over and over again. Or pray in tongues until he leaves without fear, anger, or negative emotions. If he insists and stays, I keep the thought lightly in my mind of what I commanded him to do. I say you've been told what to do, go in the name of Jesus! It's also important to fight with your heart, not your mind. Because the spirit of God is in the heart, not in the intellectual.

It's important that you don't have fear in your heart and are confident that he has to leave. If this is difficult for you, try imagining your heart in neutral and hover there. Or pretend the emotion is full of air; imagine laying on it deflating it. It's basically faith that he has to leave! If you have fear in your heart, it cancels that faith.

I met a spiritual warrior grandma, and I was still learning spiritual warfare and was struggling with it. The thought came to me, what is the difference between me and this small grandma. She's a smaller person, yet she can combat demons. Do you think size or age matters when confronting demons? It doesn't! What matters is your measure of faith and resolve against the devil. But don't succumb to his diversion tactics while fighting. Faith is a condition of the heart!

I met someone who had a definite demonic attack against them, and they lived in it. I tried to challenge them to fight it, but time was limited to talk. They had sleep deprivation. They said a keyword to me that I knew was a demonic attack. They would wake up in a scare all the time. So this spirit was harassing with fear. In time, their situation changed, and they could get to sleep, but this shifted to another symptom: they got really weird, disturbed, and suspicious over simple matters. We didn't know this person that well; we met once and had a few passing phone conversations. So I suspect the devil shifted the fear into a different form. The devil is smart. He can modify his tactics to conform to changes.

I believe that sometimes illnesses can be caused by demons. Have you ever seen someone being prayed for and the symptoms get worse; sound familiar. The devil's last stand, or his last attempt to keep his ground. Discouraging people from having faith to be healed by intensifying the ailment. It will take what I described earlier to push through this low-down tactic. Keeping your faith intact is the key. When this happens, the direction of the prayer has to be directed at the harassing demon leaving.

Another thing I do is imagine I have a spiritual sword. I imagine taking that sword and using it against him! Anything is possible in your imagination, just imagine nothing can touch you. If the devil throws a projectile at you, imagine stopping it in mid-air and sending it right back at him. This is basically a faith aid to help you, but it's probably happening in the spirit as well. The devil doesn't like fire, so imagine him burning. These things might not work instantly, but use them as part of the process. Don't let yourself get worn out. Just keep wrestling, and he will get weaker and weaker. In time, he won't want to come back!

When I feel resistance from the enemy increase, and he puts up a stronger fight; I get encouraged because I know he's just about defeated! He knows it too; that's why he's fighting harder. He does this to try to stay by trying to get you to back down. You just need to keep your faith and not waver through his increased attack, knowing that he is defeated. Like a fighter plane with a lock on its target, keep on his tail; he can't shake you unless you lose faith.

The devil hates the sound of water. So get a water fountain, because water falling has all the tones from low to high. Have you ever noticed that it's peaceful near moving waters? Also, worship music playing all day and night, even if it's just barely audible, helps.

Know your spiritual boundaries, what you have authority over

We have an enemy, and his name is Satan. He has an army of fallen angels under him referred to as demons. They of themselves have no authority to do anything. The only way they have authority is if it's given to them by man through sin or consent. When Adam was on earth, he had dominion over everything. But satan snuck in and tempted his wife and him to eat the forbidden fruit. This is his tactic and how he gets or steals authority. If he can get man to sin or allow him in, then he has rights and can come into the situation and try to get you to do more.

It's the devil's constant mission to try to gain access by any means possible. He will stop at nothing to get access. There is nothing too low for him to try. He will try to find your weakness and pick at it. There are many demons; each have their own specialty. So, for each sin, there is a demon that's dedicated and strong in that area. It's not only sins that the devil can gain access, it can be negative emotions as well. Like depression, anger, fear, lust, etc.. If he knows you're weak in an area of emotions, then he will try to push that negative emotion on you. Once he gets you to participate with that negative emotion, he has access. The devil also can see/smell negative energies and attract to them.

It doesn't necessarily mean that he goes inside of the person. He could just simply be around a person pushing them. What you should do in that situation is resist the negative thoughts and be neutral. If it's sin, then repent of the sin and ask God to cleanse you.

Sometimes, when the devil has been given access for a long time, he doesn't want to leave. It says in Eph 6:12 that you have to wrestle with principalities and powers, that means wrestle with them. You know there's an unclean spirit around when there is an icky feeling in your heart. Many people think this icky feeling is them having a bad emotion or day. But it often can be the demonic energy pressing in. That icky feeling is not coming from you, but is separate from you pushing in from the outside by demonic pressures.

One way to get him to go is to say: in the name of Jesus, the devil has to leave over and over again (See Topic "Devil's last stand and strong demon submission" page 178). But I must warn you, you only have the right to tell him to go if you have authority in that situation or given permission. "It's like a police officer from Georgia going to Toronto and exercising authority there; they don't have that authority" (paraphrased Rick Joyner). If you're out of your authority and you fight against him, but he has been given the right to be there by someone else. That demon can follow and harass you. Sometimes even physically harm you in extreme situations. It is very important that you know what you have authority over. If you live in an apartment building, you have authority only over your apartment. If you own a land, you only have authority over that land.

There are a few exceptions to this: 1. If God tells you to do it. 2. You can pray for it; in prayer, you are not commanding demons, but talking to God about it. But be careful in even this; you might be tasked with the heavy intercession (yucky feeling) involved in that situation. And don't do it on location. 3. If you have been permitted to be somewhere like if you rent a hotel room, land, house, or apartment. You are granted spiritual rights over the portion that you are allotted. 4. You have the right to keep them off you, like a small bubble around you; unless you're in a situation you shouldn't be in!

So far, I have explained how the enemy can affect you personally, but there are different layers of the demonic. The first layer is small demons that harass people like you or me. The next layer up could be over an entire neighborhood or town. Then one over each county. Then over an entire state or multiple states. Another over an entire nation. But it depends on the level of participation in each of those levels.

First off, each individual has authority over their lands and possessions. A neighborhood is a collection of people. If the enemy can get many people to participate in the same or similar thing, then he can put an oppression or stronghold over an entire neighborhood or town; depending on the level of participation. The next layer could be a governor or a collection of participation in an entire county, state, or country. The spiritual climate will depend on the level of cooperation with the enemy in any portion of land or lands.

When I go to different states, each state has a different spiritual feel. Many factors attribute to this, including leadership of the state and counties or the people in them. The devil tries to link his dominion to as big of an area as he is allowed. A network of demons could be working together to oppress a land. It depends on the amount of cooperation across those lands. Like for instance, the state of Utah is predominately Mormon, so they have 1. Mormon people 2. Mormon leaders in office of the county and state that are sympathetic to their causes. If an entire town participates in Mormonism, then that spirit will have dominance over that city.

It's like mixed soup; if you have predominantly one kind of spirit in an area, then that is what you will feel. Everybody helps flavor the spiritual soup. But if there are predominantly peaceful people who live in an area; then everybody has added peace to that soup. If you have a complete mix of both, then you will have an average feeling. The same goes for large scales as well. Everybody adds their portion to the soup, and whatever is more dominant will be the spiritual climate of that area.

Now, just like in the scripture Eph 6:12, there are bigger and bigger demons. "For we wrestle not against flesh and blood, but against principalities, against powers, against the rulers of the darkness of this world, against spiritual wickedness in high places." That's referring to greater and greater ranks of demons; principalities, powers, and rulers. In Matt 12:45, there are demons more wicked than others.

The demonic has a well-structured army; there are ranks amongst them, no doubt by their strengths. Certain demons have authority over other demons, ones that are stronger and bigger. These greater and bigger demons are often assigned to larger areas, like cities, counties, states, and countries.

The amount of power and rights that they have is entirely related to how much man participates with them. If most of the people in a town are depressed, that town will be depressed. Because the devil found people in that town to participate in it. Then he started pushing that energy around to others that also participated.

If the Governor of a state allows a particular type of sin in a state, and people in that state participate with it, this will affect the entire state spiritually. It is more of an average or a sum of everybody in larger areas. What people do as a majority in that town, state, or nation affects that respective area.

Know what you have authority to do and not do. Sometimes God will grant a person authority over something they don't normally have authority over. But sometimes not, sometimes it's not the right timing, or maybe it will never be. You have to know for sure if God is asking you to. Otherwise, you could get yourself into trouble and be attacked either spiritually or physically.

I had a vision once when thinking about this. I saw two armies, one soldier from our army, went to the enemy army by themselves and told that army that they have all power and authority and to submit; of course, they will get harmed. It was about the right timing and being cleared to do it with His protection.

So know your boundaries and stay within them. Rom 8:37-39 Col 1:16 Col 2:15

Hidden Demons / Familiar spirit

I had an experience where we were invited to visit a leader in ministry's home and felt and saw things that shouldn't be there. You might think this is a super religious guy who doesn't have much spirit. But no, this guy and his wife are really good people and are not religious. But in fact, are on board with the new things in God. Maybe they're doing exactly what God wants them to do and are in the will of God. But here's what happened when we arrived. The second we parked in their driveway, there was this terrible spiritual feeling. When we get into their house and start our meeting, I'm sitting in the background listening, and the spiritual feeling is still there. It's just a terrible spiritual choking feeling in my spirit. All seemed well in the natural, but in the spirit, it was highly choking. To my perception, these people were very nice and good. They were about 60 something years old. All the talk was good, and they seemed to know their stuff and talked the talk, but the spiritual atmosphere was saying something completely different. Now they had their adult son staying with them for the time, and they also lived in a housing development which may have something to do with that. But they should be able to hold their spiritual boundaries better than that. All I knew is the entire time I had this terrible spiritual feeling. I felt led to do some spiritual warfare since I was there quietly. As I proceeded, the feeling became less, but the Holy Spirit told me to stop when I got close to finalizing it. The Holy Spirit said to me, "they need to finish it." That makes sense because if I were to defeat all the demons. When I was gone, they could just come right back and worse. These people needed to learn to defend themselves; otherwise, it's fruitless. The guy said at some point, "I'm not concerned about demons because I know I have all power in Jesus." This is true, but sometimes you have to wrestle with principalities and powers, not ignore them or pray a 2-second prayer against them.

    The reason I'm writing this topic is because it was a major wake-up call for me, and the condition of many Christians out there. These are called familiar spirits; they are around because people don't know any better or because of disbelief of the realities of demons.

    The reality may be harsh, but if you disbelieve they exist or in their influence, they can potentially walk all over you. The devil tries to come in, and when he's allowed by participation, he won't leave until he is ousted. Sometimes simple actions can be enough to let him in. Sometimes the devil comes in just to come in. If there are no defenses in the spirit, he can do that. Especially if someone doesn't believe that this is possible and ignores the spiritual feelings, thinking it's their emotions. They assume it's something else, where in fact, it's a demon. Now it's not to say these people are possessed. It's just saying the devil has found a way in and is just puking up the atmosphere, choking them out spiritually. It says in Eph 6:12, wrestle with principalities and powers. That's not a patty cake prayer that says, okay demons go, and they're gone. No, often these demons won't leave until you wrestle them out!

    This process can take a while, and with persistence, they will leave. You also have to 100 percent it! If you feel even 1% demon left, you have to keep fighting it until they leave. Because when the devil knows you're fighting them and winning, he will try to subside his negative power and wait for you to stop, then reinsert himself. Keep going until you feel at total peace.

    Don't slumber and let the demons just sit around. Kick them out and keep them out. Otherwise, they will just keep choking you spiritually. This sometimes isn't an easy procedure, especially if you don't know how to fight very well. For me, it actually took one experience of being harassed by a demon for maybe 6 months to a year to finally have victory over it. It was subtle harassment, but after that experience, I became aware of how to kick them out. Sometimes it happens without a rhyme or a reason. You just have to deal with it. (See Topic "Devil's last stand and strong demon submission" page 178)

Wake up Christians, don't sit back and believe that demons are pushovers in the name of Jesus. Sometimes you have to wrestle with them by being persistent and standing in the faith without fear or negative emotions. He tries to get you to not believe by his persistence. Just keep pushing and standing. Demons are real and sometimes are real buggers to get rid of. It's not fair I know, but it's real.

Once you have them gone, then peace will reside unless you open the door for the enemy to come back in whatever that might be. If you keep yourself from opening the door to the enemy, then he will stay out for the most part. But pay attention to your spirit if it feels yucky again, then fight it out again. Sometimes the devil will try to push bad energy; just be aware of it.

Wake up, demons may be in your living room, and it's so familiar to you that you don't know better. Perhaps you feel it, but don't think it's that, but something else.

Even if you don't believe me. Pray through the yucky feeling and get through it. Pray in tongues and keep pressing and pressing until the feeling goes away. All that matters is that yucky feeling in your heart goes away and is replaced with rest and peace. The emptiness is gone, and God fills your heart with is His peace.

Intercessors

An Intercessor is someone who prays for people, places, or whatever is needed. The definition of intercede is to intervene for another. So it's the job of the intercessor to pray as they feel led for places or people; they often treat prayer as a lifestyle. I'm not talking about nuns here; I'm talking about regular people whom God has commissioned to be warriors of prayer.

Often they feel what is called a burden of prayer. They feel a heaviness in their heart impressed by the Holy Spirit to pray; it often is a yucky feeling. Then they pray and pray, often in tongues, until they feel a full release of peace. God uses these people in the battle against the enemy to fight His battles. They are like the soldiers in an army. They are all over the world mixed in and can be beckoned to pray for the purposes of God by the Holy Spirit as necessary. (See Topics "Sticky Emotions and Demonic Pressure" page 161, "Devil's last stand and strong demon submission" page 178, and "Know your spiritual boundaries, what you have authority over" page 180). They are a required part of God's army.

I met a pastor that thought all you have to say is in the name of Jesus demons leave, and it's done. This is a common thing. They think demons are all pushovers and all run away like a bunch of scared cats, not so! This is negligence on their behalf. Yes, sometimes they can leave that easily, but most of the time, you have to fight them tooth and nail to get them to leave; it's a process Eph 6:12, Luke 9:40.

Intercessors are an integral part of God's army. They are also an important part of ministries. Because once you become publicly or spiritually known by the enemy, then you are painting a bull's eye on your ministry. The enemy desires to ruin or destroy anything that's of God's kingdom. Once a ministry is noticed, the enemy will organize and attack because it comes against his kingdom of darkness. He will stop at nothing to tear it down in any way he can. He will look for weak points and do whatever it takes to derail it or snuff it out. He's looking for an opening of any kind to divide and conquer.

The intercessor's job is to keep this enemy attack from pressing in. The enemy doesn't always need an opening. There may be neighbors that cause spiritual issues, and that presses in his putrid spirit to suffocate life. The enemy likes to devour any life to pacify and extinguish it. It's important for intercessors to clean house on a continual basis.

If there are no intercessors to do this job, then the enemy can push his way in and choke out the spirit. Some pastors say the glory of God will push away the enemy and keep him out; in a way this is true, but not totally. If your borders are not guarded, then the enemy will come in and smother that life out because it ruins his kingdom of darkness.

Demons are very active and will do everything they possibly can to tear down this life. Intercessors are required to keep the demonic harassment off and away through prayer and intercession.

It's like an army. If you had no defenses, then the enemy can waltz right in and do whatever they want. This is a battlefront; it needs to be guarded spiritually. Now I'm not saying that people need to be there taking watches all the time, just that they keep the enemy out of the territory as needed.

The enemy sees the light and points his army to attack it and snuff it out if he can. People of prayer, like that army, need to have defenses to prevent the enemy from attacking that light. Intercessors also can be interceding in their homes for local, county, state, country, or world events.

It is also possible for any Christian to get a prayer burden, where they feel a heaviness and pray through it. God can use anybody to intercede to deal with issues. So it's a common thing, but this doesn't mean they're an intercessor. For intercessors, it's their life.

The Holy Spirit is the orchestrator of this harmony of prayer. He often uses an entire network of people at the same time to accomplish whatever task that needs to be accomplished. They do not know that they're all praying at the same time. It could be something in your personal life, or it could be something that's happening in the world. Only God knows 1Tim 2:1.

I want your Heart, not your religiousness

One day I was enjoying my personal time with God and was looking out a window and saw a cloud in the sky that looked like a Pharisee, with a long beard and twirly hairs and so forth. Then I heard the Lord say to me: "It is foolishness, all I want is their hearts, not their religiousness." It's like someone who does all the actions to say that I love you, but their heart is not in it or is somewhere else. Jesus says in Matt 15:8-9: "These people draw near to me with their mouth, and honor me with their lips, but their heart is far from me. And in vain do they worship me, teaching as doctrine rules made by men."

The Pharisees got a little carried away. They were making laws upon laws to make sure that they would not break even the tiniest of God's commands, but they neglected the heart behind the original Laws of God. They were really for our benefit so that we might get closer to Him.

Many think that legalism only refers to the Pharisees, but don't realize it also refers to us. Many of us have developed our own religious laws and have forgotten the heart behind it. Many think that if someone doesn't agree with their doctrinal standpoint that they're not as favored by God. We make things way too complicated. Some have even become like modern-day Pharisees.

God never intended for us to divide into many different denominations; that was our own doing. If we don't see eye to eye and believe the same things, what does it matter? God is going to do it His way anyway. God doesn't mind if we don't know all things perfectly; that's what grace is for.

God is not looking to see if we believe everything correctly. He's looking at the condition of our hearts. He's looking to get your heart in the right place, not your mind. He wants you to have a pure heart, then go from there. He wants us, not our religious practices. It says, "For I desired mercy, and not sacrifice; and the knowledge of God more than burnt offerings." Hosea 6:6, Matt 9:13, Matt 12:7. Mark 12:33 "To Love Him with all the heart, And with all the understanding, with all the soul, And with all the strength, And to Love His neighbor as Himself, is more important than all whole burnt offerings and sacrifices."

He wants us to pursue Him, to be Holy even as He is Holy. But God will show you what you are to work on or sacrifice. He doesn't want you to do a ritual, just to do it. Like in Matt 6:7: "Do not use vain repetitions as the heathen do. For they think that they will be heard for their many words." You can have more effect by saying a few heartfelt words than thousands said out of ritual.

Let's look at a few things that could be considered ritual. Going to church just to go to church; God knows your heart. Do you go just to go? Where is the heart in that? God is not looking for your attendance, he's looking for your heart. Because if you're going just to go, then your heart is somewhere else, and you're just coming out of duty. It is good to try to do what you're supposed to do, but put some heart into it.

Another thing is singing without heart. Do you sing the words, but your heart is somewhere else? Jesus said, "These people draw near to me with their mouth, and honor me with their lips; but their heart is far from me. And in vain do they worship me" Matt 15:8-9. God knows your heart. It's like giving someone a cold plate of food. "I know thy works, that thou art neither cold nor hot: I would thou wert cold or hot. So then because thou art lukewarm, and neither cold nor hot, I will spue thee out of my mouth" Rev 3:15-16. These are just a few examples.

Let's say your heart is into it; were not the Pharisee's zealots for what they believed? The devil knows if He can't stop you, he will try to push you too far. Going too far is just as bad as going too little. Jesus rebuked the Pharisees because they went too far, and their hearts were in the wrong place. They were trying to make the ways of God too complicated. Enter the gates of heaven as a child, why, because it's simple, not complicated. Stay on this narrow path, don't do too little, and don't do too much, or you Will fall into a ditch II Cor 3:17.

The Harvest

"The harvest indeed is plentiful, but the laborers are few. Pray therefore that the Lord of the harvest will send out laborers into His harvest." Matt 9:37-38

There is a harvest coming where the sheep and the goats will be separated. The harvest is coming where the good and bad fruits will be determined. On which side will you be? Hot, cold, or lukewarm. The time of judgment is coming to determine whether you are hot or cold.

Someone had a vision that I read that talks about a person going through many tests. In the end, there was this field by a river with a bunch of people laying on the ground passed out. He was told to go get a cup of water for one of them, and He repeated it a couple of times. Finally, the person who was in bad shape was now on their feet. They got themselves a cup, hat, or anything fillable and helped others to get a drink. This continued and continued until there were many up. They in turn, would help others get water.

In the final quest book, the torch and the sword by Rick Joyner. They were surrounded by countless enemies and they were guarding a river that the enemy wanted to destroy. Then one of the leaders in the group said to them, fill up your vessel with water and offer it to the enemy. They thought this sounds like an odd request. This army is about to attack us, but they went ahead and did it. The enemy army was shocked and didn't know what to do. They stood there for a second, then went ahead and drank the water. As soon as they drank it, they realized their thirst and wanted more. They continued bringing them more and more water, but then the demand became so much. They had to just point to the river to have them help themselves. Not all of the enemy army agreed to drink. After a while, the countenances of the enemy changed, and they started to help others drink.

In both visions, the water represents God's living water, life, and heart healing. The harvest will involve us helping others get a drink and a taste of the real living God. Once they have tasted the real, they will realize what they are really missing. We help others get the healing that they need, then they will help other people. This is the harvest. The goal is to get as many good fruits as we possibly can before time is up.

This is not referring to saving souls. It's talking about helping fellow Christians from their lukewarm, lack of life state. Their lack of real relationship with the living God; instead of their religious belief of what they think He is. God wants you to be hot, not lukewarm or cold. He wants your sincere devotion to Him, but some of us are not willing to go the distance. We will only go so far with Him, but with something that we love, it stops us. Ask yourself, is your heart into it, or are you doing it just out of duty to not feel guilty?

In this harvest, we will be required to help each other grow in strength to equip others, so they in turn, can help others. The dawning of the age is coming, and at that time, the sheep will be separated from the goats. This doesn't mean you have to have a perfect understanding of the correct doctrine.

You are judged according to your fruits. This includes pastors and leadership. Nobody is exempt from this; your fruits are not how many people you have in your church. Your fruits are your obedience to Him and your level of dying to self. Because what is inside will come out. If your tree is good, it will bear good fruits. If your tree is bad, then you will bear bad fruits.

Many will show up to the Judgment seat thinking they did wonders for God, but Jesus will paint them an entirely different picture. They may enter the humble gate and be the lowest in the kingdom. Many will show up at the Judgment seat expecting to hear the words well done good and faithful servant. But will instead hear something completely different. This applies to everybody, from the average Joe to the most top-ranking church leader.

God is having grace in this upcoming revival, which may be our last chance to change and stay there, to be hot and not lukewarm. Someone said once revival is really the last-ditch effort for repentance. God is having mercy on us to give us a little more time to become hot.

Overcoming Lust

I feel to write about this because it really is a big deal, and it plagues many Christians today. It is a topic that's often ignored, yet it's one of the biggest issues. Because there is shame, and it's embarrassing to talk about. If it wasn't an issue, then why are there so many leaders who have been exposed in this? They don't want to be lustful, and they resist it until a temptation comes along, then give in. God gave men and women sexual drives, and this sexual drive sometimes is overwhelming and frustrating. What we need to do is learn to tame it, as I'm sure most Christians are already trying to do. We need to learn to tame our eyes to not be tempted.

When I was a teenager, I was told by my youth leaders in a meeting especially designed to help in this matter; it's not the first look, it's the second and third look. I didn't think much of this at the time, but it really was the key. This is the start of it, the trigger point. It all starts from this point on. Once you entertain it, it starts from there, and the temptation grows. What you need to do is learn to stop it before it starts. The starting point is when you look at someone either in person, internet, movies, or TV. Suddenly, without warning, you see something that arouses that lust. What you need to do is to learn to stop it before it starts, and don't look the second time. Another thing I needed to stop was when I was watching videos, I would be subconsciously looking for anything sexy; even the smallest of details. If anything triggered that response, I would go back and look at it. If you are looking for it, then you are entertaining lust already.

It's true the first time isn't the problem. When you arouse lust, it grows in your heart. If you see something, then ponder it, this is also the 2nd time. Lust grows in your heart, and you start looking for the next thing that's lustful. I call this seeking because you are already entertaining lustful thoughts in your mind. Making a small excuse to find something mild to satisfy that lust and cheat your current resistance towards it. When you find that something, then that lust grows until you give in. It's like a fire. You need to quench it before it has a chance to grow any more. So the key is to stop it before it starts, to get through your temptation, and tell yourself that's enough. In that process, you may be strong at first, but the temptation works itself, trying to break your resolve. You need to keep that strength and not let it try to work its way through that strength that you give in. The battle is truly in your mind, don't let it slip around your defenses. You need to be the master of your thoughts and keep it out of your mind!

In the long run, if you participate with it on a regular basis, then you become hardened to it. Only greater lusts can satisfy you. Another thing you need to do is to find someone who will hold you accountable, and tell them your issue and have them check in with you from time to time on the matter. This way, you know you can't because this person will hold you accountable. I also discovered that I didn't like how my spirit was sucked out of life soon afterward. Because the enemy is granted access to your heart, and he literally steals your life. Being forced to deal with approaching a lifeless heart and having to fill it again with life is a lengthy, annoying process.

Really, what is going on is the demon of Lust is jumping on you or harassing you until you give in. So imagine taking that thought like a piece of trash and throwing it out as soon as it comes in. This was not overcome easily by me; it's a great battle for the mind, and a stronghold that holds many Christians today.

I have had a long and hard battle with it myself. I used to not be able to go 1 day without lusting, but each time I would sincerely be sorry and repent. Then the Lord confronted me on it one day through a dream; it showed that I looked through lustful material, and then I went on like nothing happened.

(Warning: discussion of male anatomy function) I think it's harder for men because physically our body was designed to produce semen. It builds up and produces a sexual pressure that is difficult to ignore. It takes many days for it to settle down. This is probably why men are more lustful. This pressure is directly linked to your thoughts. If you think about lustful things in your mind, then your body will apply sexual pressure to the prostate (maybe there's a form of this in women too, I don't know). So you need to keep these thoughts out of your mind and the prostate will calm down in a short time. If you master this, then the sexual pressure won't be as bad. The battle is truly in your mind; your body is reacting to your thoughts!

But it's not always this; you may want to lust because you're having a bad day, emotions, or frustrations. You need to learn to resolve those emotions. If you are married, this is ok, but don't pursue un-Godly means to resolve your frustrations.

We often don't want to talk about this and just push it away. But the problem is that the issue still exists. So I find it critical to talk about it, because something that is swept under the rug doesn't go away; it's still there in secret.

It's a stronghold that the enemy has on you. It really is like someone who is coming off of cigarettes. You try hard not to lust, but suddenly, a picture on TV, movie, or the internet will come in front of you, and the demonic spirit of lust will jump on you and keep hounding you with it relentlessly.

In our travels, there was this group of people. There was this woman who had breast implants in the group. She was saved and redeemed and that was probably the past, but there was a comment by one of the leaders there. He said when looking at her, he either has to look at her head or her feet. The thing is, the woman wore some slightly questionable clothes. You might say, why can't you control what you think. It's not that, it's when you look at a person you see all of them at once. It's hard to not see just one part of them. The next time you look at someone, think about this, and you will see what I mean. It's frustrating to be forced to look at this all the time. It would be different if she wore more appropriate attire. So if you're someone who wears questionable attire; I think it's your responsibility to present yourself in an appropriate manner.

I started lusting somewhere about 10-13 years of age and would not be able to go much more than a week without lusting. If not taken care of, someone could keep lusting their entire life, as seen in some well-known ministers. So this is nothing to ignore like it has been.

I'm not talking about pagans here; I'm talking about Christians. It's not that one goes out of their way to get a pornographic movie. It's watching TV, movies, or internet where unexpected lustful images come up. Once you take steps to get out of lust, the enemy will not want to let go of you that easily. You must keep strong, tame your eyes, and learn to stop the fire before it starts. "But I say unto you, that whosoever looketh on a woman to lust after her hath committed adultery with her already in his heart" Matthew 5:28.

It's like a sting when you see that image. What I realized was that this sting fades after about 5 minutes, and it's not as intense. But the desire may still be there. You need to decide to not get restung, but to stop it! The fire is dimmed to a small flame, but you need to snuff it out completely; because it can start up again if you fuel it.

If you're watching a movie by yourself and something comes up, do not go back, just keep going. Get past the sting! You need to determine before the movie starts to just roll past anything that pops up. I heard of a father who quit lust because he concluded these women are somebody else's daughter.

One time, when I was repentant about being lustful, I asked the Lord what he thinks when he sees a woman like this. He responded to me: "I wonder if I can adopt them." Meaning they probably have emptiness or pain in their heart that they do this. Jesus wants to adopt, heal, and save them. This really touched me. I feel when Jesus Speaks, it's absolute wisdom and beautiful! I know this because He has spoken to me a few times. When He speaks, you know what he's saying is right and beautiful. Even if it's a correction, I am in awe of His words.

Suicide

There's a demonic spirit of suicide. He looks for an opportunity of a painful experience to suggest the idea. When a painful experience happens, whatever it might be, it feels impossible to overcome at that moment. It's an incredible amount of pain, and you feel unfairly treated. I know this because I have been there in this kind of pain, and the devil has suggested to me to do such.

This might be an embarrassing topic to talk about, but it's real. A lot of Christians and normal people go through it, so I find it very important to talk about this. I have heard Christians threaten suicide. I understand the pain because I have been there; emotional pain is the hardest to heal.

The pain that you feel and the situation you are in will be remedied in time. You just need to give it some time. Also, the pain of correction or being poorly treated, threatening suicide is a power play or manipulation for power. I know you're hurt, but suicide is not the easy way out. What you need to do is ask God to heal your pain and take it. And try to remedy the situation the best you can. <u>Things in life have a way of working themselves out</u>. I heard of a situation where a girl was going to commit suicide because she was pregnant and her father was giving her grief about it. But someone caught her before she did it and prevented it. Then many years later, that same girl, now a woman, found them and told them that she had a husband and several children; they saved her that day.

That girl was going to kill herself because before her stood a difficult road with a lot of uncertainties. This all seems too difficult to handle, but it's not worth ending your life!

What you need to do is to have enough courage to face whatever you feel is so terrible; go through it the best you can. Often one will make great pain over uncertainties. <u>Life has a way of becoming better in time just get through it</u>. Nothing in this life is worth killing yourself over, because life has a way of working itself out in time. Yes, they're very painful, but in time, that pain will heal. You need to learn to just plow through the pain and get through it; the situation will get better in time.

Ask God for help. If you're reading this and don't know Jesus, you need to get to know Him because He's the healer! He will heal your heart and emotional pains (See Topic "Salvation message" page 202).

If life gives you lemons, make lemonade; just make the best of the situation. You will have to modify and change your expectations. In time, you will look back at it and realize that it didn't turn out as bad as you thought it would! It worked itself out just fine in the end.

Also, you need to not participate with the demon behind it; you need to stop thinking thoughts that would feed this demon. Because if you participate with it, then it will keep on (See Topic "Stuff happens in life" page 122).

The thing that helped me the most get out of it, and I don't know if it's true or not, but I heard that if someone commits suicide that they go to hell for it. It was enough to scare me straight. But I wonder if it's true or not because my mom had a vision of someone's father who committed suicide many decades ago, being in heaven. And I seen a video of someone going to heaven and seeing someone talking to someone at a table who committed suicide, trying to convince them to stay with them in heaven. So I'm unsure; this is just what worked for me. I apologize for the shock factor. Maybe this is something someone invented a long time ago to stop suicide, but I figure it's not worth the risk if it is by chance true.

Life has a way of working things out, in the end after all the dust is settled and time has passed, your situation will get better, so please just hang in there and plow through it the best you can, do all you can do to try to remedy the situation the best you can, then that's all you can do. I know waiting for the result can be painful, but please take heart and hang in there.

Seek Jesus for his heart healing. Consider worshiping with headphones to potent worship. Tell Jesus all about it and every feeling you have on the matter; get it all out and cry and heal yourself. Matthew 28:20 "I am with you always." Seek the wonderful heart healing like only Jesus can give, ask him to heal your heart, and wait upon Him to do it with an open heart. When it happens, you will not be able to help but to cry. It's so wonderful.

Matt 11:28-30 "Come unto me, all ye that labour and are heavy laden, and I will give you rest. Take my yoke upon you, and learn of me; for I am meek and lowly in heart: and ye shall find rest unto your souls."

Depression

Things happen in life that are not always the way we would hope, but it's our choice how we approach it. We should make the best of the situation and go on. Where do your emotions go in this process? It's a choice. Yes, you might be down about it, but going into depression is the next step down.

Depression is negative energy that the enemy can smell and exploit. It's an energy that drags you down and the spiritual environment around you. The devil will come in and try to keep you in this negative emotion and push this energy upon you. 1 Pet 5:8 I have gotten into some myself, but I have to say that's enough and decide to turn off this negative energy and get back into the life of God.

This emotion chokes out the Lord because you have chosen to be in this mud puddle. I have felt this energy; it's very undesirable and dark energy. It's a choice to stop participating in it; you have to change your expectations and turn from it, then rebuild your spiritual life. There's a demonic spirit that specializes in depression. You need to be careful that he's not choking out your spiritual life.

Once I chose not to be depressed, I prayed in tongues and worked my way out of it. It's not that I don't like the result; I change my expectations and put up with the undesired results. Things in life have a way of working themselves out in time. You need to just plow through it and go on (See Topics "Emotional Pain" page 123, and "Stuff happens in life" page 122).

Salvation attack

I had a bad experience where I was excited to learn spiritual dynamics and decided to watch videos about hell, hoping that I would glean something that would help me spiritually. It had an effect on me I didn't expect and took me years of recovery to come back to some semblance of peace. These videos had things to say that shook me to my core. I'm now wondering if the enemy has planted some books and videos on the internet that talk about Jesus giving tours of hell, saying things that make you doubt your own salvation. Yes, Jesus can give tours of hell, but I'm wondering if the devil has planted false ones to try to ruin Christians. Watching these videos scared me so much I questioned was there certain things I did that would be considered hell worthy.

I went through basically years of pain and anguish over the matter. It was a long and painful experience for me. In that process, I wanted to find out what salvation was for myself by reading the New and Old Testament and starting from scratch.

Jesus gave the keys to Peter; what he locked or unlocked was also done in heaven. It was that scripture about Peter having a vision of unclean things, and God said eat, but Peter said no. God said don't call unclean that which I have cleansed; which was referring to the gentiles. And Paul's simple messages about simple salvation. But in the Old Testament, there was Joel 2:32 "whoever calls on the name of the Lord shall be saved," and Isaiah 53.

I recommend <u>not</u> watching hell videos because they say some pretty nasty stuff. But I continually saw the numbers 316 everywhere I went, even my new house number. I took this as God trying to speak to me of the scripture John 3:16 "For God so loved the world that He gave His only begotten Son, that whoever believes in Him should not perish but have everlasting life." This is Jesus himself saying these words, not a man. But I still think there are a few lines to not cross for salvation. Like unforgiveness and unrepentant sins are big ones.

I think as long as you believe in Jesus and are trying to do the right things and pursue godliness, then He will see that and honor it. God sees if we're trying.

With all this in mind, I think it has calmed my fears down, but Jesus isn't a pushover. He still wants us to accomplish all that we can. He will be angry with us if we fail to do a good job here on earth. But I think as long as you believe in Jesus and try to live a Christian life, that is the bare minimum. But God doesn't want us to stop at the bare minimum! He wants us to go as far as we can.

When I was having my fears about salvation, I was angry at God for being so harsh as I thought. I even wondered why we serve God and why we worship Him. But I knew this was a bad thing to think as a Christian, so I kept it in check and contemplated the solutions to my errors. The reason for this response was the incredible pain I was feeling; I didn't know what to do with it. I felt trapped by this salvation attack.

The conclusion that I came up with that helped me stop being so upset with God was that God is family. You came from Him, so He is your Father. You might be upset with your real parents. It happens, but you still love them. I will stick in there with Him. Job 13:15 "Though He slay me, yet will I trust in Him."

In this process, I was desperate for God to just give me the answer. I found out that God is really subtle. His answers to me were very subtle! One wants rock-solid answers; God doesn't really do that unless it's critical. I think He wanted to build in me strength, so He allowed me to go through this trial so I would come out stronger on the other side. I wanted a very absolute answer that I truly knew I was okay. He was very subtle in His response. But He slowly instilled into me strength on the matter.

Another thing that goes on in the Christian world is some Christian groups will put fear on people that if you don't do certain things, you're in big trouble. This is fear-based! Yes, He wants things from us, but He doesn't use fear to do it. This is the enemy's tool! But this is not an excuse to be lackadaisical in your walk; God wants us to pursue Him the best we can. Fear is anti-love; these are the enemy's tactics. If you had a relationship with someone, and it was based on fear; would this really be a relationship? God is love, yet He is also the lion; the lion and the lamb. There's a balance in this, not too lenient and not too stringent either.

(Warning: graphic detail - blood) Years later, after all this was resolved, I had an experience. I was using a knife to work on a project, and it accidentally poked into my wrist a little. The result was very aggressive. I didn't know better at the time, but I thought I could die. I called out to Jesus and said: please forgive me for all that I have done, and named a few things; please forgive me for anything that I may have forgotten or hidden sins in me, and I forgive everyone. All of a sudden, while I was saying these things, I felt an unbelievable peace come over me like I have never experienced before. I felt like he heard me, and even if I did die, I was going to be okay. This experience was profound for me and has changed how I feel about death. This peace was so powerful it lasted for 3 days. The accident was way off to the side of my wrist, and covering it was all that was needed for it to clot (Caution: Do not attempt this. One may need to call 911 in this situation). Out of this experience, I felt that Jesus made himself real to me and that in death He will be there to help you through it; He will catch you (if it's unintentional). This was one of the most profound experiences of my life.

The Impressionable mind looking for acceptance/rejection

I write this because of an experience that I had when I was a teenager. Me and my parents switched churches. There was this young man my age, that asked me if I wanted to be in a gang he was making that only had one other member so far. I would be the third. He told me he was part of a well-known gang where he used to live. So I accepted his offer because it sounded appealing. After a matter of time, he showed me how to be a gangster: how to steal, how to dress, how to walk, how to treat people depending on who they were, and sometimes just simply how they wore their hat. My training on how to be a gangster was somewhat brief because we moved to a new church again later. I'm glad because it took me a couple of years and getting in trouble a few times before I shook the habit.

Had I stayed in it longer, it would have probably taken me longer to recover. Thankfully, his gang was very separated from any real gang, or it would have been much worse for me. They teach to steal, sin, and abuse people like it was nothing; basically, anything they feel like doing, they do. This is more of an extreme example of influence than most, but the principle is the same.

The young mind is very impressionable. The young person wants to be accepted by their peers, so they will seek out who's willing to accept them. Maybe part of that is played out by what type of personality they have as well. When the influence of the kids around them is bad, the person who's looking for acceptance may go with that bad influence.

What they're really looking for is Love; to be loved by someone (accepted).

They will do almost anything to get it. But if that young person already has acceptance somewhere else, they might be less likely to join that bad influence.

Here are a few more examples. I know a teenager that didn't have very many friends and was home-schooled. One of the neighbor's teenagers became his friend, and they liked to skateboard, so he decided to also. Another example is, when I was a young teenager before my semi gang experience, I wasn't very popular in school. There was this group of popular kids that liked Christian heavy metal (Christian school). I found I was able to sing their song very well, and they thought that was funny, so I was accepted in that way. I took up Christian heavy metal and acted like those kids.

It's not the skateboarding, heavy metal, or whatever that they're after; it's love and acceptance. You'll find that they might do just about anything to be accepted, especially if that is the only way to be accepted. That's why I was willing to join one of the worst types of groups there are. Perhaps if they were presented with a real alternative that's acceptable to them, like a church youth group (a cool one), they might have a better chance of not going the wrong way. They need to go to a youth group that has the power of God moving. Where God can touch their heart with His spirit, and they find real acceptance and love. Then they may have a good chance of resisting the bad influence elsewhere. But I really feel the touch from God is a big part of it.

I read that it's good for a parent to let their children know what they believe is right and wrong. Also, I think it might be better to remove them from the bad influence and put them somewhere else. That happened to me with the gang. I was thankfully separated, but the influence was strongly still in me. It took a couple of years for me to finally be free of it.

When I was younger, I was picked on and low on the social order at school. This affected me greatly; I became sad and wouldn't smile, but very rarely, and had a gloom about me. It's not being accepted by most that really hurts young people. I had one friend, but that made little difference when I was being picked on by most.

For some reason, it's cool and fun for kids to pick on others. They might say they were just kidding, but it seems that the young mind is very sensitive to rejection. It cuts deep. That's why they're willing to do anything to be accepted. It takes them out of the rejection and into acceptance. But someone who's not picked on will do what the crowd does to avoid being rejected. Because if they go against peer pressure, they will reject or pick on them.

To a child or teen, that's a pain far too great to accept, so they go with the crowd. This dynamic, in the more extreme sense, is school shootings. They get picked on and rejected by everybody, including the girls. They're surrounded by rejection and feel completely unloved and unwanted, going into a deep depression. The other kids rip on them day after day, and the pain builds and builds. So much so, they feel there is no release to the pain but to hurt those who hurt them. There needs to be a strong intervention into the picking on of children. I do not condone these actions but am seeking a solution to this serious problem. I have personally experienced the pain of being picked on in school and the accumulative emotional pain as a result.

This dynamic is nothing new; it has been growing and growing for countless years. This evil has gotten greater and greater; this is only the latest birth of this evil. It's ridiculous that it takes for people to be killed first for this terrible dynamic to finally be looked into. It has just plain been ignored for probably centuries. This is a demonic dynamic, and the devil cultivated it in schools today. It's like their own little kingdom to see who's on top, a competition, by ranks of popularity.

When I came out of the world of school and went to a technical college, it was like night and day. I was treated like an equal by most, and there was no pecking order of popularity. For some reason, the adult world is entirely different. Kids don't want to associate with unpopular kids for fear of being branded as a lesser. This even goes into dating as well. A popular person will not date an unpopular person; this cuts deep. In the adult world, all of that is removed. More of an equalness exists, at least for the most part.

I went to a different school every two years in my young life. This as well was detrimental to being accepted. Every new school I went to got a little better, but I was always picked on. Then I found acceptance in being in heavy metal. A few years later, I was influenced by the gang experience then separated from it. I then moved to a school in the country, still a lower rank in the social, but slightly better again. I found some acceptance in being unique. Then finally going to Technical College changed my life.

At some point, my sister convinced me to go to a big youth group at a mega-church. The first time I was there, the Holy Spirit touched me greatly. I still had a gloom about me, but there was love. This helped me to open up, along with multiple friends and acceptance.

Writing these things is a form of release for me, and I felt it might be beneficial to someone to know how I was delivered from rejection. But it's important to realize that this does go on in the child's kingdom of school. They make the rules of who's accepted and who is not. Your rank in this kingdom is determined by how popular you are. You are treated according to that rank. Schools should have anti-bullying policies that go more into the treating of people as lessers and the picking on of people. Maybe they should have a class that talks about this and addresses what it does to people. That it's not all fun and games; it truly ruins people's lives and shapes who they are as adults! 1 Corinthians 13:13, Isaiah 49:15-16

Salvation message

If you're reading this, and you don't have a personal relationship with Jesus. You have this emptiness in your heart that you try to fill with many things in this world. None of it really satisfies the emptiness inside of you. This is because only Jesus can fill the emptiness with His peace and love.

Let me ask you a question; if you were to die today, where would you go? Do you know? Many people say I'm a good person, and I will go to heaven because I'm good and do good works. Being a good person doesn't get you into heaven for this reason; God is perfect (holy), and we in this life are defiantly not perfect. Any sin whatsoever can not be in His presence. God knows this, so he made a fix for this, Jesus! Jesus can wash those sins from our spirit that we will be blameless when we die because He covered them and washed them from us. All it takes to receive this forgiveness is to: believe in Jesus, admit your sins to him, forgive everyone who has wronged you in any way (Matthew 6:14 "For if you forgive other people when they sin against you, your heavenly Father will also forgive you"), and live a Godly Christian life.

It says in 1 John 5:12-13: "Whoever has the Son has life; whoever does not have the Son of God does not have life. I write these things to you who believe in the name of the Son of God so that you may know that you have eternal life."

It's a common misunderstanding, that if you've been baptized or do good works, you will make it to heaven. Jesus said in John 3:3: "Verily, verily, I say unto thee, Except a man be born again, he cannot see the kingdom of God." it's not by works that you make it to heaven, but its way simpler. All you have

to do to know His peace and make it into heaven is to believe that Jesus Is the Son of God, ask Him into your life, ask Him to forgive you of all your sins, and forgive others. John 3:16 "For God so loved the world, that He gave His only begotten Son, that whosoever believeth in Him should not perish, but have everlasting life." Romans 10:9 (LEB)
"That if you confess with your mouth, Jesus is Lord and believe in your heart that God raised Him from the dead you will be saved."

Romans 3:23 says for all have sinned and fall short of the glory of God, that includes everyone, including Christians. The only difference being a Christian is being forgiven of them through Jesus, by what He did for us on the cross. All you have to do is accept this sacrifice for your sins.

In the following, this is Jesus speaking, and you are that sheep. "What do you think? If a man has a hundred sheep, and one of them goes astray, does he not leave the ninety-nine and go to the mountains to seek the one that is straying? And if he should find it, assuredly, I say to you, he rejoices more over that sheep than over the ninety-nine that did not go astray. Even so, it is not the will of your Father who is in heaven that one of these little ones should perish." Matt 18:12

Jesus wants you to come to Him and rejoices over you. Jesus is willing to forgive your darkest sins no matter what they are, and replace your pain with His peace. Some people think they're too far gone to be saved, but if you're willing to change and accept this, then you are not too far gone. God is not an angry God like many seem to think; he is a God of love. Sure, God can get angry, but it's temporary, not all the time. Just like a parent can get angry at their children, they still love them. Ezekiel 18:25-32 " when the wicked turns away from his wickedness that he has committed and does that which is lawful and righteous, he shall save his soul alive."

Ask Jesus to make Himself real to you, but it's not give me a sign or make this happen, then I'll believe. It's in ways that He chooses that are subtle. If you want to have Jesus's peace in your heart and know that you are going to heaven when you die, all you have to do is pray this prayer with sincerity and live the Christian life.

Pray this prayer

Jesus, I come before you now. I ask you to come into my life, forgive me of all my sin. I denounce satan and all his works. I confess Jesus as the Lord of my life. I believe that Jesus is the son of God and that he rose from the dead to wash me of my sins. I forgive everyone who has wronged me and release it to you. Thank you, Jesus, for saving me. I ask that you make yourself real to me and fill me with your peace in the name of Jesus.

That's it, if you prayed this prayer with sincerity, and try to live a Godly life, then you will know that you will go to heaven when you die!

Read the Bible, starting with the books of 1 John, 2 John, and 3 John. Also, find what is called a spirit-filled church. Not Lutheran, Baptist, Catholic, etc.., but spirit-filled. And find one that has spirit-filled worship, where you feel His presence in the room touching your heart. Healing your emotions, hurts, and filling you with peace when you sing. An example of heart-felt worship would be this song: (do an internet search) Oceans Where Feet May Fail by Hillsong United, on May 31, 2013. Congratulations I'll see you in heaven one day!

Recommended Books

I recommend Rick Joyner's 3 Final Quest series books: "The Final Quest," "The Call," and "The Torch and the Sword," or the all three in one book is called "Final Quest Trilogy." Also, Anna Rountree's "The Heavens Opened," and "the Priestly Bride," or both in one book, "Heaven Awaits the Bride."

All 5 of these books are full open visions. It isn't them coming up with it, it's God coming up with the events in those books, and they are just transcribing them into their books. The entire time it's Jesus, Angels, or God directing what's being shown, said, and done. There are many themes; it's like spending the day with God. In these books, He takes them places and shows them things about current and future events. These books are like taking a journey with God through their eyes. This is true meat. It's a very deep revelation and is challenging in a good way.

www.ingramcontent.com/pod-product-compliance
Lightning Source LLC
Chambersburg PA
CBHW062034290426
44109CB00026B/2622